Confucius

Titles in the *Bloomsbury Library of Educational Thought* Series:

St Thomas Aquinas, *Vivian Boland OP*
Aristotle, *Alexander Moseley*
St Augustine, *Ryan N. S. Topping*
Pierre Bourdieu, *Michael James Grenfell*
Jerome Bruner, *David R. Olson*
Confucius, *Charlene Tan*
John Dewey, *Richard Pring*
Michel Foucault, *Lynn Fendler*
Paulo Freire, *Daniel Schugurensky*
John Holt, *Roland Meighan*
John Locke, *Alexander Moseley*
Loris Malaguzzi and the Reggio Emilia Experience, *Kathy Hall, Mary Horgan, Anna Ridgway, Rosaleen Murphy, Maura Cunneen and Denice Cunningham*
Maria Montessori, *Marion O'Donnell*
A. S. Neill, *Richard Bailey*
John Henry Newman, *James Arthur and Guy Nicholls*
Robert Owen, *Robert A. Davis and Frank O'Hagan*
R. S. Peters, *Stefaan E. Cuypers and Christopher Martin*
Jean Piaget, *Richard Kohler*
Plato, *Robin Barrow*
Jean-Jacques Rousseau, *Jürgen Oelkers*
Rudolf Steiner, *Heiner Ullrich*
Leo Tolstoy, *Daniel Moulin*
Lev Vygotsky, *René van der Veer*
E. G. West, *James Tooley*
Mary Wollstonecraft, *Susan Laird*

Series Editor: Richard Bailey is a writer and researcher in education and sport. A former teacher in both primary and secondary schools and a teacher trainer, he has been Professor at a number of leading Universities in the UK. He now lives and works in Germany.

Members of the Advisory Board

Robin Barrow, Professor of Philosophy, Simon Fraser University, Canada.

Peter Gronn, Professor of Education, Head of Faculty, University of Cambridge, UK.

Kathy Hall, Professor of Education and Head of the School of Education at University College Cork, Ireland.

Stephen Heyneman, Professor of International Educational Policy at the College of Education and Human Development, Vanderbilt University, USA.

Yung-Shi Lin, President Emeritus and Professor, Department of Education and Institute of Graduate Studies, Taipei Municipal University of Education, Republic of China, Taiwan.

Gary McCulloch, Head of Department of Humanities and Social Sciences at the Institute of Education, University of London, UK.

Jürgen Oelkers, Professor of Education at the University of Zurich, Switzerland.

Richard Pring, Emeritus Professor at the Department of Education, and Emeritus Fellow of Green Templeton College, University of Oxford, UK.

Harvey Siegel, Professor and Chair of the Department of Philosophy, University of Miami, USA.

Richard Smith, Professor of Education, University of Durham, UK.

Zhou Zuoyu, Professor, Faculty of Education, Beijing Normal University, People's Republic of China.

Confucius

CHARLENE TAN

Bloomsbury Library of Educational Thought
Series Editor: Richard Bailey

BLOOMSBURY
LONDON • NEW DELHI • NEW YORK • SYDNEY

Bloomsbury Academic
An imprint of Bloomsbury Publishing Plc

50 Bedford Square	1385 Broadway
London	New York
WC1B 3DP	NY 10018
UK	USA

www.bloomsbury.com

First published 2013 by Continuum International Publishing Group
Paperback edition first published 2014 by Bloomsbury Academic

© Charlene Tan, 2013

All rights reserved. No part of this publication may be reproduced or transmitted in any form or by any means, electronic or mechanical, including photocopying, recording, or any information storage or retrieval system, without prior permission in writing from the publishers.

Charlene Tan has asserted her right under the Copyright, Designs and Patents Act, 1988, to be identified as Authors of this work.

No responsibility for loss caused to any individual or organization acting on or refraining from action as a result of the material in this publication can be accepted by Bloomsbury Academic or the author.

British Library Cataloguing-in-Publication Data
A catalogue record for this book is available from the British Library.

ISBN: PB: 978-1-4725-1498-1

Library of Congress Cataloguing-in-Publication Data
A catalogue record for this book is available from the Library of Congress.

Design by Newgen Knowledge Works (P) Ltd., Chennai, India
Printed and bound in Great Britain

To my husband Lim Pin (twb)

Contents

Series Editor's Preface ix
Foreword xi
Acknowledgements xv

Introduction 1

Part 1 Intellectual Biography

1 Confucius' Life, Personality and Influence 17

Part 2 Critical Exposition of Confucius' Work

2 The Concept of *Li* 31
3 The Concepts of *Dao* and *He* 51
4 The Concept of *Ren* 74
5 The Concept of *Junzi* 103
6 The Concepts of *Xue*, *Wen* and *Si* 123

Part 3 The Relevance of Confucius' Work Today

7 Confucius and Twenty-First-Century Education 191
8 Conclusion 219

References 241
Index 259

Series Editor's Preface

Most of the books in this series take the form of what might be called 'philosophical biography' in the area of educational studies. Their shared purpose, simply put, is to understand the thoughts and practices of certain educational philosophers.

Straightaway, this project is confronted with some potential difficulties. As even a cursory reading of the list of thinkers whose names provide the titles within the series will testify, many are not ordinarily considered philosophers. Some can be more sensibly located in other areas of the academy – sociology, economics, psychology and so on. Others seem unsuited to the label because their contribution to education is primarily in terms of its practice. In the narrow, disciplinary sense, then, many of the subjects of this series are clearly not philosophers. In another sense, however, and this is the sense employed by Jean-Paul Sartre in his own attempts in the genre, a philosophical biography can be written about anyone whose thought is important and interesting. In this sense, I suggest, each of the thinkers acknowledged in this series are philosophers.

Implicit within the *Bloomsbury Library of Educational Thought* is an assertion that theories and the practices that follow from them (and equally, practices and the theories that lie implicitly within them) are vitally important for education. By gathering together the ideas of some of the most important and interesting educational thinkers, from the Ancient Greeks to contemporary scholars, the series has the ambitious task of providing an accessible yet authoritative resource for a generation of students and practitioners.

It will always be possible to question the list of key thinkers that are represented in this series. Some may question the inclusion of certain thinkers; some may disagree with the exclusion of others. That is inevitably going to be the case. There is no suggestion that the list of thinkers represented within the *Bloomsbury Library of Educational Thought* is in any way definitive. What is incontestable is that these thinkers have fascinating ideas about education, and that taken together, the Library can act as a powerful source of information and inspiration for those committed to the study of education.

Charlene Tan's volume on 'Confucius' fulfils the ambitions of these series very well. Her subject will be known – at least by name – by most readers, yet the influence and relevance of Confucius is often overlooked, especially in the West. Is it fair to say that Confucius is too closely associated with Chinese philosophy? And, for that matter, with a China of the past? Tan confronts these concerns, and makes the persuasive case that anyone who aspires to be familiar with key political, social and educational thinkers must know something about Confucius.

So, at one level, this book can be read as a clear and accessible introduction to a hugely significant thinker. At another, Tan's remarkable book offers the reader the opportunity to look at educational theory and practice through new lenses. Aside from its value as a volume with the *Bloomsbury Library of Educational Thought*, this book stands as an outstanding contribution to educational thinking, in its own right.

Richard Bailey
Series Editor

Foreword

Confucius' teachings in the *Analects* (or the *Lunyu* in Chinese) are very much a living tradition of Chinese societies in China, Taiwan (Republic of China), Hong Kong and elsewhere, and of other East Asian societies like Japan and South Korea. They are also relevant to the modern world.

When he took office as the Premier of Taiwan in February 2013, Jiang Yi-huah acknowledged the deep responsibility which he was about to shoulder by citing a verse from the *Analects* (passage 8.3) and which originated from the *Book of Poetry* (*Shi Jing*): 'I feel apprehensive and cautious, as if I'm balancing on the brink of a deep gulf, as if I'm treading on thin ice.' While stating the need for reform and innovation in his government's aspiration to make Taiwan 'a democratic society of prosperity and propriety', Jiang cited another passage from the first chapter of the *Analects* (1.15): Confucius' disciple Zigong asks what he thinks of the saying, 'Poor without being obsequious, wealthy without being arrogant'? Confucius replies, 'That will do, but better still "Poor yet delighting in the Way, wealthy yet observant of the rites".'

Explaining that Confucius is proposing a higher ideal in which he hopes that the poor pursue the best way to live and the rich pay attention to their spiritual needs, Jiang said: 'Personally, I consider this attitude a spiritual asset of Chinese society's Confucian tradition which applies to all eras and governmental systems . . . We need to think about how to make concepts of freedom and democracy that originated in the West flourish here in Taiwan, and how to integrate them with the Confucian culture we already have, so that democracy constitutes not only competition but also respect for differing views and rational dialogue. I believe this is an opportunity for change, not only in our national policy, but also in our cultural and political atmospheres. This ideal may be too lofty, but if nobody pursues it, we will always be confined to reacting to challenges to current policies' (*Executive Yuan of the Republic of China* Press Release, 19 February 2013).

Premier Jiang Yi-huah holds a PhD in Political Science from Yale University and before taking government office, was a Professor at the National Taiwan University where he was known to be strict and also caring about his students. One of his academic specializations is the thought of Hannah Arendt. His admirers say he exemplifies Confucian virtues such as modesty, propriety, sincerity, justice, respect and compassion towards others, and an attitude towards learning which includes giving room for the opinions and perspectives of others. His statement above reflects the thinking of a contemporary scholar-official steeped in the Confucian tradition (he learned the Confucian classics from a Master when he was a student) as well as in the Western democratic tradition, striving to integrate and practice what he has learned from both. This example shows us that the thinking of Confucius can inspire and be publicly relevant today.

The appreciation of its relevance is not limited to scholars and government officials, however. Indeed, the ideas of Confucius pervade the daily lives of ordinary citizens. On the same day as I write this foreword (14 March 2013), there is an online news video report from the *China Times* in Taiwan of some erroneous quotations of the *Analects* displayed in a Confucian temple, with angry parents openly complaining that their children cannot be properly educated given that the errors are misleading and distort Confucius' teachings.

In mainland China, the popular author Yu Dan's *Insights on the Analects* sold more than three million copies within four months after its publication in November 2006. It seems that Confucius has been undergoing a popular revival and this is perhaps indicative of the need to fill a spiritual vacuum amidst the almost overnight transformation of China from a socialist to a capitalist society in the last few decades (C. C. Ni, 'China turns to Confucius, with a modern twist', *Los Angeles Times,* 7 May 2007, www.latimes.com).

In *Confucius*, Charlene Tan focuses on the educational import and contemporary relevance to education of Confucius' teachings, discussing the text which best represents his thought, the *Analects*. Noting the many distorting appropriations of Confucius, including those of the management gurus, she carefully puts the *Analects* back into the proper social, moral and educational contexts and lucidly explains the interlocking concepts involved in Confucius' philosophy.

Writing as an educationist and as a philosopher of education, Professor Tan relates her explanation of Confucius' philosophy to issues about educational philosophy and value systems. For instance, she dispels the common idea that Confucius is a pedantic moralizer. The 'Confucianism' as expounded by its founder is not just about rote learning and top-down methods of instruction, nor is it just about the teaching and learning of 'key competencies'. Confucius' educational philosophy integrates the aesthetic, moral and spiritual aspects of the individual. Instead of just the focus on competencies, he offers a rich educational policy based on 'spiritual literacy' and character development.

What impresses me most about this book is its depth of scholarship. In articulating the life of Confucius, his thinking as a whole, and the concepts of his philosophy in particular, Charlene Tan provides detailed readings of the *Analects* and supplements these with readings from other traditional texts where necessary. While endorsing Confucius' philosophy as a whole, she is also aware of its shortcomings. She critically engages the writings of other contemporary scholars and provides cogent and original interpretations, combining these with the pertinent use of empirical findings in the educational field.

Charlene Tan expertly combines sound educational philosophy with original and illuminating scholarship on Confucianism. This is a fine piece of work and brings to mind the carved jade mentioned in the second half of the conversation between Confucius and his disciple Zigong referred to above. After Confucius modifies or 'innovates' upon his saying, Zigong cites a couple of lines from the *Book of Poetry* (or the *Odes*):

> Like bone cut, like horn polished,
> Like jade carved, like stone ground.
> 'Is not what you have said a case in point?'

The Master said, 'Si (Zigong's informal name), only with (someone) like you can one discuss the *Odes*. Tell such a (person) something and he can see its relevance to what he has not been told' (D. C. Lau, Trans.,

Confucius – The Analects. The original Chinese is gender-neutral. I have replaced 'a man' with 'person' and 'someone').

Kim-chong Chong
Division of Humanities
The Hong Kong University of
Science and Technology

Acknowledgements

My sentiments for this section are summed up by these words of Confucius: 'To love is better than just to know, and to find joy is better than just to love' (*Analects*, 6.20). Indeed, I've obtained not just precious knowledge of Confucius' work in the course of writing this book, but also love and joy because of the kind assistance I have received from the following persons.

First, I thank Associate Professor Lee Ong Kim and Associate Professor Ng Pak Tee of the National Institute of Education for approving my no-pay leave and research grant so that I can work full-time on this book. I also thank Professor Jeu-Jenq Yuann of the Department of Philosophy, National Taiwan University, as well as Professor Zheng Yongnian and Mr Lye Liang Fook of the East Asian Institute, National University of Singapore, for supporting this research through my fellowships at their institutions in 2012.

I am very grateful to Professor Kim-chong Chong. A Confucian scholar, he has given me valuable feedback on my drafts and supported my academic pursuit for over 20 years. My husband and I are particularly grateful to him and his wife, Dr Kathy Ku, for graciously hosting us when we visited Taiwan in 2012, especially accompanying us to the Confucius temple in Tainan. Special thanks also go to Richard Bailey, Rosie Pattinson, Claire Cooper and other staff at Bloomsbury, as well as Srikanth Srinivasan of Newgen Knowledge Works for their editorial support. I also thank my good friend Bee Leng for sacrificially assisting me with the research and translation, Elizabeth for her dedicated and expert proofreading despite her busy schedule, and Kim, Karen, Lucille, Connie and Sharon for their words of encouragement.

Finally, my deep gratitude goes to my parents who brought me up in the best of Confucian tradition; I learn from and see in them the bond of family, the value of education, and the virtues of love, sacrifice and hard work. I also thank my loving husband Lim Pin for being my Valley of Achor. All the persons mentioned are not in any way responsible for any mistakes found in this book, which are wholly mine.

Soli Deo Gloria
Charlene Hwee Phio Tan (陳惠萍)
Singapore
December 2012

Introduction

Figure 1.1 A Confucius temple in Taiwan

The world celebrated Confucius' 2,563rd birthday anniversary on 28 September 2012. Yes, Confucius has been around *that long*. Since Confucius' demise in the fifth century BCE, much has been written about his life, work and influence. Confucius temples (such as the one shown in Figure 1.1) and Confucius institutes have been established all over the world to preserve his teachings. An internet search on 'Confucius' and 'Confucianism' easily yields 15 million hits. There are also thousands of books, book chapters and articles published on Confucius, his followers and their teachings, in both English and Chinese. The EBSCO database lists over 7,000 articles on Confucius and Confucianism while the

Chinese database *Wanfang Data* (万方数据 *Wanfang shuju*) records over 17,000 articles on the same keywords.[1]

So do we need another book on Confucius?

My answer to the above question is 'yes'. To explain my position, I would like to highlight three trends in the current literature on Confucius, Confucius' education and Confucian education.

Confucius as an ancient master?

The first trend is a somewhat pejorative view of Confucian education. Confucius' views on education, often summarily reduced to 'Confucian education', are perceived as 'bad' teaching that is out of touch with the twenty-first century. Such an education is interpreted variously to be about textual transmission, rote learning, memorization without understanding, didactic teaching, suppression of individuality, and neglect of critical thinking, creativity and other forms of higher-order thinking.

For example, Aoki (2008) asserts that '[i]n contrast to Western education in which students are encouraged to engage in debate, Confucian education tends to emphasize rote learning and memorization … finding a good teacher and imitating his words and deeds' (p. 35). Han and Scull (2010), commenting on 'Confucian Heritage Cultures' (Asian societies that are apparently influenced by Confucian culture), claim that these societies share the following key philosophical tenets and schooling practices (p. 603) (also see Aguinis & Roth, 2005; Dahlin & Watkins, 2000; Hui, 2005; Kim, 2005a, 2005b; Wong, 2001):

- Transmission of knowledge via teacher-centredness;
- Uncommon usage of the interactive process;
- Top-down method;
- Bias towards obedience: students do not ask questions and interrupt the flow of instruction; they often talk only when asked;
- Rote memorization; and
- More hours of homework and cram schools after school.

Somehow, a prevalent perception today is that Confucius' teachings on education are undesirable and even detrimental to students' learning and growth. Confucius is often portrayed as a bookish, no-nonsense and stoic *shifu* (师傅 master) trapped in the milieu of ancient China. Is the above a fair and accurate description of Confucius and his teachings? A textual study of the *Analects* (论语 *Lunyu*) – a compilation of the sayings and conduct of Confucius – will reveal the opposite, as I shall show later.

Confucius as a moral teacher?

A second trend in the current literature, in contrast to the first trend, highlights the positive aspects of Confucius' teachings. This trend does not necessarily refute the general perception that Confucius' teachings are pedagogically outdated; what it does instead is to stress that Confucius' *moral* or *ethical* teachings are still relevant today.[2] By limiting Confucius' contribution to the moral/ethical arena, this trend draws our attention to Confucius as a great moral teacher. For example, Starr (1930) claims that Confucius 'was primarily a teacher of ethics' (p. 7, as cited in Radcliffe, 1989, p. 219). Huang (2011) posits that 'the education that Confucius had in mind is primarily *moral* education, as his goal was to help his students to become virtuous persons' (p. 141, italics in the original). Likewise, Li (2003) asserts that the 'concern of Confucius was not academic, not mind oriented, but moral in nature' and that 'the Confucian model is about moral striving' (pp. 146–7).

The tendency to classify Confucius' teachings as moral teachings is also reflected in the proliferation of popular books, comics and even television shows, where writers and presenters expound 'Confucius' wisdom' to the masses (e.g. see Fu, 2002; Fu, Guo & Kong, 2008; Yu, 2007, 2008; Wang et al., 2010; Fukuda, 2012 Fu, 2010; Watanabe, 2011; Chang, 2012; Lin et al., 2012). Among the more well-known personalities are Fu Peirong (傅佩榮) from the National Taiwan University and Yu Dan (于丹) from the Beijing Normal University.[3]

While I agree that Confucius is concerned with ethical issues, seeing as he has argued for a specific ethical perspective, I do not think that Confucius is *only* interested in morality and moral education. A problem with limiting Confucius' teachings to the moral dimension is that it presents a truncated version of Confucius' education. It is important to acknowledge that Confucius' ethical perspective is not merely moral but is intricately linked to spiritual and aesthetic considerations. Rather than reducing his teachings to 'moral' or 'ethical' dimensions, Confucius' philosophy is more accurately described as 'spiritual-ethical-aesthetic', as I shall explain in subsequent chapters.[4] I am also reluctant to use the term 'moral education' for Confucius' teachings as such a term may be narrowly understood to be a stand-alone subject taught in many modern schools, instead of a holistic approach to values inculcation that is infused into the total curriculum.

Confucius as a teaching and management guru?

The third trend, like the second trend, underscores the positive aspects of Confucius' teachings. Unlike the first trend, the third trend rejects the assumption that Confucius' educational thought is obsolete and deleterious, recognizing that there is much we can learn from Confucius in education, management and other fields. This trend delineates the good teaching methods, effective leadership and exemplary management styles allegedly found in Confucius' teachings. However, this approach tends to reduce Confucius' teachings largely to skills, strategies and techniques for teachers, managers and leaders. In short, Confucius is marketed as a teaching or management guru.

An example is an article by Low (2010) where he identifies the 'successful teaching ways' of Confucius. These include: 'revise, review and be reflective', 'be aware of the common errors in educating students', 'deliver and teach according to the needs of the students', 'prevent bad habits before they arise', 'understand motivations to learn and be self-motivating', 'ensure timeliness, reveal relevant examples and tell stories or show visuals at appropriate time', 'check orderliness', and 'generate stimulation', and 'use the right side of the brain too!'. Another writer Cummins (1983) concurs that Confucius 'conceptualised many psychological principles, such as habit, modeling, inquiry, peer influence, individual differences, readiness, sequencing, intuition, and performance-based education' (p. 60).

Self-help books in Chinese on Confucius' educational thought have also hit the bookshelves, with titles such as *Learn to be a Teacher like Confucius* (跟孔子学当老师 *Gen Kongzi xuedang laoshi*) (Zhou, 2008), *Learn to Have the Wisdom of a Teacher like Confucius*

(学孔子当老师的智慧 *Xue Kongzi dang laoshi de zhihui*) (Gao, 2011) and *Dear Teacher Confucius* (亲爱的孔子老师 *Qinai de Kongzi laoshi*) (Wu, 2010).

Besides books, there are also other publications applying Confucius' teachings to education in the context of a knowledge-based economy and globalization. Examples include Confucius' teachings as applied to modern education (Wang, 2006), action research (Elliott & Tsai, 2008), lifelong learning (Sun, 2008; Kyung, 2009; Bai, 2011), modern vocational education (Chen & Wang, 2011), education for talented performance (Wu, 2006), and teacher quality needed for the modern world (Peng, 2010). Moving in tandem with the literature on education are publications relating Confucius' teachings to the fields of management and leadership, with the aim of producing successful leaders, managers and companies (e.g. Bi, Ehrich & Ehrich, 2012; Chan, 2008; Fernandez, 2004; Ip, 2009; Liu, 2010; Romar, 2002, 2004; Wang & Hu, 2010; Woods & Lamond, 2011).

Another interesting phenomenon is the mushrooming of articles written by academics from China who attempt to use Confucius' teachings to justify China's current educational reforms. These educational reforms are implemented under the banner of 'quality-oriented education' (素質教育 *suzhi jiaoyu*) that emphasizes a shift from textual transmission, didactic teaching, rote learning and memorization to student-centred teaching, higher-order thinking and real-life application (for a discussion of curriculum reforms in Shanghai, see Tan, 2011, 2012a, 2013). In supporting these reforms in China, many Chinese academics turn to Confucius' exhortations to 'teach without discrimination' (有教无类 *youjiao wulei*, literally 'teach without category'), practise 'customized teaching' (因材施教 *yincai shijiao*, literally 'teach according to aptitude') and other 'modern' aspects of Confucius' teachings (e.g. Chen & Huang, 2005; Li, 2010; Liu, 2011; Ping, 2011; Zhang, 2007; Zhou, 2005. There are hundreds of such articles in the *Wanfang Data* database).[5]

I agree with Low (2010), Cummins (1983) and others that Confucius was indeed progressive in advocating the aforementioned 'successful teaching ways', 'psychological principles' and leadership principles. These are generally sound advice and I am all for applying the wisdom of Confucius (as well as other ancient philosophers such as Socrates and Aristotle) to contemporary issues and challenges. Accordingly, I shall elaborate on the relevance of Confucius' work in Part 3 of this book.

That said, my concern is the tendency (consciously or unconsciously) for educators and readers to oversimplify or worse, misrepresent Confucius' teachings. A danger is to take particular sayings and actions of Confucius out of context, thus robbing them of their original philosophical, spiritual or metaphysical underpinnings. In the above-cited literature highlighting the contemporary relevance of Confucius' educational thought, a number of questions have been ignored or under-explored. For example, why does Confucius advocate using 'the right side of the brain too'? Is the dictum to 'revise, review and be reflective' meant only for academic achievement? What is the philosophical significance of modelling and cultivating habit? What does it mean to have the 'wisdom' of Confucius? And perhaps the most fundamental question of all: what is the point of education, according to Confucius?

Let me further elaborate on the danger of oversimplifying Confucius' teachings using his concept of *li* – usually translated as 'ritual' or 'propriety' (I shall postpone an exposition of this term to Part 2). Romar, in discussing the views of Peter F. Drucker (the latter widely acknowledged as the founder of modern American management), maintains:

> Ritual (*li*) is the mechanism that permits the roles to be performed correctly because ritual is a process that allows for a collective activity to be successfully concluded. Confucians view social success through the carrying out of interdependent relationships in a prescribed manner. It requires the participants both to execute their part correctly and to apply the proper attitudes while doing so (Graham, 1989, p. 18). Therefore, a ritual can be viewed as a process of social interaction designed to achieve a collective good. Drucker easily updated the Confucian use of ritual to apply to the modern organisation with its specialised tasks organised into specialised functions. The success of the organisation is based upon each individual fulfilling their role and tasks in a prescribed way and with an attitude that will be mutually beneficial to both those they relate to immediately and the entire organisation as well. (p. 205)[6]

We can see from the above that *li* is regarded primarily as a mechanism and process of social interaction designed to achieve a collective good. The 'collective good', in this case, is the success of a profit-making company. In my view, however, this understanding of *li* appears reductionist and ignores the philosophical foundation of and original context for *li*. Much more needs to be said about what Confucius means by *li* as 'the mechanism that permits the roles to be performed correctly', 'interdependent relationships' and 'collective good' *beyond* the economic considerations of a profit-making company. Bemoaning the dilution of modern adaptations of Confucius' teachings, Louie (2011) maintains that 'because Confucius has in the last sixty years come to stand for practically *anything*, it has enabled academics and politicians to advance a set of "core Confucian values" for the contemporary world that is at best highly conservative and at worst schizophrenic' (p. 80, also see Dirlik, 1995).

Overall, we can observe, from the three trends on Confucius' teachings, a tendency to select and highlight aspects of his teachings without adequately considering their deeper philosophical underpinnings.[7] There is therefore a need to revisit and re-examine Confucius' teachings to get a more complete picture of his work before we can draw out its relevance for the twenty-first century.

Research approach, method and outline of the book

At the outset, it is necessary to make two clarifications about the scope of this book. First, this book focuses on Confucius and not Confucianism as a whole. The latter is a broad and all-encompassing concept that includes not just the ideas of Confucius but also those of his followers such as Mencius (孟子) and Xunzi (荀子), the Neo-Confucians, policymakers in East Asian societies, and contemporary Confucian scholars and educators.[8] This book discusses the work of Confucius as presented in the *Analects* (论语 *Lunyu*), with a focus on the *educational implications* of his work. This means that this book does not discuss at length Confucius' political thought (such as his views on human rights and democracy), metaphysical views (such as his concepts of human nature and heaven) etc. While I shall provide the intellectual biography of

Confucius, it is necessarily brief, with the larger portion of the book focusing on his work and its relevance for twenty-first century education. Readers are encouraged to peruse the extensive body of literature on a detailed biography and other teachings of Confucius and Confucianism.[9]

The second clarification concerns the definition of 'Confucius' education'. In line with the distinction between Confucius and Confucianism, I distinguish 'Confucius' education' from 'Confucian education'. The former refers specifically to Confucius' educational thought as presented in the *Analects*, while the latter refers to all forms and aspects of education that are associated with Confucianism as an ideology and system.

As mentioned, this book expounds Confucius' work as presented in the *Analects*. Literally means 'compiled sayings', the *Analects* is a collection of the sayings and conduct of Confucius and his disciples.[10] The process of collating Confucius' teachings started shortly after his death; his sayings were recorded in little 'books', which were subsequently collated to make up what we know today as the *Analects* (Ames & Rosemont, 1998). As the *Analects* was compiled a few centuries after Confucius' death, it is not surprising that there have been controversies over its authenticity.

For example, Brooks and Brooks (1998) argue that the chapters of the *Analects* represent discrete strata with later interpolations, and that the work was composed over a much longer period of time than has been generally accepted. They assert that the *Analects* 'contain[s] only a core of sayings by the historical Confucius, to which were added layers of attributed sayings and conversations invented by his successors to update their heritage, and to address the new needs of changing times' (p. vii). In response to Brooks and Brooks' claim, Slingerland (2001) counters,

> I will say that I find their position to be extremely speculative. Though the various strata no doubt represent different time periods and somewhat different concerns, they display enough consistency in terminological use and philosophical and religious conceptualisation to allow us to treat the text as a genuine representation of the state of the 'School of Confucius' before the innovations of Mencius and Xunzi. The probable later date of last chapters in the *Analects* (esp.

chaps. 15–20) should be kept in mind throughout the discussion that follows, but this should not affect the substance of the arguments made. (p. 98, also see Slingerland, 2000)

Arguing along the same line is Shun (1993) who posits that '[u]ntil there is philological evidence for the inauthenticity of certain passages, it does not seem misguided to take the text as a whole, and to attempt to find an interpretation of Confucius' conception . . . which can make sense of all the relevant passages' (p. 459). Another Confucian scholar Li (2007) adds that 'while we cannot rule out the possibility of original textual inconsistency we should at least try to read the text in a coherent manner, on the basis of the principle of charity if on nothing else' (p. 324).

I share the views of Slingerland (2001), Shun (1993) and Li (2007) that we should assume that all the chapters in the *Analects* represent Confucius' teachings, that all the chapters form one complete text, and that we can obtain a generally coherent reading from the chapters. In any case, my focus is not on Confucius as a historical figure; nor am I using the *Analects* as a source to authenticate the historicity of Confucius. Rather, I am interested in studying Confucius as a *philosophical* figure whose sayings attributed to him were passed down to us in the *Analects*. Here, I agree with Li (2007) that 'if such attempts [to read the text in a coherent manner] cannot be taken as a reduction to Confucius' own thought, they at least can be seen as reconstructions that may help us understand Confucianism' (p. 324).

The *Analects* is not an easy book to translate. As noted by Zhu (2009, p. 34), it is written in classical or literary Chinese (文言文 *wenyan wen*) where there are often missing contents, contexts, syntactic functions (subjects, objects, predicates, modifiers, complements, etc.) and word classes (verbs, prepositions, pronouns, articles, conjunctions, etc.). The brevity and compactness of every character, coupled with the use of rich idioms and aphorisms, make understanding and translating the book challenging. Compounding the challenge is the fact that the *Analects* is not a systematic treatise on Confucius' thought, but a collection of the conversations between Confucius and his disciples in a variety of real-life situations. Hence, in interpreting the book, we need to consider variables such as the person(s) involved, the specific context, the issue at hand etc., all of which affect Confucius' replies and reactions. (I shall give examples of such instances in subsequent chapters.)

All the translations in the *Analects* from Chinese into English were done by me, unless otherwise stated. In my translation, I have tried to preserve the original meaning and word pattern as much as possible. Any additions to the translation for the purpose of clarification are marked by square brackets. All the English translations are preceded by the original Chinese passages for easy reference. I have consulted, in different ways and to varying degrees, a number of translated works and commentaries of the *Analects* in both Chinese and English. The primary translated works in Chinese that I consulted are Yang (1980) (reproduced in Liu & Yang, 2009), Sun (1993), Yang (2010) and Fu (2011a); those in English are Lau (1979) (reproduced in Liu & Yang, 2009), Ames and Rosemont (1998) and Slingerland (2003). All subsequent references to these translators refer to the above-mentioned texts, unless otherwise stated. Besides consulting the above texts, I have also consulted, to a lesser extent, other translated works, as will be evident in subsequent discussions.

A challenge I face in my translation concerns the use of gender-specific references. Given that the classical script in the *Analects* is gender-neutral, I have tried to use gender-neutral pronouns in my translations where possible, except in instances where doing so would lead to awkward phrasing.[11] In such cases, I usually opted for the male pronoun to ensure a smooth and consistent reading of the *Analects*. However, I have used both male and female pronouns in my discussion of the *Analects*. All the non-English words are italicized, and I have used the *pinyin* (拼音) system of transliteration for Chinese characters, except in cases of citations from secondary sources where the original system of transliteration is preserved.

This book is meant primarily for those with no background knowledge of Confucius' teachings and the Chinese language. To make the reading clear and accessible, I have avoided adding to the main text of this book the detailed and advanced discussions and debates among Confucian scholars on various aspects of Confucius' work. However, being aware of the value of these discussions and debates, I have included them in the notes, wherever applicable, for interested readers. Following Yao (2000), I have adopted both the insider and outsider perspectives in writing this book: an insider perspective as an ethnic Chinese who has been socialized into a Confucian culture, and an outsider perspective as a philosopher and educator who studies and teaches Confucius' work. I do not claim that this book offers a definitive explanation of the *Analects*, nor do I assume that my interpretation of it will be uncontroversial. My intention is to offer modern readers a systematic exposition of the educational thought and contemporary relevance of Confucius through a textual study of the *Analects*. In doing so, I hope to continue the long tradition of understanding, discussing and valuing the wisdom from the ancient past.

This book is divided into three main parts. Part 1 focuses on the intellectual biography of Confucius where I outline his life, personality and influence. Part 2 forms the bulk of the book where I expound Confucius' key concepts. Part 3 examines the relevance of Confucius' work for education in the twenty-first century.

Notes

1 Throughout the chapters, I shall use Chinese in its traditional form (繁体字 *fantizi*) rather than in its simplified form (简体字 *jiantizi*) as the former is more aligned with the formal classical style (文言文 *wenyanwen*) found in the *Analects*.
2 I have used 'moral' and 'ethical' interchangeably in this section based on the understanding that the terms 'ethics' and 'morality' originally refer to the same thing. The word 'ethics' is a transliteration of the Greek word *ethikos*, while the word 'morality' is from the Latin word *moralis*, which is the Latin translation of *ethikos* (Yu, 1998, p. 342). However, for the rest of the book, I shall use the word 'ethical' instead of 'moral' as far as possible. This is because the word 'moral' has, through the passage of time, obtained certain connotations in Western moral philosophy that may be incompatible with ancient Chinese thought. This has been pointed out by a number of Confucian scholars. For instance, Ames and Rosemont (1998) observe that 'the term "morality" in contemporary English, and particularly in post-Kantian ethics, is linked intimately with a number of other terms: "freedom" "liberty," "choice," "ought," "individual," "reason," "autonomy," "dilemma," "objective," "subjective." *None* of these English terms has a close analogue in classical Chinese' (pp. 53–4, italics in the original). Ivanhoe (2007) similarly maintains that 'morality', unlike ethics, implies that the self is a rational, free and autonomous agent of choice (p. 33). Lai (1995) concurs that 'there is no equivalent of the term "moral" in classical Chinese. The definition of abstract and metaphysical concepts without simultaneously considering their practical manifestations is nonexistent in the classical Confucian tradition' (p. 249).
3 Interestingly, Yu Dan has been criticized by academics such as Daniel Bell for allegedly presenting a highly selective, depoliticized and even distorted version of Confucius' teachings (Fan, 2007; Bell, 2008a). I agree with Bell's general point that Yu Dan has left out the political teachings of Confucius but I disagree with some of Bell's critiques of Yu Dan's interpretation of Confucius, in particular the issue of whether anyone can be a *junzi*. I shall postpone this discussion to the concluding chapter.
4 Lai (1995) makes the same point when she observes that it 'seriously narrows the Confucian enterprise to think of it merely as a moral philosophy and consequently to characterise it according to the categories appropriate only to moral philosophy in the Western philosophical tradition' (p. 254).

5 Louie (1984) avers that 'because the Chinese leadership now feels the necessity to train as quickly as possible a new generation of scientists and technicians to modernise the country, almost all articles on Confucian education now try to prove that he had stressed developing the individual talents of the students' (p. 34).
6 I am not claiming that Drucker will agree with Romar's interpretation of him (Drucker). My concern is not about Drucker's views of Confucianism per se, but about the propensity of writers to borrow and adapt Confucius' ideas in the areas of management and leadership.
7 I am not asserting that *every* writer who discusses Confucius' educational thought has ignored its philosophical underpinnings. Authors who have premised their discussion of Confucius' concepts on a philosophical appreciation of his ideas include Hall and Ames (1987), Kim (2003) and Elliot and Tsai (2008).
8 Different writers have adopted different terms to describe different strands of Confucianism. For example, Fukuyama (1995a) and Tu (1998) distinguish between *political* Confucianism and *philosophical* Confucianism. The former refers to the attempts of various groups to politicize Confucian ethical values in the service of other non-ethical purposes, while the latter refers to the Confucian intent to infuse politics with morality through personal cultivation of the self (Tu, 1984). Yao (1999), on the other hand, suggests that 'traditional Confucianism is consciously divided into two parts, "Confucianism as the source of moral values" and "Confucianism as the structure of a traditional society", which correspond, to some extent, to Ninian Smart's distinction between "doctrinal Confucianism" and "religious Confucianism" (Smart, 1989, p. 104), and to Modern New Confucians' distinction between "the Confucian tradition" or "idealistic and cultural Confucianism," and "the Confucian China" or "dynamic and social Confucianism" (Li, 1994, pp. 340–345)' (p. 31).
9 For useful readings on Confucius' biography, see Creel (1949); Dawson (1982); Clements (2004); Chin (2007); Lin (2009); Nylan and Wilson (2010); and Luo (2011). For a useful introduction to the teachings and evolution of Confucianism, see Yao (2000); Du (2008); and Rainey (2010). On various aspects of Confucius' philosophy and Confucianism published in Chinese, see Wang, Zeng and Yang (1982); Tang (1997); Shandongsheng ruxue yanjiu jidi (山东省儒学研究基地) and Qufu shifan daxue kongzi wenhua xueyuan (曲阜师范大学孔子文化学院) (2001); Zhang and Wang (2004); Tan (2006); Hu et al. (2008); Lin (2009); and Chen (2011). On various aspects of Confucius' philosophy and Confucianism published in English, see Slote and De Vos (1998); Yao (2000); Van Norden (2002); Bell (2008b); Rainey (2010); and Yu, Tao and Ivanhoe (2010).
10 Brooks and Brooks (1998) argue for the use of the term 'protégé' instead of 'disciple' as they claim that the latter 'implies a relationship which arose

only later, as the Confucian school became more organised' (p. 11). I shall use the terms 'disciple', 'protégé' and 'student' interchangeably to refer to a follower of Confucius, with no suggestion of Confucianism as an organized school during Confucius' time.

11 Although the classical script in the *Analects* is gender-neutral, it is arguable that Confucius, as a man of his time, had a male audience, disciple or ruler in mind. Women during his time were generally denied the opportunity to receive an education, hold official appointments, seek employment and interact freely with men outside their family circles. A debate among scholars and educators is whether (and if so, the extent to which) Confucius' teachings apply to women. I shall revisit this topic in the last chapter.

Part 1
Intellectual Biography

Chapter 1
Confucius' Life, Personality and Influence

Much has been written about the life of Confucius. There are even films produced on his life, the latest being a 2010 movie starring Hongkong celebrity Chow Yun-fat.[1] The numerous claims about the life of Confucius range from what is plausible, such as Confucius having up to 3,000 disciples; to what is dubious, such as Confucius receiving instruction from Laozi (老子) who is the founder of Daoism (道教); and what is ridiculous, such as Confucius being abandoned as an infant and nursed by a tiger (Luo, 2011). Csikszentmihalyi (2002) points out how Confucius had been wildly eulogized by the time of the Han dynasty (206 BCE–220 AD):

> Confucius was thought to have possessed superhuman abilities, have displayed visible marks placed by Heaven that proved his destiny to rule as king, have transmitted esoteric teachings and prophecies to his disciples, and have been sanguine about serving the ghosts and spirits. Because of these qualities, Confucius was seen and treated increasingly as a divinity. (p. 135)

This section introduces readers to a brief background of the life, personality and influence of Confucius. The primary traditional sources on Confucius' life are the *Analects*, *Zuo Commentary* (左傳 *Zuozhuan*), *Records of the Historian* (史記 *Shiji*) and *The School Sayings of Confucius* (孔子家語 *Kongzi jiayu*). I have already introduced the *Analects* in the previous chapter. Here, I shall briefly discuss the other three sources in chronological order.

First, the *Zuo Commentary* chronicles the history of the Spring and Autumn period (c. 722–468 BCE). It provides useful historical, social and cultural information on life during Confucius' time. (To read this book in Chinese, see Yang, 1990; for the translated version in English, see Legge,

1960.) The sayings of Confucius were also recorded in *The School Sayings of Confucius,* a book that was written by Wang Su during the Wei period (220–265 BCE). The authenticity of the book, however, was questioned by scholars as early as in the Song dynasty (960–1276 CE). It is believed that the book contains those sections that were rejected as not reliable enough to be included in the *Analects* (Ji, 2010, p. 8). (To read this book in Chinese, see Ji, 2010; Wang & Wang, 2011; for the translated version of sections of the book in English, see Kramers, 1950.) Finally, the *Records of the Historian* was written by court historian Sima Qian (c. 145 BCE–86 BCE) during the Han dynasty. Besides containing the history of ancient China, the book also includes a section on the biography of Confucius. Given that it was written many centuries after the death of Confucius, some scholars have doubted its historical accuracy. (To read this book in Chinese, see Sima Qian, 2010; for the translated version in English as well as a good discussion of the book's historical reliability, see Watson, 1958.)

I have consulted the relevant sections of the *Analects, Zuo Commentary, Records of the Historian* and *The School Sayings of Confucius* in preparing this chapter on the intellectual biography of Confucius. But I decided not to rely much on the last three sources mentioned above due to reasonable doubts over their accuracy and authenticity on Confucius' life, coupled with a lack of any objective means to adjudicate the various claims about Confucius. What I have done instead is to incorporate selected information from the above-mentioned references where applicable but focus primarily on the *Analects* as it is regarded as the most reliable among the sources. This means that my write-up of Confucius' biography is necessarily brief. But the brevity will not hinder us from acquiring a sufficient understanding of Confucius' life and personality, so as to appreciate his work later.

Confucius' life

The name 'Confucius' was coined by Jesuit missionaries who went to China in the sixteenth century. 'Confucius' is a Latinized version of *Kong Fuzi* (孔夫子) that means 'Kong Master'. Chinese today call Confucius *Kong Fuzi* or *Kongzi* (孔子) for short; he was simply addressed as

Fuzi (夫子 Master) in the *Analects*. His real name is *Kongqiu* (孔丘) where 'Kong' is his family name and 'Qiu' is his given name. He is also known as *Zhongni* (仲尼) that is his alternative Chinese name (also known as 'Chinese style name') given to adults in ancient China.

Confucius (c. 551–479 BCE) came from the Lu state that is near Qufu of Shandong province in China today. It is probable that Confucius belonged to the *shi* (士) class – a group of learned people sandwiched between the aristocrats and the common people who sought to be employed as court officials and teachers. His father was a military officer in the Lu state and died when Confucius was about 3 years old, leaving Confucius to the sole care of his mother. We are told in the *Analects* that Confucius grew up poor and learned many menial skills at a tender age (9.6) to support the family. Huang (2011) claims that 'Confucius also knows martial arts, he can run fast enough to catch a rabbit, he is so strong that he can raise the city gate with his hands and he can fish, hunt, raise cows and horses, do accounting, and organise funerals (also see Cai, 1982, p. 6; Kuang, 1990, p. 307)' (p. 149). The *Records of the Historian* informs us that Confucius was interested in *li* (often translated as rites or ritual propriety but more accurately understood as normative human behaviours; I shall elaborate on this in the next chapter) from a young age as he often played games using various ritual vessels.

Confucius was married but not much is known about his wife. But we know from the *Analects* that he had at least one son (17.10) and one daughter (5.1) (all subsequent references of passages are taken from the *Analects*, unless otherwise stated). The Spring and Autumn Period (c. 722–468 BCE) that Confucius grew up in, was a period rife with political and social turmoil, with rulers of different states vying for power and control. Appalled by the political and social chaos in his time, Confucius hoped to restore order and harmony by spreading his teachings and serving in the government. He desired to replace the prevailing harsh rule by law and punishment with rule by virtue (2.3), through reviving the practices of the sage-kings from the Zhou dynasty (3.14, 8.20, 8.21, 9.5). Confucius was not only well-versed in scholarship; the *Records of the Historian* claims that he taught his disciple Ranyou military skills that enabled the latter to lead the army of the state of Lu to defeat the army from the state of Qi.

At about the age of 50, he was appointed the Minister of Public Works and later the Minister of Crime in the state of Lu but he left his position a few years later. According to the *Records of the Historian*, Confucius was disappointed that the court officials in the state of Lu did not adhere to proper behaviour and that the Duke had neglected his state duties. Aware that he could not make much headway serving in the court of Lu, Confucius resigned himself to travelling to various neighbouring states such as Chen (5.22), Qi (7.14) and Wei (7.15) where he repeatedly failed to assume official position in court. The *Records of the Historian* claims that he and his disciples were welcome in the state of Wei by Duke Ling but they left after ten months when the Duke neglected state affairs because of his old age.

Confucius' inability to carve out a successful career as a minister is noted in the *Analects*, where someone asked why Confucius did not participate in government (2.21), and another person commented that Confucius did not hold an official position (3.24). On Confucius' part, he was also selective about serving in a state; for example, he chose not to take up an official position in the state of Wei (7.15), probably due to the unstable political developments there. Schiller (2011, pp. 504–6) points out that there was a power struggle in the state of Wei during that period among Duchess Nanzi (who was a concubine of Duke Ling), Prince Kuai-kui (who was the son of the Duke) and Duke Chu (who was the Duke's son), culminating in the victory of Duke Chu.

The *Analects* offers us interesting snippets of Confucius' encounters and experiences in the various states. He visited the state of Qi, where he was enthralled by the *shao* music played by a royal musician (7.14). He also went to the state of Wei, where he met the beautiful and infamous Nanzi who was the concubine of the Duke Ling (6.28). While travelling from the state of Wei to the state of Chen, Confucius was captured by the people of Kuang due to a case of mistaken identity (9.5). His life was again endangered in the state of Song when Huan Tui, the military minister of Song, sought to kill him (7.23). We also know that Confucius experienced hardships and setbacks in life, such as suffering from a serious illnesses (9.12) and coping with the death of his son Boyu (11.8) and his favourite disciple Yanhui (11.8, 11.10).

Throughout his travelling, Confucius was accompanied by a loyal band of disciples who served and protected him while learning from him. After spending 14 years travelling from state to state, he returned to the state of Lu at around 484 BCE in his late sixties where he spent his remaining years teaching. It was during that period that Confucius revised the *Ya* and *Song*, sections in the *Book of Songs* (詩 *Shi*, also known as the *Book of Odes*), where he probably set the poetry to fit the music. Besides the *Book of Songs*, it is also plausible that he edited other classical texts such as the *Book of Documents* (書 *Shu*, also known as the *Book of History*) and the *Spring and Autumn Annals* (春秋 *Chunqiu*). He passed away at the age of 72, and his disciples mourned his passing.

Confucius' personality

Confucius was described in the *Analects* as gentle yet serious, awe-inspiring yet not severe, respectful yet at ease (7.38). Rather than being stoic and restrained, Confucius was an expressive man who was unafraid to show his emotions. That was evident especially in his overwhelming grief over the death of his favourite disciple, Yanhui (11.9, 11.10, also see 6.10 for his reaction towards another disciple).[2] Eschewing dogmatism and self-centredness (9.4), he came across as amiable, kind, respectful, modest and obliging (1.10). His kindness was noted in a number of instances as recorded in the *Analects*. For example, he offered to take care of the funeral arrangements of a friend who died without any surviving relatives (10.22), and was sensitive to assist a blind musician in his movements (15.42). On another occasion, when Confucius' household steward refused a payment of 900 measures of grain, Confucius persuaded him to accept the payment so that he could distribute the grain to needy people in the neighbourhood (6.5).

Confucius' compassion was also evident in his care and concern for his disciples. When his disciple Boniu became seriously ill, Confucius held the latter's hand and lamented why such a state had befallen him (6.10). The *Zuo Commentary* also records Confucius shedding tears over the death of Zichan, exclaiming that Zichan was a specimen of the love transmitted from the ancients. His modesty could be seen in his denial that he possessed wisdom (9.8), and had achieved the ideal of a *junzi* (君子 literally a 'gentleman') (7.33) or that of a sage (7.34). That he valued integrity was evident in an episode where he fell gravely ill. A disciple had arranged for some disciples to dress as official retainers to serve Confucius as if he was a lord. Although the disciple did this with the good intention to honour Confucius, he was chastised by Confucius who told him that one should not be pretentious and fool heaven (9.12).

Confucius was one who enjoyed simple pleasures and joys in life. For example, he talked about the joy gleaned from learning (1.1), from spending time with friends and disciples (1.1, 11.26) and from music (7.14, 7.32). He also enjoyed light-hearted moments with his disciples (e.g. 5.7, 17.4), where their relationship was marked by warmth, spontaneity and affection. Confucius encouraged questions from his students and even allowed them to disagree and correct him. For example, Confucius agreed with Ziyou's correction of one of his remarks (17.4). In another instance, upon learning that Zilu objected to his meeting a woman of ill repute, Confucius appeased him by swearing an oath of innocence, instead of chastising him for his insolence (6.28).[3]

He also expressed a strong interest in current affairs and did not shy away from correcting the political leaders of his generation (e.g. 3.1, 3.2, 3.6, 3.10, 5.18, 12.18). He expressed confidence that he was able to improve the sociopolitical conditions in any state within one year and deliver results within three years (13.10). Despite his political ambition, he did not believe that one could contribute to society only by assuming public office. When asked why he was not employed in government, he replied that being filial to one's parents and friendly to one's brothers were tantamount to participating in government (2.21). Describing his aspirations, he said that he wished to bring comfort to the old, inspire trust in his friends and cherish the young (5.26).

It is interesting to note that Confucius uttered and did certain things that were considered unconventional and even radical. For example, he gave his daughter in marriage to Gong-ye Chang despite knowing that the latter had a criminal record, on the basis that he (Gong-ye Chang) was innocent of the crime (5.1). Confucius was also not shy to ask many questions upon entering the Grand Ancestral Hall (3.15). Such behaviour was uncommon at that time and unbecoming of a teacher as it reflected his ignorance; this point was evident in the response of someone who remarked, 'Who said this son of a man from the Zou village understands *li* [禮 normative human behaviours]? On entering the

Grand Ancestral Hall he asks questions about everything.' To that, Confucius replied that asking questions itself was the right thing to do – a response that was so unconventional that it confounded many (I shall elaborate on this passage in the chapter on *li*).

A key concept noted by Confucius is heaven (天 *tian*). Confucius believed in the existence of heaven and ascribed anthropomorphic characteristics to it. He claimed that it was heaven that had given him virtue (7.23), preserved his life from danger (9.5) and understood him (14.35). Slingerland (2003) explains that 'heaven is viewed as the source of normativity in the universe, the all-powerful Being who, when pleased with proper ritual conduct, charges its representative on earth with the Mandate to rule, as well as the power of virtue that made realising the Mandate possible' (p. 239). Confucius' faith in heaven, however, did not extend to a corresponding belief in spirits, ghosts and superstitions. He was not interested to discuss the supernatural or the issue of life after death, advocating instead that we should keep a distance from ghosts and spirits (6.22, also see 7.21, 11.12).

In contrast to his reluctance to discuss and speculate on other-worldly matters such as religious and supernatural topics, Confucius had much to say about this-worldly concerns, especially normative behaviours, human relationships and education. He ingeniously borrowed the common terms of his times, particularly *li* (禮 rites or ritual propriety), *ren* (仁 humanity) and *junzi* (君子 gentleman), and assigned to them novel and rich interpretations and implications. I shall elaborate on these terms in subsequent chapters. Departing from tradition where the aristocrats were deemed to be superior to the common people, Confucius advocated judging a person based on one's ethical character rather than status, family background, or other exogenous factors. That was why Confucius praised Zhonggong for his virtue despite his humble family background (6.6). Related to his emphasis on one's ethical character was his reminder that we should focus on self-cultivation and not be too concerned with what others think of us (1.16). In the same vein, he cautioned his disciples against seeking personal gain, materialism and power at the expense of doing the right thing (4.5, 7.12, 7.16, 9.1).

In the area of education, Confucius was a model of learning and teaching. He proclaimed that he loved learning (5.28, 7.20), set his mind on learning at the age of 15 (2.4), and was keen to teach others (7.2).

Well-versed in ceremonial rituals and scrupulous about observing them (e.g. 3.12), he propagated living a life that was totally guided by *li* (normative human behaviours) (12.1). He also appreciated the arts and humanities especially poetry, claiming in the *Zuo Commentary* that words are essential for human beings to know their own thoughts, express themselves and advance in life. Highlighting a symbiotic relationship between learning and teaching, he taught that a teacher should constantly review and built on what he or she had learned (2.11).

Confucius was also known for being a pioneer in offering private education to the masses. That was significant as private education was available only to aristocrats at that time. Confucius revolutionalized education by stating that he taught without social discrimination (15.39), and that he was willing to accept anyone who was keen to learn (7.7, 7.8). Confucius taught his students four areas of learning: *Culture* (文 *wen*), *Conduct* (行 *xing*), *Dutifulness* (忠 *zhong*) and *Trustworthiness* (信 *xin*) (7.25). The learning of *Culture* involves the 'six arts' (六藝 *liuyi*) – a set of subjects or domains of learning that was learned by students in ancient China. They are *li* (禮 *li*), music (樂 *yue*), archery (射 *she*), charioteering (御 *yu*), calligraphy or writing (書 *shu*) and mathematics (數 *shu*). (I shall elaborate on these concepts in Chapter 6.)

Confucius' influence

After Confucius' death, his grandson Kongli (also known as Zisi) continued Confucius' teaching by founding the School of Zisi and writing a Confucian classic known as *Zhongyong* (中庸). Confucius' teachings were further developed and propagated by Mencius (c. 372–289 BCE) and Xunzi (c. 312–230 BCE). Internally, the Confucian School was divided into eight sects, each with their doctrines and practices. Externally, Confucius' teachings faced competition from other schools of thought such as Legalism, Moism, Taoism, and Buddhism in China.[4] Confucianism was subsequently sidelined when the Qin rulers (c. 221–207 BCE) endorsed Legalism that promoted the rule by law and punishment, rather than rule by virtue as advocated by Confucius.

However, Confucianism's fortune changed during the Han dynasty when it was privileged as the state ideology by emperor Han Wudi

(140–87 BCE). It was also during the Han dynasty (206 BCE–220 CE) (and continued till the Qing dynasty, 1644–1911 CE) that the *Analects* was included as one of the 'Four Books' (四書 *Sishu*) that aspiring scholars needed to study for the Chinese imperial exam.[5] In subsequent dynasties after the Han dynasty, Confucianism remained prominent but continued to face stiff competition from Buddhism and Taoism. Confucianism reached another apex during the Song dynasty (960–1279 CE) in the form of Neo-Confucianism – essentially a fusion of Confucianism with Buddhist and Taoist ideas. Following the 1911 revolution, Confucianism was variously praised, exalted, sidelined and castigated. It came under attack in the May Fourth Movement in 1919 under the slogan 'Down with Confucius and sons', and again during the Cultural Revolution (1966–76) where Confucianism was seen as a threat to socialism.[6] But Confucianism proved to be resilient as it continued to evolve and assimilate diverse ideas to entrench itself permanently in the psyche and worldview of the Chinese today.

The twentieth century also witnessed the rise of New-Confucianism or 'Modern New Confucianism'. The focus of this ideology is on 'modernizing' Confucianism so that it might be a living tradition and factor for economic success in modern East Asia (Yao, 2000, p. 247; also see Tu, 1996a). Another interesting development since the 1990s is the rise of Post-Confucianism and its variants such as 'Postmodern Neo-Confucianism', 'Post-Neo Confucianism', and 'New Neo-Confucianism'. Despite their different names, they share a common critique of modernity, coupled with a realization that Confucianism must embrace modernization in order to survive and thrive (Tian, 2009).

Although Confucianism is no longer the state ideology in China, it has indelibly shaped the sociocultural values and practices of the Chinese, not only in China but also in other parts of the world.[7] Confucius' teachings have spread beyond China to Vietnam, Korea and Japan, and subsequently to other parts of East Asia and South-east Asia. Today, societies that are strongly influenced by Confucian ideals, practices and way of life, such as Japan, Korea, Taiwan, and Singapore, are known as 'Confucian Heritage Cultures' (or CHC for short) (Tu, 1993, 1996a, b; also see collection of essays in Slote and De Vos, 1998; Yao, 1999; Reid, 1999; Hahm, 2004; Chen, 2011). Tu (1996b) highlights the following 'Confucian concerns' in East Asian societies: self-cultivation, regulation of the family, social civility, moral education, well-being of the people, governance of the state, and universal peace (pp. 1, 7).[8] With the rise of China as an economic power, Confucianism is currently enjoying a worldwide interest and revival. There are now more than 300 Confucius Institutes in at least 96 countries and regions (Fan, 2007; Na, 2012; Starr, 2009). Supported by the Chinese government, these institutes aim to promote Chinese language and culture, including Confucius' teachings. The international appeal of Confucius' teachings makes a study of his educational thought from the *Analects* instructive and timely.

Having discussed the life, personality and influence of Confucius, we shall proceed to explore his work in Part 2 of the book.

Notes

1 For a good narrative of the life of Confucius, see Clements (2004); Chin (2007); and Nylan and Wilson (2010). For a critical review of the movie, see Cai and Sun (2011).
2 For an interesting account of the relationship between Confucius and his disciples, see Shi (2010). Shi explains that his account is constructed from the *Records of the Historian*, *Zuo Commentary*, *Mencius*, and *Xunzi*. For a detailed description of Confucius' disciples, see Fu (2011).
3 On the relationship between Confucius and his students, Elstein (2009) observes: 'There is not an absolute distinction drawn where the master is an authority figure and the student submits to his authority. Kongzi [Confucius] treats his students as near-equals more than as subordinates. A better understanding of the master-student relationship in the *Analects* will show that there is not an unbridgeable gap between Kongzi and his students: Kongzi can learn from them as well as they from him' (p. 144).
4 On the competition Confucianism had to face against rival ideologies, Ivanhoe (1991) explains: 'While I do not want to deny its [Confucianism's] profound role in the history of Chinese thought, it is simply wrong and misleading to lend the impression that it was without sophisticated and successful competitors. These competitors have deeply influenced and at times dominated Confucianism, even in the early "classic" period' (p. 68). Also see Schwartz (1985) on the history of competing schools of thought in ancient China.
5 Besides the *Analects*, the other three books are *Mencius* (孟子 *Mengzi*), *The Great Learning* (大学 *Daxue*) and *The Doctrine of the Mean* (中庸 *Zhongyong*). In addition to the *Four Books*, scholars in ancient times had to read the *Five Classics* (五經 *wujing*) that comprises *The Book of History* (書 *Shu*), *The Book of Songs* (詩 *Shi*), *The Book of Rites* (禮 *Li*), *The Book of Changes* (易 *Yi*) and *The Book of the Spring and Autumn Annals* (春秋 *Chunqiu*).
6 For a good discussion of the Chinese communist regime's representation of Confucius before, during and after the Cultural Revolution (1966, 1976), see Zhang and Schwartz (1997). For a discussion of the trajectory of Confucianism in China from 1949 to the present time, see Louie (2011). For a critical discussion of the revival of Confucianism and its relationship with socialism in China today, see Bell (2010).

7 For a discussion of the influence and development of Confucian thought in modern China, see Louie (1984); De Bary (1995); Hui (2005); and Bell (2008a).
8 On the cultural influences of Confucianism among ethnic Chinese in the workplace, see Hofstede and Bond (1988); and Robertson and Hoffman (2000). For a discussion of the impact of Confucianism from sixteenth to eighteenth century Europe, see Rowbotham (1945); and Yu (2009).

Part 2

Critical Exposition of Confucius' Work

Chapter 2

The Concept of *Li*

Figure 2.1 An incense burner and a bell used during ceremonial rituals in ancient China

Introduction

Confucius' work is so rich that there are many possible ways to explore his ideas and their significance. The most helpful way, in my view, is to begin with the concept of *li* (禮). Mentioned over 70 times in the *Analects*, *li* is one of the most-cited and widely-discussed Confucian concepts in the text.[1] *Li* is etymologically linked to religious sacrifices; the photo above shows an incense burner and a bell that were traditionally used in ceremonial rituals in ancient China (Figure 2.1). Although *li* has an inherent religious origin, Confucius ingeniously reinterprets the term in a novel and radical way. In doing so, he aims to make *li* a universal concept that forms an integral part of human life, and not merely in the field of religious sacrifices. *Li* has been variously translated as 'rites', 'ritual propriety', 'rules of propriety' and 'ceremony' etc.¹ Given the diverse ways in which *li* is understood, I shall leave this concept un-translated throughout the book. Despite the different translations, the bottom line, as agreed on by most scholars, is that *li* is intended by Confucius to encompass specific human behaviours that are widely upheld as 'proper', 'acceptable', 'good' and 'prescriptive'.² What these human behaviours are, and why they are prescriptive, are the topics for this chapter.

This chapter begins by discussing two types of *li* that are mentioned in the *Analects*: (1) *li* that is understood and practised by the masses, particularly the political leaders, during Confucius' time; and (2) *li* that is expounded and advocated by Confucius. I shall call the first type of *li* the *prevailing li* and the second type *Confucius' li*. Let us begin by understanding the *prevailing li* and Confucius' critique of it, followed by a discussion of *Confucius' li*.

The prevailing *li*

The prevailing li refers to the *li* that was understood and practised by the masses, particularly the political leaders of the various states, during Confucius' time. The *prevailing li* primarily comprises ceremonial rituals and rules of propriety. Confucius often speaks disappointingly of the *li* that was practised by his contemporaries. An example is 3:10:

3.10 子曰：'禘自既灌而往者，吾不欲觀之矣。'

The Master said, 'As for the *di* sacrifice that follows the opening libation, I do not desire to watch it.'

In the above verse, Confucius commented on the *di* sacrifice that was performed by the princes of Lu state. The 'opening libation' referred to the segment of the ritual where sacrificial wine was offered to the ancestors who were represented by impersonators, usually children (Yang, 1980, p. 28). The *di* sacrifice was not just any ordinary sacrifice; it was an imperial ancestral sacrifice that should only be performed by the emperor of the Zhou dynasty. But the princes of Lu who were obviously not emperors brazenly appropriated it for themselves. Confucius, in claiming that he had no desire to watch it, was objecting to the Lu aristocrats' arrogant abuse of *li*.

The above verse was not the only occasion where Confucius expressed his disapproval of the political leaders' observance of *li*. Various forms of ceremonial rituals belonging to the emperor were flagrantly and widely abused by the princes during Confucius' time. Another example is 3.2:

3.2 三家者以《雍》徹。

子曰：'相維辟公，天子穆穆'，奚取於三家之堂？'

The Three Families had the *yong* ode performed when [the sacrificial implements] were being cleared.

The Master said, '[quoting the ode] "Assisting were the various lords, the Son of Heaven solemn and dignified". What relevance does this have to the ancestral hall of the Three Families?'

The Three Families of Lu, namely Meng-sun, Shu-sun and Ji-sun, had audaciously appropriated an ode that was meant for the Son of Heaven who was the emperor. That prompted Confucius' rhetorical question about the application of the ode to the Lu rulers who were evidently not emperors. The above example shows that Confucius was upset, not so much with the *manner* in which the *li* was carried out (e.g. how and when to offer the wine), but with the *relevance* of *li* to the participants for that occasion. On other occasions, however, Confucius also objects to the way in which the lords performed *li*, as seen in another verse:

3.1 孔子謂季氏，'八佾舞於庭，是可忍也，孰不可忍也？'

Confucius said of the Ji family, 'They use eight rows of eight dancers to perform in the courtyard; if this can be tolerated, what cannot be?'

Unlike the case of the Lu princes who should not have performed the *di* sacrifice, the Ji rulers were permitted to use dancers in observing the ceremonial ritual. But where they erred was the choice of using eight rows of dancers, a practice that was the sole prerogative of the emperor. The Ji lords, being of a lower social status, were only entitled to four rows of dancers (Yang, 1980, p. 24).

We see from the earlier examples that Confucius was critical of *the prevailing li* as understood and practised by the political leaders. He essentially objected to the *form* of *li*, both in terms of whether the appropriate ritual was observed and how the ritual should be carried out. Besides the form, Confucius was also aggrieved with the *substance* (or the lack of it) of *the prevailing li*. An example is the following verse:

3.26 子曰：'居上不寬，爲禮不敬，臨喪不哀，吾何以觀之哉？'

The Master said, 'One who in occupying high office is not tolerant, who in observing *li* is not respectful, and who in overseeing the mourning rites does not grieve – how could I bear to look upon such a person?'

Here, Confucius lamented that the rulers (those who occupied high office) lacked the essential values and attitudes that should accompany the proper observance of *li*; namely, tolerance, respect and genuine grief.[3]

The political leaders were not the only ones who practised and perpetuated *the prevailing li*. Confucius also criticized the masses for their wrong understanding and abuse of *li*. Take the case of *xiao* (孝) or filial piety. When asked what filial piety is, Confucius replied as follows:

2.5 孟懿子問孝。

子曰：'無違。'

樊遲御，子告之曰：'孟孫問孝於我，我對曰，無違。'

樊遲曰：'何謂也？'

子曰：'生， ；死，葬之以禮，祭之以禮。'

Meng Yizi asked about filial piety.

The Master replied, 'Do not violate.'

Fan Chi was driving [the Master's chariot] and the Master said to him, 'Meng Yizi asked me about filial piety, and I replied, "Do not violate."'

Fan Chi asked, 'What does that mean?'

The Master replied, 'While your parents are alive, serve them according to *li*; when they are dead, bury them according to *li*, and offer sacrifice to them according to *li*.'

But what is being filial to one's parents according to *li*? For a start, we know the masses' interpretation of filial piety from Confucius' observation below:

2.7 子游問孝。

子曰：'今之孝者，是謂能養。至於犬馬，皆能有養；不敬，何以別乎？'

Ziyou asked about filial piety.

The Master replied, 'Nowadays a filial person means one who provides for his parents. But even dogs and horses are provided for. If you show no respect [towards your parents], what is the difference?'

The majority of people who lived during Confucius' time viewed filial piety principally as providing for one's parents materially; feelings of respect for parents were often not taken into account. This limited understanding of filial piety, according to Confucius, makes a human being no better than animals. To Confucius, filial piety needs to be accompanied by not just the form ('serve them', 'bury them', 'offer sacrifice to them') but also the substance of appropriate values, attitudes and dispositions.

Overall, *the prevailing li* is characterized by external and perfunctory observance of *li*. There is little emphasis on the appropriateness of a particular ceremony for the participants as well as the emotional engagement and ethical considerations underlying the observance of *li*. So slipshod was the observance of *li* that Confucius avers that the masses would view anyone who desires to conscientiously observe every detail of *li* as obsequious:[4]

3.18 子曰：'事君盡禮，人以爲諂也。'

The Master said, 'If you serve your lord based on every detail of *li*, people will think that you are obsequious.'

Confucius' *li*

Confucius advocates that the *li* that everyone should observe is not *the prevailing li*; *li* should be more than just ceremonial rituals and specific rules of propriety. This is evident in his comment below:

17.11 子曰：'禮云禮云，玉帛云乎哉？'

The Master said, 'In talking about *li*, are we [merely] talking about jade and silk?'

The 'jade and silk' are items commonly used in ceremonial observances. Confucius' rhetorical question suggests that *li* is more than just a rigid and outward observance of the rites and rituals. What else, then, does *li* constitute? Confucius answers this question in his response to his disciple's question on *li*:

12.1 子曰：'非禮勿視，非禮勿聽，非禮勿言，非禮勿動。'

The Master replied, 'Do not look if it is not in accordance with *li*; do not listen if it is not in accordance with *li*; do not speak if it is not in accordance with *li*; do not move if it is not in accordance with *li*.'[5]

I have translated the expression '非禮' (*feili*) literally as 'if it is not in accordance with *li*'; other scholars have translated it as 'unless it is in accordance with *li*'.[6] Either way, Confucius' point is that we should look, listen, speak and move – in short, engage in all human activities – in accordance with *li*. Confucius' prescriptive prohibitions ('do not . . .') remind us that *li* carries a *normative* force: *li* is about living one's life deliberately and meaningfully according to a certain standard. Based on 12.1, I propose that *li* is best understood as follows:

Li refers to the totality of normative human behaviours that are accompanied by corresponding attitudes and values for all aspects of one's life.[7]

To further understand *li*, it is necessary for us to clarify what we (and Confucius) mean by 'normative'. Three observations can be made here. First, the word 'normative' comes from the root word 'norm'. By 'norm', Confucius does not mean a strict set of rules or laws. Nowhere in the *Analects* do we find Confucius prescribing a set of do's and don'ts to govern and control his students' every movement. Rather, he talks about an ideal standard or pattern to guide people in their everyday conduct. Another way to understand a norm is to see it as a *discourse* or a social process of constructing shared meanings that instruct a community on the proper form and purpose of given practices (Tan, 2011). Accordingly, a life that is guided by *li* is one that is lived according to one or more norms that unite a group of people around shared meanings and practices.

Second, 'normativity' is not only about 'displaying socially acceptable' behaviours; it also includes the desirable values and attitudes that should accompany the normative behaviours. Given that our actions stem from our thoughts and feelings, our behaviours cannot be separate from our attitudes and values. By 'attitudes', I refer to a person's overall predisposition towards objects, people and/or situations; 'values', on the other hand, refers to the totality of beliefs and qualities that a person deems important for oneself and others. Attitudes and values are essential in shaping a person's mental habits and emotional inclinations, which in turn affect his or her behaviours. As such, *li* is more than an outward performance of rituals (represented by 'jade and silk' in 12.1); it involves the total experience of a human being where one's values, attitudes and behaviours are harmonized.[8]

Third, as noted earlier, 'normativity' prescribes to a community that which is 'good', 'proper', 'correct' and 'desirable'. In other words, the behaviours, attitudes and values demonstrated by a person who observes *li* are what he or she, as well as everyone else within a community, *ought* to do; *li* focuses on 'what should be' (prescriptive) rather than 'what is'

⟵─────────────────⟶

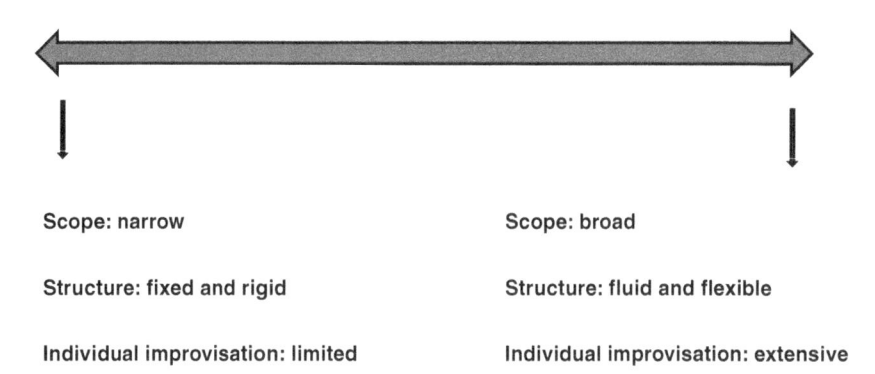

Scope: narrow	Scope: broad
Structure: fixed and rigid	Structure: fluid and flexible
Individual improvisation: limited	Individual improvisation: extensive

Figure 2.2 A continuum of Confucius' *li*

(descriptive). The prescriptive nature of *li* provides a standard not only for living one's life, but also for evaluating and improving the behaviours, attitudes and values of others and ourselves in society.

Understanding Confucius' *li*

We can further understand Confucius' *li* from three angles: the scope, structure and degree of individual improvisation allowed. The continuum above (Figure 2.2) illustrates the range of Confucius' *li*:[9]

The 'scope' refers to the extent of subject matter that *li* deals with; the 'structure' refers to the process and form involved when one observes *li*; and 'individual improvisation' refers to the degree to which one may exercise one's discretion and judgement when observing *li*. Let me explain the continuum by starting with the left side. This type of *li* covers instances of *li* where the scope is relatively narrow and the structure is relatively fixed and rigid. At the same time, there is limited room for individual improvisation in observing *li*. An analogy for this type of *li* is classical orchestral music where musicians generally have to stick strictly to the music score, without the option of changing the notes or rhythm.

Examples of *li* that are narrow in scope, relatively fixed and rigid in structure and give little room for individual improvisation are ceremonial rituals such as the *di* imperial ancestral sacrifice (3.10) and performance of the *yong* ode with eight rows of eight dancers (3.2). Other examples recorded in the *Analects* include observing mourning rituals (3.4), performing sacrifices to the spirits (3.12), sacrificing a live sheep at the announcement of the new moon (3.17), using the proper pronunciation when reciting the *Book of Songs* and *Book of History* (7.18), knowing where and when to prostrate (9.3) and offering the appropriate greeting during a game of archery (3.7).[10] What unites the above instances of *li* is the demand for observers to adhere closely to the predetermined purpose, process and form of *li*. The political leaders, such as the Lu family and the Three Families, were castigated by Confucius precisely because of their presumptuous attempt to 'improvise' when observing these instances of *li*; that is why they ended up misappropriating and violating *li* instead.

But Confucius' notion of *li* is not confined to the type of *li* discussed above; he also highlights other types of *li*, particularly those that lie on the right side of the continuum. This type of *li* is characterized by being relatively broad in scope as well as fluid and flexible in structure. At the same time, the observers of *li* are at liberty and even expected to improvise by exercising their discretion and judgement while observing *li*. An analogy is jazz music where the musicians, though guided by a melody and some basic chords, are free to improvise as they play.[11] It is this category of *li* that is the focal point in 12.1, where Confucius speaks of not doing anything (looking, listening, speaking and moving) unless it is in accordance with *li*. The actions of looking, listening, speaking and moving represent the totality of one's behaviours, thoughts and feelings in everyday life. In the *Analects*, we find examples of Confucius observing this type of *li* through his daily activities such as conversing with someone (10.2, 10.15), receiving gifts (10.23), mounting and riding in the carriage (10.26), manifesting context-appropriate facial expressions and movements (10.3, 10.4), sitting (10.12), eating (10.10) and even kneeling and sleeping (10.24) etc.[12] By emphasizing the need to act in accordance with *li*, Confucius is not talking about conducting ourselves based on a rigid and fixed set of rules all the time. This is because it is practically impossible for anyone to base his or her *every* conscious activity on a set of rules, unless one is a robot! Confucius' point, rather, is that we need to live a life that is guided by *li* which serves as a normative pattern, and living such a life entails that we exercise our individual discretion and judgement appropriately in different contexts according to *li*.[13] Echoing the need for individual improvisation, we are told in the *Analects* that Confucius rejects certainty and dogmatism (毋必，毋固) (9.4), hates inflexibility (疾固也) (14.32) and chooses to pursue what is good and works well (擇其善者) (7.28).

The need to exercise one's discretion and judgement in observing *li* is further exemplified in the following incident:

11.22 子路問：'聞斯行諸？'

子曰：'有父兄在，如之何其聞斯行之？'

冉有問：'"聞斯行諸？'

子曰：'聞斯行之。'

公西華曰：'由也問聞斯行諸，子曰，"有父兄在"，
求也問聞斯行諸，子曰，"聞斯行之"。赤也惑，敢問。'

子曰：'求也退，故進之；由也兼人，故退之。'

Zilu asked, 'Upon hearing something, should I act upon it?'

The Master said, 'Your father and elder brothers are still alive. So how could you, upon hearing something, act upon it?'

Then Ranyou asked, 'Upon hearing something, should I act upon it?'

The Master said, 'Upon hearing something, act upon it.'

Gongxi Hua said, 'When Zilu asked, "Upon hearing something, should I act upon it?" You said, "Your father and elder brothers are still alive." But when Ranyou asked, "Upon hearing something, should I act upon it?" You said, "Upon hearing something, act upon it." I am confused and I would like to ask about this.'

The Master said, 'Ranyou holds back, so I urged him on. Zilu has the energy of two persons, so I reined him in.'

Here is a situation where two disciples asked Confucius the same question about whether they should put into practice what they have heard. Confucius gave them diametrically opposing answers because he was sensitive to the contrasting temperaments of his disciples – Ranyou is diffident while Zilu is impulsive. His advice to his disciples was therefore carefully tailored to suit their specific personality traits. What I wish to highlight here is not so much the fact that Confucius gave opposing replies to the two disciples (which is an interesting point in itself), but that he gave different *justifications* to his replies. Confucius could have explained to Zilu that given his impulsive nature, he (Zilu) should delay acting upon what he has heard and take time to ponder over it. Conversely, Confucius could have encouraged Ranyou to act upon what he has heard because doing so would help him to overcome his diffidence.

But Confucius chose instead to convince Zilu not to act because his father and elder brothers were still alive. Lau (1979) aptly brings out the normative force of Confucius' justification for Zilu in his translation: 'As your father and elder brothers are still alive, *you are hardly in a position immediately to put into practice what you have heard*' (italics added). The justification of not acting based on familial consideration reminds us of Confucius' teaching in 2.5, quoted earlier, that filial piety entails serving one's parents according to *li*. Following 2.5, Confucius' justification for Zilu therefore should be understood as an instance of practising filial piety. Zilu is advised not to act on what he has heard because doing so would mean that he has yet to consult his father and elder brothers, and hence is being disrespectful towards them. The prescriptive nature of *li* rendered this justification strong enough to dissuade Zilu from acting on what he has heard.

In contrast to Zilu, Confucius did not give the same justification for Ranyou. By prodding Ranyou on to act on what he has heard, in contradistinction to the advice given to Zilu, is Confucius encouraging Ranyou to be unfilial towards his elders in a flagrant violation of *li*? Surely not. Confucius views Ranyou's action of acting upon what he has heard as an observance of *li*, just as Zilu's non-action is an observance of *li*. Confucius' antipodal responses to his two disciples imply that *li* should not be observed in a rigid and dogmatic way, and that different people may legitimately observe *li* by responding to the *same* situation differently. A proper observance of *li* must take into consideration the specific context, profile of the observers and the needs of the parties involved.

Let me further elaborate on this type of *li* with an example that is familiar to many of us: the art of making small talk. Apart from observing basic social etiquette such as greeting the person (saying 'hello' in English or another appropriate language, getting the person's name or title right etc.) and maintaining the right body language (establishing eye contact, giving a slight bow, not frowning etc.), there is no manual dictating what we should say, how we should respond, how to keep the conversation going and when to end the conversation. That there is no fixed formula for making good small talk is because it really depends on many contingent factors, such as who the person is (gender, age, social status etc.), one's relationship with that person (a good friend? an acquaintance? one's superior?), and the context in which the small talk takes place (in one's home? at a social event? at a job interview?). As such, a person who makes small talk needs to exercise one's discernment and discretion to know how to conduct oneself appropriately in accordance with *li*.

We should not underestimate the extent of individual improvisation in one's observance of *li*. Even for ceremonial rituals – those that lie on the left side of the continuum of *li* – where the room for individual improvisation is limited, some modifications of *li* are still possible and acceptable under certain circumstances. Confucius himself demonstrated this point, as follows:

9.3　子曰：'麻冕，禮也；今也純，儉，吾從眾。拜下，禮也；今拜乎上，泰也。雖違眾，吾從下。'

The Master said, 'A linen ceremonial cap is prescribed by *li*. Nowadays, a silk cap is used instead; this is frugal and I follow the majority on this. To prostrate oneself before ascending [the steps to the hall] is prescribed by *li*. Nowadays, one prostrates oneself [only] after ascending [the steps to the hall]; this is arrogant. Although this goes against the majority, I prostrate myself before ascending [the steps to the hall].'

Two instances are recorded in 9.3. In the first instance, Confucius approved the masses' modification of *li* by substituting the material used for the ceremonial cap. In the second instance, however, he rejected following the majority by adhering to the traditional practice of prostrating oneself before entering the hall.

We can identify two principles of the proper observance of *li* based on 9.3. First, the observance of *li* is neither unchanging nor static, but evolves over time. This is evident in the case of choosing a cheaper material for the ceremonial cap. Second, the observance of *li* has an intrinsic *ethical* dimension.[14] Confucius is careful about modifying *li* on the basis of strong ethical justification, namely the value of frugality in the first instance and the value of reverence in the second instance. It is for the same reason that Confucius chastised the rulers of his time – they had modified the ceremonial rituals not out of a sense of frugality, reverence or other ethical principles, but out of presumptuousness and arrogance. To Confucius, the spirit behind the observance of *li* is as important as the observance of *li* itself.[15]

The pervasive nature of *li* as implied in the continuum explains why Confucius highlights the socializing function of *li* for human beings as members of a community. For example, he teaches that 'I take a stand by observing *li*' (立於禮) (8.8); that 'someone who does not understand *li* has no way of taking a stand' (不知禮，無以立也) (20.3); and that 'if you do not study *li*, you will be at a loss as to where to stand' (不學禮，無以立) (16.13). The expression 'where to stand' refers to knowing how to conduct oneself and perform one's social roles in a community.[16] It is through observing *li* – internalizing and manifesting normative behaviours and corresponding values and attitudes in our personal and public life – that we can 'take a stand' in society.[17]

Confucius further elaborates on how *li* enables a person to 'take a stand' by avoiding the vices of lethargy, timidity, rowdiness and rudeness:

8.2 子曰：'恭而無禮則勞，慎而無禮則葸，勇而無禮則亂，直而無禮則絞。'

The Master said, 'Deference without *li* is labour; caution without *li* is timidity; courage without *li* is rowdiness; candour without *li* is rudeness.'

Besides guiding us in our daily interactions, *li* is also instrumental for good government. Confucius explains as follows:

4.13 子曰：'能以禮讓爲國乎？何有？不能以禮讓爲國，如禮何？'

> The Master said, 'If a person is able to govern a state through observing *li* and showing deference, what more is needed? But if the person is unable to govern a state through observing *li* and showing deference, of what use is *li*?'

Confucius' point is that without a spirit of deference, the outward observance of *li* will be reduced to mere formalism. Note that the *li* needed in governing a state is not merely the performance of ceremonial rituals, where the scope is narrow, the structure is fixed and rigid, and the room for individual improvisation is limited (cf. *li* that lies on the left side of the continuum). To achieve social order in a state, a ruler would need, on top of a proper observance of ceremonial rituals, disposition and ability in exercising his discretion and judgement to do what is right in accordance with *li*.

Not only should a ruler observe *li*, he also needs to ensure that his people order themselves according to *li*. Addressing rulers, Confucius advises as follows:

> 2.3 子曰:'道之以政, 齊之以刑, 民免而無恥; 道之以德, 齊之以禮, 有恥且格。'
>
> The Master said, 'Lead [the common people] with policies, and keep them in line with punishments, and the common people will avoid punishments but will be without a sense of shame. Lead [the common people] with virtue, and keep them in line through *li*, and they will have a sense of shame and order themselves.'

Here, Confucius contrasts two types of government: rule by law through punishment, and rule by virtue through *li*. Confucius views the latter as effective for transforming not only the people's behaviour, but also their character. Social order is obtained when the people are capable of and intrinsically motivated to ordering their lives in accordance with *li*. When people know and act according to *li*, they will naturally feel ashamed if their behaviour deviates from *li*, with or without the fear of punishment. Besides this 'voice of conscience', the fact that everyone is able to evaluate and correct one another based on the common yardstick of *li* also produces an external pressure for all to conform to *li*.

It should be clear by now that in order for *li* to provide internal motivation and external pressure for values inculcation and social conformity, it cannot be confined to ceremonial rituals alone (the type of *li* that lies on the left side of the continuum). Other types of *li*, especially those concerning our everyday activities (looking, listening, speaking and moving) are part and parcel of the whole package of *li*. A proper observance of *li* requires a careful consideration of the specific context, conditions and parties involved. Given that *li* encompasses all aspects of human life, individual engagement, deliberation and application are indispensable to the observance of *li*.[18] I shall return to the topic of the importance of individual discretion when I discuss the concept of *yi* (義 appropriateness or rightness) in a later chapter.[19]

I need to clarify here that I am *not* proposing that we adopt an 'anything goes' approach to observing *li*. Nor am I suggesting that we are free to interpret, modify and even discard all cases of *li* at our whims and fancies. My point, rather, is that there exists a wide spectrum of instances of *li* that vary in their scope, structure and degree of individual discretion. Between the two ends of the continuum of *li* are other types of *li* that differ from and overlap with one another in terms of their scope, structure and degree of individual improvisation. Despite the varying scope, structure and degree of individual improvisation allowed, all instances of *li* are united in comprising the norm that guides all human beings – from rulers to the common people – to conduct themselves appropriately.[20]

Attitudes and values

Thus far, we have seen how Confucius' *li* comprises a wide spectrum of *li* that differs in terms of the scope, structure and room of individual improvisation allowed. Regardless of the types of *li* along the continuum, all observance of *li* must be accompanied by *desirable attitudes and values*. This point has already been alluded to in our earlier discussion. For example, we saw how Confucius criticized rulers of his time who lacked tolerance, respect and genuine grief while observing *li* (3.26). We also noted Confucius' emphasis on the importance of respect in filial piety and deference in governing a state. In this regard, *Confucius' li* is antithetical to *the prevailing li* as the latter lacks appropriate emotional engagement and ethical considerations.

Confucius frequently underscores the need for appropriate attitudes and values to accompany the observance of *li*.[21] He teaches that we should 'love *li*' (好禮) and not just observe *li* (see 1.15, 13.4, 14.41). He explains that the basis of *li* is one's emotional engagement and ethical consideration rather than mere formality:

3.4　林放問禮之本。

子曰：'大哉問! 禮, 與其奢也, 寧儉; 喪, 與其易也, 寧戚。'

Lin Fang asked about the basis of observing *li*.

The Master replied, 'What a great question! In observing *li*, it is better to be modest than extravagant; in mourning, it is better to be sorrowful than fastidious.'

We note from the passage above that Confucius highlights the importance of modesty and genuine sorrow in one's observance of *li*. Confucius is against any observance of *li* that glorifies pride ('extravagant'), and is insincere and fastidious. Confucius believes that true virtue stems from within a person, and is not just an outward display of piety. In fact, Confucius calls a person who pretends to be virtuous a 'thief of virtue' (德之賊也) (17.13) – someone who takes something that does not belong to him, in this case, virtue.

The primacy placed on appropriate attitudes and values for the proper observance of *li* explains why Confucius avers in 3.12, 'If I do not [participate in a] sacrifice [in my spirit], it is as if I have not sacrificed [at all]' (吾不與祭, 如不祭). It also helps us to understand why Confucius did something that appeared unusual at first glance:

3.15　子入太廟, 每事問。

或曰：'孰謂鄹人之子知禮乎? 入太廟, 每事問。'

子聞之, 曰：'是禮也。'

When the Master entered the Grand Ancestral Hall, he asked questions about everything.

Someone said, 'Who said that this son of man from Zou village knows *li*? On entering the Grand Ancestral Hall, he asked questions about everything.'

When the Master heard of this, he said, 'The asking of questions is *li*.' (also see 10.21)

At that time, someone of Confucius' stature (a teacher who belongs to the *shi* 士 or learned class) was expected to know much, or at least some basic information, about the Grand Ancestral Hall and the observance of *li* inside the hall. That Confucius asked questions about everything was indeed surprising; it prompted someone to justifiably conclude that Confucius was ignorant. But what is interesting was Confucius' explanation: he had asked many questions not because he did not know the answers, but because asking questions was itself part of observing *li*. Confucius' point is that the act of asking questions demonstrates one's attitude and value of sincerity, attentiveness, humility, and most importantly, the love of *li*. That Confucius was criticized and misunderstood by his contemporaries indicates that most people during his time did not understand the necessity and importance of possessing appropriate attitudes and values as an integral part of observing *li*.[22]

The centrality of appropriate attitudes and values for the observance of *li* is further reflected in another incident. Zilu, a disciple of Confucius, boasted of what he was able to achieve if he were given the opportunity to govern a state:

11.26 '千乘之國, 攝乎大國之間, 加之以師旅, 因之以饑饉; 由也爲之, 比及三年, 可使有勇, 且知方也。'

'Let me govern a state of a thousand chariots. Even if I am situated among great neighbouring states, coupled with invading foreign armies and famine in my state, I am able, at the end of three years, to give the people courage and realization of the right direction.'

Confucius responded to Zilu mildly by smiling and not saying anything, suggesting that he was displeased with Zilu's answer. Later, when conversing with another disciple, Confucius explained his cryptic response to Zilu: 'In governing a state you need [to observe] *li*, [yet] [there was] no deference in [his] speech, [hence] I smiled [at him]' (爲國以禮，其言不讓，是故哂之). Confucius' point is that Zilu's lack of deference undermines his boastful claim about governing a state successfully, since good governance requires one to possess deference – the very quality Zilu lacks. Zilu fails to see that our observance of *li* includes not just what we say but also *the spirit* in which we say it. He also fails to see that one's intention and its outcome may be good ('to give the people courage and realization of the right direction'), but they remain inadequate if they are not accompanied by appropriate values and attitudes. Confucius' insightful remark signifies that the observance of *li* necessarily involves not just normative behaviours, but also appropriate attitudes and values.

The inseparability of one's attitudes, values and behaviours is further illustrated in another episode. Upon seeing a disciple sitting with his legs spread out while waiting for him – a flippant and disrespectful posture during Confucius' time – Confucius chastised him and said, 'To be young and not have modesty and respect, to grow up and not have anything to pass on, and to grow old and not die [with dignity], such a person is a thief' (幼而不孫弟，長而無述焉，老而不死，是爲賊) (14.43). From his disciple's sitting position, Confucius inferred that he lacked modesty and respect, and extrapolated his potential development. Such a person would be unable to contribute to society ('to grow up and not have anything to pass on'), live a graceful life ('to grow old and not die with dignity'), and be a burden to society ('a thief'). This example amplifies Confucius' teaching that one's actions, thoughts and feelings are intertwined: a person whose actions violate *li* is likely to be deficient in certain desirable attitudes and values.

There is one more thing I need to add about *li*, and that concerns the different senses in which it is used in the *Analects*. Confucius uses two senses of *li*: a *general* sense and a *specific* sense. Consider the two verses cited earlier:

3.4 林放問禮之本。

子曰：'大哉問! 禮，與其奢也，寧儉; 喪，與其易也，寧戚。'

Lin Fang asked about the basis of observing *li*.

The Master replied, 'What a great question! In observing *li*, it is better to be modest than extravagant; in mourning, it is better to be sorrowful than fastidious.'

4.13 子曰: '能以禮讓爲國乎？何有？'

The Master said, 'If a person is able to govern a state through observing *li* and showing deference, what [more] is needed? But if the person is unable to govern a state through observing *li* and showing deference, of what use is *li*?'

In both cases, *li* is the subject matter. However, in the first verse (3.4), appropriate attitudes and values such as modesty and sincerity are *essential components* of observing *li*. In the second verse (4.13), however, Confucius talks about observing *li and* showing deference, as if they are two separate issues. Confucius seems to imply in 4.13 that observing *li* need not be accompanied by appropriate attitudes and values such as deference. How does one reconcile the apparent discrepancy between the two verses?

The key to unravel the mystery is to understand that Confucius is using the term *li* in two distinct senses. In the first case (3.4), *li* is understood as a general term that encompasses not just normative behaviours, but also appropriate attitudes and values. In the second case (4.13), however, Confucius is using *li* in the specific or narrow sense, referring only to normative behaviours. The two senses are not contradictory. The *essence* of *li* necessarily comprises an integration of normative behaviours, attitudes and values. Yet, this general and encompassing meaning of *li* does not preclude other instances where *li* is used in a more restricted sense for Confucius to achieve a specific purpose.[23] Confucius occasionally switched to a specific sense of *li* to assist the listeners, who are new to his interpretation of *li* vis-à-vis the prevailing *li*, to appreciate the need for certain attitudes and values. In 4.13, for example, Confucius used the specific sense of *li* to highlight the essential virtue of deference in governing a state. Given that many rulers during Confucius' time lacked deference, as evident in their usurping the emperor's ceremonial rituals and using laws to subjugate the people, Confucius wanted to emphasize the quality of deference when one observed *li*.[24] Recognizing these two senses of *li* helps us to make sense of Confucius' sayings in the *Analects*, which may at times appear confusing and contradictory.

Conclusion

We have explored in this chapter Confucius' concept of *li* and learned that it refers to normative human behaviours that are accompanied by appropriate attitudes and value for all aspects of one's life. We have also seen how *Confucius' li* is contrasted with *the prevailing li*, especially in the former's accent on the harmonization of one's behaviours, attitudes and values. For the rest of this book, I shall use *li* to refer only to *Confucius' li*, unless stated otherwise.

The pervasiveness of *li* in our everyday life is illustrated in an interesting practice I noticed when I visited the Confucius Temple in Taiwan and the Confucius Institute in Singapore. Apparently the staff at both venues had printed the character *li* (禮 in traditional Chinese script in Taiwan, 礼 in simplified Chinese script in Singapore) and pasted the character on the wall of their toilets. The message is that members of the public should extend their practice of *li* by keeping the toilets clean! Given that *li* is ubiquitous and carries a normative force, a question remains: what is the *norm* that *li* is based on, according to Confucius? This will be answered in the next chapter.

Chapter 3
The Concepts of *Dao* and *He*

If you visit a Confucius Temple in Taiwan, you may notice a statue of an owl decorating the roof of the temple. Legend has it that the wild and intemperate owls stopped to listen to Confucius' teachings and subsequently became tame and peaceful. Presumably they learned to observe *li*! The verity of the legend aside, this story highlights the transforming power of *li* for human beings (and animals).

We have discussed in the previous chapter that *li* refers to the totality of normative human behaviours that are accompanied by corresponding attitudes and values for all aspects of one's life. I have pointed out that the 'norm' that *li* is based on does not refer to a rigid and fixed set of rules or laws that controls and restricts human conduct. Although some categories of *li* such as ceremonial rituals are observed based on specific regulations (e.g. how many rows of dancers to use, when to prostrate in a sacred hall), *li* is more than just observing traditional rites. The 'norm' propagated by Confucius is better understood as an ideal pattern and discourse that guides human beings in their daily lives. But what exactly is this 'norm' advocated by Confucius? This chapter answers this question by introducing two Confucian concepts, *dao* (way) and *he* (harmony), and elucidating their connection to *li*.

Understanding the norm: Zhou *Li*

It is helpful to begin our discussion by making three general observations about *li* and the norm that *li* is based on. First, *li* did not originate from Confucius. He states in 7.1 that '[I] transmit but do not make; [I] trust in and love antiquity' (述而不作，信而好古).[1] Second, the norm championed by Confucius was not the norm that was understood and adhered to by the masses and political leaders during Confucius' time. Otherwise, Confucius would not have been aggrieved by the way the rulers and people transgressed *li*. Third, the norm Confucius had in mind was described as from 'antiquity'. This refers to the era before Confucius' time, namely the Xia, Shang and Zhou dynasties where sage-kings such as Yao, Shun (8.18, 8.19, 8.20) and Yu (8.21) lived.[2] Confucius praised these sage-kings because of their normative behaviours and accompanying attitudes and values, as elaborated in passages such as the following:

8.21 子曰：'禹，吾無間然矣。菲飲食而致孝乎鬼神，惡衣服而致美乎黻冕，卑宮室而盡力乎溝洫。禹，吾無間然矣。'

The Master said, 'As for Yu, I can find no fault with him. He has meagre drink and food yet he was filial in his offerings to the ancestral spirits and gods. His clothes were coarse yet [his ceremonial] robes and caps were splendid. His dwelling was humble yet he devoted all his energy to the [building of] canals and ditches. As for Yu, I can find no fault [with him].'

Confucius regards Yu as faultless because the latter has observed *li* completely and faithfully. First, Yu's observance of ceremonial rituals was seen in his devotion to the gods and spirits of his ancestors, as well as his diligent wearing of splendid ceremonial robes and cap. At the same time, Yu did not neglect the observance of *li* in other areas of his life. He conducted his private life in accordance with *li* by living frugally, thereby illustrating Confucius' teaching that 'in observing *li*, it is better to be modest than extravagant' (3.4). As a ruler, Yu also conducted his public life in accordance with *li* by building drain canals and irrigation ditches to benefit the people. Overall, Yu's actions were accompanied by modesty, self-sacrifice and love for others.

Among the earlier dynasties (Xia, Shang and Zhou), Confucius singled out the Zhou dynasty (about 1122 BCE) as being the best in terms of the rulers' observance of *li*. He declared that 'I follow the Zhou' (吾從周) (3.14) and that 'Zhou's virtue can be said to be the highest of all' (周之德，其可謂至德也已矣) (8. 20, also see 17.5). So highly did

Confucius regard the Duke of Zhou (who was also the founder of Lu state where Confucius came from) that he lamented that 'How I have regressed! It has been a long time since I dreamt of the Duke of Zhou' (甚矣吾衰也！久矣吾不復夢見周公) (7.5). Other virtuous rulers from the Zhou dynasty include King Wen and King Wu (cf. 8.20, 9.5).[3]

It is important to note that Confucius praised the Zhou dynasty not because it had single-handedly created and promoted *li*. Rather, the Zhou dynasty learned and adapted *li* from two earlier dynasties (Xia and Shang), as noted by Confucius:

3.14 子曰：'周監於二代，郁郁乎文哉！吾從周。'

The Master said, 'Zhou [dynasty] has before it the two Ages. How rich in culture! I follow the Zhou.'[4]

Not only did the Zhou dynasty learn from previous dynasties, the Shang (also known as Yin) dynasty also adopted *li* from its predecessor. As noted by Confucius in 2.23: 'Yin [dynasty] built on the [observance of] *li* of the Xia [dynasty], the alterations can be known; the Zhou [dynasty] built on the [observance of] *li* of the Yin [dynasty], the alternations can be known' (殷因於夏禮，所損益，可知也；周因於殷禮，所損益，可知也). Another noteworthy point is that Confucius does not just recommend following Zhou's *li*; he advises rulers who wish to govern a state effectively to judiciously select the observance of *li* from various dynasties. This is noted in the following passage:[5]

15.11 顏淵問爲邦。

子曰：'行夏之時，乘殷之輅，服周之冕，樂則《韶》《舞》。
放鄭聲，遠佞人。鄭聲淫，佞人殆。'

Yenhui asked about governing a state.

The Master replied, 'Follow the calendar of the Xia [dynasty], ride on the carriage of the Yin [dynasty], wear the [ceremonial] cap of the Zhou [dynasty], [and] play the *shao* and *wu* [music]. Abandon the tunes of Zheng [state], [and] keep glib people at a distance. The tunes of Zheng [state] are lewd and glib people are dangerous.' (cf. 3.25 and 7.14 on the beauty and felicity of the *shao* music)[6]

The continuation of the observance of *li* through the successive dynasties before Confucius' time points to the existence of a discourse – a social process of constructing shared meanings that seek to instruct a community on the proper form and purpose of given practices. This discourse is expressed through the 'norm' propagated by Confucius. More can be said about the norm by examining the concepts of *tian* (heaven) and *dao* (Way) – the topic of the next section.

The genesis of *li*: *Tian* (Heaven) and *Dao* (Way)

We have noted that the norm that *li* is based on is essentially that of the Zhou dynasty, which in turn was inherited and adapted from earlier dynasties. But this raises the question: where did the sage-kings and heroes during Zhou and other previous dynasties learn about the norm? A clue is given in Confucius' comment on the three dynasties (Xia, Shang and Zhou):

15.25 子曰：'吾之於人也，誰毀誰譽？如有所譽者，其有所試矣。斯民也，三代之所以直道而行也。'

The Master said, 'When it comes to other people, whom have I condemned, and whom have I praised? If a person is praised, [it is because the person] has been put to the test. [That is why] the people of the Three Dynasties acted based on the straight Way.'

The Chinese character for 'Way' is '道' (*dao*). The adjective 'straight' (直 *zhi*) highlights the unbroken continuation of the Way down the three dynasties.[7] But what exactly is the Way? The following verse on the sage-king Yao is informative:

8.19 子曰：'大哉堯之爲君也！巍巍乎！唯天爲大，唯堯則之。蕩蕩乎，民無能名焉。巍巍乎其有成功也，煥乎其有文章！'

The Master said, 'How great was Yao as a ruler! How majestic! Only heaven is great, and only Yao modeled himself upon it. [His grace was so] extensive that the common people could not find words [to praise him]. How majestic in his success and brilliant in his cultural accomplishments!' (see also 8.18, 8.20, 8.21)

Yao was considered majestic and great because he modelled himself upon *tian* (天 heaven). It is therefore instructive for us to take a closer look at the concept of heaven and its relationship to the Way and *li*.

Confucius uses anthropomorphic terms to describe heaven in the *Analects*. In other words, heaven is perceived as a Being capable of understanding and interacting with human beings, as well as revealing its mandate or ordinance (命 *ming*) to them.[8] Confucius professed that he understood the mandate of heaven at the age of fifty (五十而知天命) (2.4). He teaches that it is possible for one to offend heaven (罪於天) (3.13), that heaven is the author of the virtue in him (天生德於予) (7.23), and that only heaven understands him (知我者其天乎) (14.35). The concept of virtue (德 *de*) here refers to the power given by heaven to a person that exalts and empowers one to influence others towards goodness. Elsewhere, Confucius discusses virtue (*de*) in the context of good governing (2.1), the company a virtuous person enjoys (4.25), and the influence of a *junzi* (noble or exemplary person; more on this later) on others (12.19).[9]

Confucius also underlines the mandate of heaven and its relationship with the Way:

14.36 子曰：'道之將行也與，命也；道之將廢也與，命也。'

The Master said, 'If the Way prevails, it is because of mandate; if the Way is discarded, it is also because of mandate.'[10]

The context for this verse was that Zilu, a disciple of Confucius, was being falsely accused and faced possible execution. Rather than being anxious about Zilu's fate, Confucius expressed his faith in heaven's mandate to ensure that the Way prevail by protecting the innocent (in this case, Zilu). That is why Confucius praised sage-king Yao and the rulers from the Xia, Shang and Zhou dynasties: they understood the mandate of heaven, modelled themselves upon it and followed the straight Way by relying on the virtue given by heaven (see 15.25, 8.19, 7.23). Simply put, to fulfil the mandate of heaven is to follow the Way by observing Zhou *li*.

As mentioned, the Zhou *li* was manifested in the normative behaviours and corresponding attitudes and values of the sage-kings such as Yao, Shun and Yu of the first three dynasties. Yao's majestic success and brilliant cultural accomplishments, for example, are evidences of his praiseworthy behaviours, attitudes and values in accordance with the Way (8.19). The primacy Confucius gives to realizing and keeping the Way is evident in the following verse where he comments on himself:

4.5 子曰：'富與貴，是人之所欲也；不以其道得之，不處也。貧與賤，是人之所惡也；不以其道得之，不去也。'

The Master said, 'Wealth and honour are what people desire. [But if they are acquired] not in accordance with the Way, I would rather not have them. Poverty and disgrace are what people hate. [But if they are avoided] not in accordance with the Way, I would rather not reject them.'

So important is following the Way that Confucius urges all to 'set [your heart-mind] on the Way' (志於道) (7.6) and 'hold fast to the good Way till death' (守死善道) (8.13). By Confucius' time, unfortunately, the Way had not been realized and upheld in the world. We know that because the *Analects* records an official remarking that 'the world has long been without the Way' (天下之無道也久矣) (3.24). We are also told that Confucius exclaimed: '[If] the Way is to be found in the world, I would not [need to] change [anything]' (天下有道，丘不與易也) (18.6).[11]

However, the good news is that the Way has not been lost completely in the world. A disciple of Confucius points out that 'the Way of [Kings] Wen and Wu has not yet fallen to the ground [but] lives in the people' (文武之道，未墜於地，在人) (19.22). More importantly, Confucius declares that the Way that was manifested in the Zhou *li* or culture now resides with him:

9.5 子畏於匡，曰：'文王既没，文不在茲乎？天之將喪斯文也，後死者不得與於斯文也；天之未喪斯文也，匡人其如予何？'

When the Master was surrounded in Kuang, he said, 'With King Wen dead, does not culture reside here [in me]? If heaven is going to destroy culture, those who come after me would not be able to have it. If heaven is not going to destroy culture, what can the people of Kuang do [to me]?'

Although heaven desires all human beings to follow the Way, it does not compel them to do so, nor does it have the power to ensure that the Way prevails on earth. It is ultimately up to human beings to realize and broaden the Way, as noted by Confucius:

15.29 子曰：'人能弘道，非道弘人。'

The Master said, 'It is human beings who are able to broaden the Way, not the Way that is able to broaden human beings.'

The word 'broaden' refers to the act of realizing, perpetuating and promoting the Way on earth to future generations.[12] The possibility of broadening the Way signifies that the Way is not predetermined or transcendental; human beings are empowered to realize the Way through their collective actions on earth.[13] That is why Confucius commended the sage-kings for acting based on the straight Way because doing so served to broaden the Way (15.25). Confucius' faith in the ability of human beings to broaden the Way and change the course of history accounts for the description of Confucius' teachings as humanistic.[14]

More about the Way: *He* (Harmony)

To further understand the Way, we need to understand another key concept expounded by Confucius: *he* (和 harmony). The achievement of harmony is the most important function of the observance of *li*, as noted in the verse below:

1.12 有子曰：'禮之用，和爲貴。先王之道，斯爲美；小大由之。'

> Master You said, 'Among the functions of *li*, harmony is the most valuable. [Harmony made] the Way of the Former Kings beautiful, and is followed alike in great and small [matters].'[15]

To broaden the Way on earth is to achieve harmony on earth. The Former Kings kept to the straight Way by observing *li*, which led to the establishment of harmony in the empire. The word 'harmony' conjures up the image of combining and arranging different musical notes to form a melodious and pleasing piece of music.[16] The aesthetic connotation of harmony is probably why the above verse describes harmony as 'beautiful'. How then does harmony function as a guiding standard for 'great and small matters'? To answer this question, we need to take a closer look at the concept of harmony by examining its internal and external aspects.

First, *internal* harmony refers to the inner peace, contentment and delight found in a person who possesses harmony. This internal harmony guides a person in her thoughts, feelings and actions in accordance with *li*.[17] The attainment of internal harmony is encapsulated in one word: joy (樂 *le*). Confucius delineates the relationship between knowledge (知 *zhi*), love (好 *hao*) and joy (樂 *le*) in this simple yet profound statement:

> 6.20 子曰：'知之者不如好之者, 好之者不如樂之者。'
>
> The Master said, 'A person who loves is better than a person who [merely] knows, and a person who finds joy is better than a person who [merely] loves.'[18]

Here, 'joy' does not refer to sensuous and transient pleasure but a deep appreciation of and great delight in something. Confucius does not stipulate the object of knowledge, love and joy in the verse. But it is reasonable to assume that he has both the Way (*dao*) and the observance of *li* in mind. On the former, we are informed that Confucius extols the value of 'being poor yet finding joy in the Way' (貧而樂道) (1.15).[19] According to 6.20, we need to go beyond having a mere cognitive awareness of (know) and affection towards (love) something, to a spontaneous delight (joy) in it. In other words, the ideal state is when we find joy in something in a natural and unself-conscious way, so much so that delighting in it has become second nature to us. In the case of the 'something' being the Way, this means we should seek to know, love *and* find joy in the Way; this is possible only by observing *li*. When we delight in the Way, we attain harmony and join the former kings in 'making the Way beautiful'. This, in turn, will result in human beings broadening the Way on earth.

The same point about joy applies when we take the object to refer to the observance of *li*. It is not enough for us to merely know or even love *li*; we also need to observe *li* by finding joy in doing so. Such a person is one who has internalized *li* to such an extent that observing *li* has become part of one's DNA and personal identity. The end result is a person who abides in *li* all the time (cf. 12.1) through the harmonization of one's thoughts, feelings and actions, thereby reflecting the beauty of the Way of the Former Kings.

It is noteworthy that Confucius stresses that the joy one obtains from observing *li* is independent of one's material comforts. It is for this reason that he praises his disciple Yanhui for being admirable:

6.11 子曰:'賢哉, 回也! 一簞食, 一瓢飲, 在陋巷, 人不堪其憂, 回也不改其樂。賢哉, 回也！'

The Master said, 'Excellent is Hui! He has a bowl of rice, a gourd of water, and lives in mean dwelling. Other people would find this sorrowful, but Hui does not let this affect his joy. Excellent is Hui!'

The verse above informs us that the joy Confucius talks about originates from within a person and is not influenced by one's external circumstances. It is a deep satisfaction that one obtains from observing *li*, through disciplining oneself in accordance with the Zhou culture, including its music. That is why Confucius urges all to 'find joy in regulating [yourself] through *li* and music' (樂節禮樂) (16.5). It is therefore not a surprise that Confucius describes himself as one who is '[so] joyful that he forgets about worry, and does not know that old age has befallen him' (樂以忘憂, 不知老之將至云爾) (7.19). This joy, in short, is what characterizes a person who possesses internal harmony.

Besides internal harmony, there is *external* harmony where a person fulfils the mandate of heaven and coexists peacefully, purposefully and joyfully with other human beings and one's surroundings in accordance with *li*.[20] Confucius himself claims that he 'understood the mandate of heaven' (知天命) (2.4). He reminds all to 'find joy in talking about the goodness of [other] people, find joy in having many excellent friends' (樂道人之善，樂多賢友) (16.5). Combining internal and external harmony is the opening verse of the *Analects*:

1.1 子曰：'學而時習之，不亦說乎？有朋自遠方來，不亦樂乎？'

The Master said, 'To learn and practise [what you have learned] from time to time, is it not a pleasure? To have friends who have come from afar, is it not a joy?'

Internal harmony is obtained when one finds pleasure in learning and application. It is interesting that Confucius describes learning and regular practice not in pragmatic terms such as 'a benefit' or 'a necessity' (although these nouns are certainly appropriate) but as 'a pleasure'. What he wishes to highlight is the joy one derives from studying and applying what one has learned. Complementing this internal harmony is external harmony as represented by the joy in meeting up with friends from afar. It is instructive that learning, regular practice and interaction with friends are all examples of *li*, given that *li* encompasses all normative behaviours (cf. 12.1). This reiterates our point that harmony is the most valuable function of *li* (1.12) since the former enables a person to find joy in observing the latter.

Spiritual-ethical-aesthetic dimension of *li*

Thus far, we have learned that the norm of *li* is the Zhou *li*, as exemplified in the paradigmatic behaviours and corresponding values and attitudes of the sage-kings. We have also noted that the ultimate purpose of *li* is to achieve harmony, both internally and externally. In this section, I would like to elaborate on how human beings could achieve internal and external harmony by observing *li* through three facets or angles: spiritual, ethical and aesthetic. These three facets are interrelated, integrated and inseparable, similar to how different facets of a diamond are individually distinguishable but come together to give the diamond its brilliance and shine. I shall use the term 'spiritual-ethical-aesthetic dimension' to underscore the interwoven nature of the three facets.[21]

For a start, it is helpful to note that the spiritual-ethical-aesthetic dimension of *li* is reflected in the life of Confucius. He describes his life path as follows:

> 2.4 子曰：'吾十有五而志于學，三十而立，四十而不惑，五十而知天命，六十而耳順，七十而從心所欲，不踰矩。'

> The Master said, 'At fifteen, I was set on learning; at thirty I took my stand; at forty I no longer doubtful; at fifty I understood the mandate of heaven; at sixty my ear was attuned; at seventy I could follow my heart-mind's desires without overstepping the line.'

Confucius understood the mandate of heaven (spiritual dimension), took his stand (i.e. observe *li*) and did not overstep the line (i.e. did not violate the boundary set by *li*) (ethical dimension), and was attuned and set on learning [the arts and humanities] as I shall explain later (aesthetic dimension). That is why he confidently proclaimed that he could follow his heart-mind's desires freely. The term 'heart-mind' (心 *xin*), rather than just 'heart', denotes the intertwining of affect and cognition. Like Confucius, we are encouraged to follow our heart-mind's desires so that our thoughts and feelings are aligned with *li*.[22] What we have is a portrait of a person who succeeds in observing *li* (not overstepping the line), not in a self-conscious, contrived or anxious manner, but in a spontaneous, genuine and relaxed way. In short, it is a picture of one who has achieved harmony.[23]

Confucius' achievement of harmony makes him a source of inspiration for others to follow suit. Unsurprisingly, one of Confucius' disciples asserts that had Confucius been a ruler of a state, he would be able to 'move [the people] and [they would] achieve harmony' (動之斯和) (19.25). To further understand the three facets of harmony, let us examine the spiritual, ethical and aesthetic facets in turn.

Spiritual facet

The spiritual facet of *li* refers to the spiritual basis for the observance of *li*. I have deliberately used the word 'spiritual' instead of 'religious' for two reasons. First, the term 'religion' usually connotes a system of beliefs involving the supernatural or afterlife, something that Confucius professes to be uninterested in. His disciples note that 'the Master did not speak of strange happenings, physical force, disorder and spirits' (子不語怪，力，亂，神) (7.21). When asked by a disciple about serving ghosts and spirits, Confucius responded: '[You are] not yet able to serve human beings, how is it possible to serve the ghosts?' (未能事人，焉能事鬼？) (11.12).

Second, the term 'spiritual' refers to the human capacity to make sense of oneself within a wider framework of meaning, and see oneself as part of a larger whole. Elsewhere, I have argued that spirituality helps a person acquire insights of enduring worth into one's personal existence, attribute meaning to one's life experiences, and value a non-material and transcendental (although not necessarily other-worldly) dimension to life (Tan, 2008, 2009a, 2009b, 2010; Tan & Wong, 2012). The spiritual dimension of *li*, accordingly, takes us beyond being merely a 'moral' person to finding one's place in the universe and achieving authentic and enduring harmony. This brings us back to our discussion on heaven and the Way. Confucius teaches that we should seek to fulfil the mandate of heaven by following the Way through observing the Zhou *li*. Harmony is grounded in the conviction that human beings have been invited and empowered by heaven to broaden the Way on earth by collectively manifesting the virtue bestowed by heaven.[24] I shall return to the spiritual dimension when I discuss Confucius' concept of the noble or exemplary human being (*junzi*) in a later chapter.

Ethical facet

While the spiritual facet focuses on achieving harmony through one's fulfilment of heaven's mandate, the ethical facet of *li* focuses on possessing harmony through regulating one's relationships with fellow human beings.[25] Confucius often uses the expression 'take a stand' to refer to conducting oneself appropriately in society by observing *li*. For example, he extols the merit of 'taking a stand through *li*' (立於禮) (8.8) and describes himself as 'taking my stand at thirty' (三十而立) (2.4). Not overstepping the line (不踰矩) (2.4) means not violating the boundary set by *li* even as one takes a stand. I shall elaborate on the relationship between 'taking a stand' and the arts and humanities when I discuss the aesthetic dimension of *li* later.

There are two aspects of the ethical facet. First, in tandem with Confucius' emphasis of the integration of one's thoughts, feelings and actions, the term 'ethical' refers not just to a person's actions and its consequences (as commonly understood in discussions on morality) but more importantly to *a person's character*.[26] Put otherwise, there should be a harmonization of one's behaviours, attitudes and values. It is precisely due to this lack of integration of actions, attitudes and values that Confucius reprimanded the rulers for observing an outward form of *li* without the substance (see previous chapter for details).

Second, the ethical facet emphasizes the *symbiotic relationship* between helping oneself and helping others to observe *li*. Confucius notes: 'In desiring to [take a] stand, one helps others to [take their] stand; in desiring to reach [a goal], one helps others to reach [their goal]' (己欲立而立人，己欲達而達人) (6.30). To 'take a stand' is to perform one's social roles in society in accordance with *li*. What Confucius is saying is that we can only observe *li* when we help others to do likewise. As such, external harmony is crucial for us to coexist and collaborate with others so as to collectively realize and broaden the Way (1.12).[27]

That said, achieving harmony with others does not mean eradicating our individual differences or coercing others to conform to one's own standards. Confucius cautions that we should 'seek harmony not sameness' (和而不同) (13.23).[28] We are further instructed in the *Analects* that 'to know and achieve harmony without being regulated by *li* will not work' (知和而和，不以禮節之，亦不可行也) (1.12). In other words, we should not seek superficial harmony (sameness) but genuine harmony (unity with diversity) by observing *li*. Genuine harmony is obtained when we possess the appropriate values and attitudes to accompany the outward observance of *li*, such as respect (敬) (3.26), modesty (儉) (3.4), deference (讓) (11.26) and virtue (德) (2.3). I shall postpone a detailed discussion of the ethical dimension of *li* to the next chapter. It suffices to note, for now, that we should not overemphasize the ethical facet of *li* or assume that this facet is more important than the spiritual or aesthetic dimensions. As noted in the preface, writers have a tendency to restrict Confucius' teachings to the ethical domain. Rejecting such a position, the thesis of this book is that the ethical dimension does not stand alone, neither is it the most important; rather, it is part of the spiritual-ethical-aesthetic dimension of *li*.

Aesthetic facet

Confucius alludes to the aesthetic facet of *li* in 1.13, when he points out that harmony 'made the Way of the Former Kings beautiful' (先王之道，斯爲美) (1.12). This facet refers to the observance of *li* that enables one to appreciate beauty, joy and ethical values through the arts and humanities.[29] Confucius notes the importance of the arts and humanities, in particular poetry and music:

> 8.8 子曰：'興於《詩》，立於禮，成於樂。'
>
> The Master said, 'Be inspired by the *Songs*, take a stand through *li*, and be complete with music.'

The verse above highlights the close relationship among poetry, *li* and music. We have already discussed how *li* enables a person to take a stand in society through normative behaviours with corresponding attitudes and values. The *Songs* here refers to the *Book of Songs* which is a compilation of Chinese poetry and one of the *Five Classics* in ancient China (see chapter 1 for details).[30] The value Confucius places on poetry and music is evident when he remarked that 'it was only when I returned from Wei [state] to Lu [state] that music was put right, and the *ya* and *song* were put into their proper order' (吾自衛反魯，然後樂正，《雅》，《頌》各得其所) (9.15).[31] It is probable that Confucius revised the *ya* and *song* which are sections in the *Songs* by properly setting the poetry to music.[32]

By juxtaposing poetry and music with *li*, Confucius foregrounds their contributions to the observance of *li*. Enjoying the arts is indispensable to one's observance of *li*; as previously mentioned, 'a person who loves is better than a person who [merely] knows, and a person who finds joy is better than a person who [merely] loves' (知之者不如好之者，好之者不如樂之者) (6.20). This joy is obtained when one is inspired by the beauty and significance of poetry and music.[33]

Let us further explore the aesthetic function of language, literature and music. On *language and literature*, Confucius avers: '[If you] do not learn the *Songs*, you will be without words' (不學《詩》，無以言) (16.13). What he means is that a person who has not studied the *Songs* is unable to communicate with and relate to others. Confucius reinforces this point when he advised his son Boyu:

17.10 子謂伯魚曰：'女爲《周南》，《召南》矣乎？人而不爲《周南》，《召南》，其猶正牆面而立也與？'

The Master said to Boyu, 'Have you studied the *Zhounan* and *Shaonan*? To be a human being and not study the *Zhounan* and *Shaonan* is like a person who stands with one's face to the wall.'

The *Zhounan* and *Shaonan* are sections from the *Songs*. Confucius' counsel to his son is that a person who does not appreciate the *Songs* is unable to interact well with others; such a person would be isolated, like a man who stands facing the wall. The action of standing reminds us of Confucius' analogy of 'taking a stand' for the observance of *li* (cf. 2.4, 6.30). A man who stands with his face to the wall is therefore one who is unable to conduct oneself in society in accordance with *li*. By drawing upon the *Songs* and other classical texts as channels for the observance of *li*, Confucius is following the straight Way (直道 *zhidao*) by relying on the wisdom of the past (cf. 15.25).[34]

How then do the *Songs* enable a person to take a stand? Confucius delineates a number of benefits of mastering the *Songs*:

17.9 子曰：'小子何莫學夫《詩》？《詩》，可以興，可以觀，可以羣，可以怨。邇之事父，遠之事君；多識於鳥獸草木之名。'

The Master said, 'Little ones, why do none of you study the *Songs*? The *Songs* can give you inspiration, observation [skill], [ability to] live with others, and [means to express] grievances. [The *Songs* enable you to] serve your father who is near, and serve your lord who is far. [You will] learn broadly about the names of birds, beasts, plants and trees.'

From the above verse, we can make two observations about the relationship between studying poetry and observing *li*. First, we see how a person can benefit from studying the *Songs* by engaging one's senses. The allusion to looking and listening ('inspiration', 'observation skills', 'learn broadly about the names of birds' etc.), speaking ('means to express grievances'), and moving ('ability to live with others', 'serving your father' and 'serving your lord' etc.) reminds us of 12.1 where Confucius exhorts all to do all things in accordance with *li*. Mastering the *Songs*, therefore, contributes directly to one's observance of *li*. Second, the verse highlights how poetry allows us to achieve internal and external harmony. Internal harmony is implied in the expression 'inspired' that suggests that a person finds pleasure and enlightenment when learning poems. External harmony is achieved when one is able to live peaceably and collaboratively with fellow human beings, including one's superiors ('ability to live with others', 'serve your lord' and 'expressing grievances') and with nature ('learn broadly about the names of birds, beasts, plants and trees').[35]

Examples of how poetry from the *Songs* could offer new meanings and insights that facilitate our observance of *li* are recorded in two passages. The first passage is a conversation between Confucius and his disciple Zixia.

3.8 子夏問曰：'"巧笑倩兮，美目盼兮，素以爲絢兮。"何謂也？'

子曰：'繪事後素。'

曰：'禮後乎？'

子曰：'起予者商也！始可與言《詩》已矣。'

Zixia asked, '"Entrancing smile with dimples, beautiful eyes so clear, colours upon the unadorned base". What is the meaning?'

The Master said, 'The plain base comes first, then the colours are applied.'

Zixia said, 'Just like *li* that comes after?'

The Master said, 'It is you who have illuminated me! It is only with someone like you that one can discuss the *Songs*.'

In the passage, Zixia was able to draw a parallel between painting on an unadorned base (plain silk) and observing *li*. Just as colours are added to an unadorned base, the observance of *li* is built upon one's basic quality (cf. 15.18. I shall elaborate on this 'basic quality' in subsequent chapters).

The second passage, like the first passage, records a conversation between Confucius and a disciple. A disciple Zigong quoted from the *Songs*: 'Like bone carved and polished, like jade cut and ground' (如切如磋，如琢如磨) (1.15). From reflecting on the process of refining raw ivory and jade, Zigong inferred that loving *li* similarly entails a long process of self-cultivation. Delighted with Zigong's insights drawn from the *Songs*, Confucius responded: 'Only with someone like you can one discuss the *Songs*; you know what is to come based on what has been said' (始可與言《詩》已矣，告諸往而知來者). The preceding shows that Confucius values the function of language (cf. 16.13) and poetry (cf. 17.10) in facilitating one's effective communication and smooth integration into society. It is palpable that Confucius does not see the learning of languages, literature and other humanities as a purely academic pursuit. Rather, such learning serves to mould one's character and guide one's outlook, life choices and role performance in society. I shall return to the topic of language when I discuss *zhengming* (rectification of names) in a later chapter.

Besides poetry, *music* is also instrumental in enabling one to appreciate beauty, joy and ethical values, thereby contributing towards one's attainment of harmony through the observance of *li*. Confucius, himself a zither player and music lover, explains the function of harmony in music (as translated by Slingerland):

3.23 子語魯大師樂，曰：'樂其可知也：始作，翕如也；從之，純如也，皦如也，繹如也，以成。'

The Master was discussing music with the Grand Music Master of Lu. He said, 'What can be known about music is this: when it first begins, it resounds with a confusing variety of notes, but as it unfolds, these notes are reconciled by means of harmony, brought into tension by means of counterpoint, and finally woven together into a seamless whole. It is in this way that music reaches its perfection.'

Other parts of the *Analects* record how music paves the way for a person to transcend the mundane and enter a realm of harmony and beauty.

Once, Confucius was so enthralled by the *shao* music that he could not appreciate the taste of meat for three months; in his words, '[I had] no idea that the joy of music could reach such heights' (不圖爲樂之至於斯也) (7.14). In the same vein, Zengxi, a disciple of Confucius, was able to express his harmonized worldview through playing his zither meditatively, portraying a picture of someone who is in tune with himself, people and nature (11.26) (I shall return to this passage in the next section).

Other than providing peace, beauty and joy, music also plays a part in ethical inculcation. Musical appreciation contributes towards ethical development in at least two ways. First, a well-composed and performed piece of music regulates our emotions by giving us a sense of *balance, concord and inspiration*. Confucius was very particular about the choice of musical pieces played, which probably explains why he was unhappy with Zilu's zither playing (11.15). According to Yang (1980, p. 120) and Slingerland (2003, p. 117), Confucius was displeased with the tune of music played by Zilu, which came across as crude and aggressive rather than gentle and refined. In contrast, he praised the 'Guan ju', which is the first of the *Songs*, for '[expressing] joy without being wanton, [expressing] sorrow without being injurious' (樂而不淫，哀而不傷) (3.20). The ethical influence of music is the reason why Confucius exhorts us to 'find joy in regulating [yourself] through *li* and music' (樂節禮樂) (16.5) and 'be complete with music' (成於樂) (8.8).

Second, the historical background of a piece of music also contains *ethical lessons* for human beings. It was based on such consideration that Confucius evaluated the *shao* music and *wu* music. On the former, he judged it to be 'perfectly beautiful and perfectly good' (盡美矣，又盡善也) because it was the court music of sage-king Shun who ascended the throne peacefully after the abdication of his predecessor (3.25). In contrast, he judged the *wu* music to be 'perfectly beautiful [but] not perfectly good' (盡美矣，未盡善也), as it was the court music of King Wu who came to the throne through military force – an act that Confucius considered to be a violation of *li*. Music is also a means to bring people together in harmony; we see this in 7.32: 'When the Master sings with others [and he finds the] singing good, [he will] surely [ask to] have [the song sung] again, then [sing] in harmony [the second time round]' (子與人歌而善，必使反之，而後和之).

The close link between music and *li* explains why Confucius relates them to social order and punishments. He notes in 13.3, '[When] matters are not accomplished, *li* and music will not flourish; [when] *li* and music do not flourish, punishments will miss the mark; [when] punishments miss the mark, the people will not know what to do [with themselves]' (事不成，則禮樂不興；禮樂不興，則刑罰不中；刑罰不中，則民無所錯手足). For *li* and music to flourish, a prerequisite is the establishment of a social order where people are able to perform their tasks smoothly. This will give them the peace of mind to focus on observing *li* and enjoying music. Socialized into a culture enriched by *li* and music, both the ruler and the people will be able to 'take their stand' in society. The ruler should therefore ensure that laws and penalties are introduced and implemented appropriately so as to complement the observance of *li*. In turn, *li* would guide the people to conduct themselves acceptably in society. That Confucius mentions music in relation to *li* reiterates the ethical influence of music in attracting people to learn and meditate on what is good and desirable as determined by *li*.[36]

The example of Zengxi

Against a backdrop of our understanding of the spiritual, ethical and aesthetic facets of *li*, it is timely to look at an illustration of the spiritual-ethical-aesthetic dimension of *li* from a passage in the *Analects*. The passage is about the conversation between Confucius and his four disciples (Zilu, Ranyou, Zihua and Zengxi) about their aspirations. The first three disciples centred their aspirations on statescraft: Zilu aspired to rule in a state of a thousand chariots, Ranyou wished to rule over a small territory, and Zihua dreamed of becoming a minor official in charge of protocol. In contrast to the other three disciples, Zengxi's answer was markedly different and, more importantly, the only one praised by Confucius. An excerpt of the conversation between Zengxi and Confucius is as follows:

11.26 '點！爾何如？'
鼓瑟希，鏗爾，舍瑟而作，對曰：'異乎三子者之撰。'

子曰:'何傷乎? 亦各言其志也。'

曰:'莫春者, 春服既成, 冠者五六人, 童子六七人, 浴乎沂, 風乎舞雩, 詠而歸。'

夫子喟然歎曰:'吾與點也!'

'Zengxi, how about you?'

Zengxi strummed the final notes on the zither, set the instrument aside and rose to his feet. 'I would choose to do something different from the other three.'

The Master said, 'What harm is there in that? Each of you is talking about your aspirations.'

'At the end of spring, after the spring clothes have been made, I would like, together with five or six adults and six or seven children, to bathe in the Yi River, to enjoy the breeze on the Rain Altar, then return home singing.'

The Master sighed deeply and said, 'I am with Zengxi!'

Zengxi's aspiration appears modest and even prosaic, in contradistinction to the grand and ambitious aspirations of the other three disciples. Given Confucius' constant refrain on the need for him and his disciples to hold an office in a state, it is surprising that Confucius chose to identify with Zengxi's aspiration. But Confucius' support for Zengxi's aspiration makes sense when we take into consideration three distinctive characteristics of Zengxi in this passage.

First, Zengxi was not insecure and anxious to prove his worth and boast about his abilities, like the other disciples. Rather, he was content with finding harmony with nature (spiritual), human relationships (ethical), and music through singing and zither playing (aesthetic). Second, the activities he dreamed of – wearing spring clothes, being with friends, bathing in the river, enjoying the breeze and singing – mundane though they may be, were all in accordance with *li* as they reflect a state of peace, balance and concord with oneself, people and nature. Third, Zengxi epitomizes someone who goes beyond knowing and loving the Way to finding joy in it; this is seen in his spontaneous and almost effortless appreciation of contentment and beauty. Overall, Zengxi's aspiration paints a charming picture of harmony through his joyful observance of *li*.[37]

Conclusion

We have learned in this chapter that the norm for *li* is Zhou *li* as exemplified in the normative behaviours and corresponding values and attitudes of the sage-kings. It is the mandate of heaven to bestow human beings, including Confucius and the sage-kings, with virtue so that the Way might prevail on earth. Given that the Way had not prevailed during Confucius' time, as evident in the rampant violation of *li* by the masses and rulers in the midst of widespread political and social chaos, Confucius' mission was to restore the Way on earth. To broaden the Way is to achieve harmony through the observance of *li*.

It is important to note that the observance of *li* as well as the joy one derives from such an endeavour does not and cannot occur overnight. To use the analogy of driving, observing *li* is unlike the achievement of earning a driver's license at a particular point in time. Rather it is more akin to the process of becoming a skilful driver that entails a lifelong pursuit. Confucius modelled this spirit of lifelong learning when he asks for more time to learn to observe *li*: 'Add a few more years to my life so that [I will have had] fifty years of study [and I] could be free of [any] serious oversight' (加我數年，五十以學易，可以無大過矣) (7.17, also see 2.4). The observance of *li* involves a long and arduous journey of self-cultivation where one goes through three stages. The three stages of the observance of *li* are based on the extent to which one has succeeded in knowing, loving and enjoying *li* (6.20).

The first stage: Knowing *li*

The first stage is that of *knowing li*, where the novice begins to 'take a stand' by learning about and reflecting on the nature and application of *li* in one's life. The content of *li* includes desirable behaviours, values and attitudes such as filial piety, respect, deference and courage. The application of *li* includes conducting oneself appropriately in accordance to the specific scope and structure of *li*, as well as the extent of individual improvisation allowed. For example, a novice will learn that she should perform a religious ritual by adhering strictly to the details, but may exercise her discretion when holding a causal conversation. Besides learning about normative behaviours, a novice is taught to strive to harmonize her actions with desirable attitudes and values in all aspects of her life. Overall, she is a beginner in the sense that she is still learning the ropes, struggling to relate different types and requirements of *li* to specific circumstances, and making inevitable mistakes along the way.

The second stage: Loving *li*

The next stage is the intermediate stage of *loving li*. The focus is on observing *li* with greater confidence, affection and enthusiasm as compared to the first stage. Unlike the novice, the intermediate learner is more well-versed and experienced in observing *li*, and more adept at exercising her own judgement to suit the needs of different contexts. The spotlight here is on learning to love *li* by being affectionate towards and intrinsically motivated to observe *li* in all aspects of her life, be it in looking, listening, speaking or moving. Her attachment to *li* is also evident in her increasingly successful harmonization of her thoughts, feelings and actions. Conscious of her mission to fulfil heaven's mandate, she works hard at broadening the Way by studying and manifesting Zhou *li*. However, at the intermediate level, she has yet to gain mastery in her observance of *li*; this is evident in her somewhat self-conscious, deliberate and obligatory effort to remind herself to act appropriately and align her thoughts, feelings and actions to *li*.

The third stage: Finding joy in *li*

The final stage is that of *finding joy in li*, where one succeeds in going beyond merely knowing and loving *li*. The expert in this stage observes *li* in a whole-hearted, holistic and spontaneous way because doing so has become part of her identity. Delighting in *li*, her attitudes, values and behaviours are integrated in her mission to fulfil heaven's mandate by broadening the Way. Appreciating the spiritual-ethical-aesthetic dimension of *li*, she is also skilful in exercising her discernment and judgement to modify her observance of *li* where necessary. Another key characteristic of the expert is her ability to exert a positive influence on people around her so that others are also inspired to observe *li*. However, this does not mean that she is perfect as she still may have occasional lapses. But she persists in observing *li* faithfully and joyfully in her lifelong quest of self-cultivation and improvement.

It is important to note that the three stages are not strictly demarcated; there are natural overlaps between the stages and it is even possible for a person to straddle between two stages. Furthermore, we should note that the exercise of individual improvisation is not limited to any one stage, but exists in all three stages. In other words, the novice, intermediate learner and expert are all expected to exercise their individual discretion and judgement where necessary because the observance of *li covers everything one does in life*. It is therefore impossible for anyone, including the novice, to avoid situations where she does not need to discern, evaluate and decide. An example, as mentioned, is that of making small talk. What distinguishes the observers of *li* in the different stages are the *varying* levels of competence and confidence, degree of knowing, loving and finding joy in observing *li*, and extent of success in observing *li*. Ultimately, what distinguishes a novice from an expert is not whether a person is at liberty to improvise her observance of *li*, but the extent to which the person is able to observe *li* appropriately, lovingly and joyfully.[38]

But there remains a question about the specific behaviours, attitudes and values required for one to observe *li*. What are these behaviours, attitudes and values? How are these behaviours, values and attitudes related to one other, and how do they come together to guide a person in practice? Is there a central and higher-order quality that sums up the normativity of *li*? These questions will form the topic of discussion in the next chapter.

Chapter 4

The Concept of *Ren*

We have learned in the previous two chapters that *li* refers to the totality of normative human behaviours that are accompanied by corresponding attitudes and values for all aspects of one's life. *Li* is based on the norm practised by the sage-kings who lived before Confucius' time, especially during the Zhou dynasty. The most important function of *li* is to achieve internal and external harmony where we find peace, concord and joy within ourselves and with people and surroundings spiritually, ethically and aesthetically.

What we have yet to explore is the question of the specific behaviours, attitudes and values required in one's observance of *li*. A quality that sums up all the normative behaviours and corresponding values and attitudes is *ren*. The Chinese character '仁' (*ren*) signifies co-humanity as it is comprised of two Chinese characters: 'human being' (人 *ren*) and 'two' (二 *er*). This idea of co-humanity or humans as interdependent of one another is a running theme in Confucius' thought. The *Analects* is replete with accounts of Confucius interacting and conversing with all kinds of people. Many paintings of Confucius also portray him, not reading or meditating by himself, but instructing his disciples or communing with people. It is therefore necessary for us to explore the concept of *ren* in order to fully understand Confucius' philosophy. Mentioned over 100 times in the *Analects*, the concept of *ren* existed prior to Confucius' time. While its exact original meaning was unclear, what we do know is that *ren* was a term historically associated with the aristocrats and rulers.[1]

Like what he did for the concept of *li*, Confucius gives *ren* a new interpretation and wider application. *Ren* has been variously translated as 'benevolence', 'goodness', 'perfect virtue', 'humaneness', 'humanity', 'authoritative conduct' etc. Given its multiple definitions and its multifaceted nature, I shall leave *ren* un-translated, as with the case of *li*, but explain its meaning and significance in the chapter. This chapter begins by clarifying the relationship between *ren* and *li*, followed by discussing the key characteristics of *ren* and its relationship with other Confucius' concepts.

Relationship between *li* and *ren*

To understand the close relationship between *li* and *ren*, we need to revisit the passage where Confucius clarifies the meaning and scope of *li*.

> 12.1 顏淵問仁。
> 子曰：'克己復禮爲仁。一日克己復禮，天下歸仁焉。爲仁由己，而由人乎哉？'
> 顏淵曰：'請問其目。'
> 子曰：'非禮勿視，非禮勿聽，非禮勿言，非禮勿動。'
> 顏淵曰：'回雖不敏，請事斯語矣。'
>
> Yanhui asked about *ren*.
>
> The Master replied, 'Overcoming the self and returning to *li* is *ren*. If a person can overcome the self and return to *li* for one day, the whole world would regard such a person as *ren*. Being *ren* comes from oneself, how could it come from other people?'
>
> Yanhui said, 'I would like to ask about the specifics.'
>
> The Master replied, 'Do not look if it is not in accordance with *li*; do not listen if it is not in accordance with *li*; do not speak if it is not in accordance with *li*; do not move if it is not in accordance with *li*.'
>
> Yanhui said, 'Although I am not quick [in learning], allow me to carry out what you have said.'

Confucius' statement about 'overcoming the self and returning to *li* is *ren*' was in response to Yanhui's query on *ren*. Confucius' point is that *ren* is achieved when we observe *li*.[2] The expression 'overcoming the self' refers to regulating and restraining one's attitudes, values and behaviours so that one does not violate *li* at all times. In other words, we should discipline ourselves by conscientiously doing everything, be it looking, listening, speaking or moving, in accordance with *li*.[3]

Confucius elaborates on *ren* in the verse that immediately follows 12.1:

12.2 仲弓問仁。

子曰：'出門如見大賓，使民如承大祭。己所不欲，勿施於人。在邦無怨，在家無怨。' 仲弓曰：'雍雖不敏，請事斯語矣。'

Zhonggong asked about *ren*.

The Master replied, 'When outdoor, behave as though you are meeting important guests; when employing the common people, behave as though you are overseeing a great sacrifice. What you do not desire for yourself, do not impose upon others. [In this way], you will have no ill will in public, and no ill will at home.'

Zhonggong replied, 'Although I am not quick [in learning], allow me to carry out what you have said.'

Confucius teaches that *ren* is about respecting others ('you are meeting important guests'), demonstrating sincerity, reverence, dutifulness ('you are overseeing a great sacrifice'), and empathy ('what you do not desire for yourself, do not impose upon others'). Confucius presents *ren* as an overarching and general quality that encompasses the more specific qualities such as respect, sincerity and empathy (I shall return to this point about *ren* being a general term later).[4] Keeping in mind our definition of *li* as normative human behaviours accompanied by appropriate attitudes and values that pervade all aspects of our lives, Confucius' point in 12.2 is that *ren* is achieved when we conduct ourselves in accordance with *li*, whether in private or public. Read together, the two verses (12.1 and 12.2) inform us that *ren* is the goal and *li* is the way to achieve it. To put it simply, *li is the means to attain ren*.[5]

Not only is observing *li* the way for one to attain *ren*, the observance of *li* is also the evidence that a person truly possesses *ren*. This point is stated in 3.3 where Confucius asks rhetorically: 'A person who is not *ren*, what [has he got] to do with *li*?' (人而不仁，如禮何?). This verse strongly suggests that a person who is *ren* is *also* one who observes *li*.[6] This interpretation makes sense when we remember that *li*, as an all-encompassing term, includes all prescriptive actions as well as desirable attitudes and values. Confucius further avers that a person who is *ren* must also be one who observes *li* – 'the whole world would regard such [a person] as *ren*' (天下歸仁焉) (12.1). A person who successfully observes *li* is necessarily one who possesses the behaviour, attitude and value of *ren*. It follows that *li* is the social-cultural expression of *ren* or to put it simply, *li is the embodiment of ren.*

The two ways in which *li* and *ren* are related – means and embodiment – are complementary and symbiotic. On the one hand, the observance of *li* provides the means for one to progressively cultivate *ren*; on the other hand, the inculcation of *ren* is evident in the extent to which one faithfully observes *li* in all aspects of life. Following our discussion of the relationship between *ren* and *li*, I propose defining *ren* as follows:

Ren defines the normativity of *li* in the sense that to observe *li* is to possess and demonstrate *ren* in all our thoughts, feelings and actions.

Two observations can be made about our definition of *ren* as the quality that defines the normativity of *li*. First, *ren* is the *central quality* that encompasses all other normative qualities in our observance of *li*.[7] All desirable qualities when we observe *li* reflect different facets of *ren*; that is why Confucius teaches in 12.2 that *ren* entails showing respect, sincerity, reverence, dutifulness and empathy. Other commendable attributes associated with *ren* in the *Analects* include courage (勇) (14.4), 'strength, decisiveness, simplicity and deliberateness in speech' (剛、毅、木、訥) (13.27), and 'tolerance, trustworthiness, diligence and generosity' (寬，信，敏，惠) (17.6). I shall return to *ren* as the central quality that encompasses all other normative qualities when I discuss the two senses of *ren* as used in the *Analects*.[8]

Second, the definition of *ren* as the defining quality for the normativity of *li* means that *ren* is not just about one's attitudes and values; it also concerns one's actions that are visible to all and sundry. In 12.2, Confucius describes *ren* not purely in terms of attitudes or values but in concrete actions, such as how one should behave in public and how one should employ others. Just as *ren* is not purely or primarily about one's attitudes and values, *li* is not purely or primarily about one's actions. As pointed out earlier, *li* was principally thought of by the rulers and people during Confucius' time as consisting of one's ritualistic and formalistic behaviours, with little consideration of one's thoughts and feelings. We have, however, already learned that one's actions, no matter how outwardly aligned with *li*, must stem from corresponding attitudes and values from within. One's affective disposition towards *li* is paramount, as Confucius stresses that we should not just observe *li* but 'love *li*' (好禮) (1.15, 13.4, 14.41).[9] It follows that a person who observes *li* is also one who possesses and manifests the harmonization of *ren* behaviours, attitudes and values. This inseparable relationship between *ren* and *li* is the reason why Confucius asks rhetorically: 'A person who is not *ren*; what has he got to do with *li*?' (人而不仁, 如禮何?) (3.3).[10]

I will further amplify the relationship between *li* and *ren* through three examples from the *Analects*. The first example is about a person who appears to observe *li* but is bereft of *ren*:

3.26 子曰: '居上不寬, 爲禮不敬, 臨喪不哀, 吾何以觀之哉? '

The Master said, 'One who in occupying high office is not tolerant, who in observing *li* is not respectful, and who in overseeing the mourning rites does not grieve – how could I bear to look upon such a person?'

Here Confucius disapproves of a person, in this case, a ruler, who appears to observe *li* but lacks tolerance, respect and sincerity. Such a person, as noted in the chapter on *li*, is observing *the prevailing li* and not *Confucius' li*. To Confucius, one who is truly observing *li* (i.e. *Confucius' li*) will naturally be tolerant, respectful and sincere – qualities that, as discussed earlier, reflect the virtue of *ren*. This example shows the inseparable relationship between *li* and *ren*: the possession of *ren* traits determines whether one is genuinely observing *li*. Without *ren*, a person who appears to observe *li* is not really observing *li*.[11]

Just as one can appear to observe *li* but lacks *ren*, it is possible for one to appear to possess *ren* but does not observe *li* outwardly. This brings us to our second example where Confucius describes one who has *ren*-related qualities, but lacks the necessary follow-up action in accordance with *li*:

> 8.2 子曰：'恭而無禮則勞，慎而無禮則葸，勇而無禮則亂，直而無禮則絞。'
>
> The Master said, 'Deference without *li* is labour; caution without *li* is timidity; courage without *li* is rowdiness; candour without *li* is rudeness.'

Here Confucius describes a person who possesses desirable qualities such as deference, caution, courage and candour – attributes that reflect *ren*. But such a person manifests behaviours that violate *li*, such as rowdiness and rudeness. A case in point is a person who is courageous but ignorant of the proper social-cultural ways to express her boldness; she might end up offending others through her aggressive or disruptive demeanour. She would be like a proverbial elephant creating havoc in a china shop. Such a person, although possessing *ren*-related qualities, has yet to fully acquire the virtue of *ren*. Desirable attitudes and values such as courage and candour do not, in themselves, imply that the possessor of these attitudes and values has achieved *ren*. The litmus test is when she is able to match the appropriate actions to these qualities. To do so, she needs *li* to inform and regulate her behaviours so that she could manifest these qualities appropriately and harmonize her behaviours with her attitudes and values.

The third example, briefly mentioned earlier, is about observing *li* in the spirit of *ren*.

> 12.2 仲弓問仁。
>
> 子曰：'出門如見大賓，使民如承大祭。己所不欲，勿施於人。在邦無怨，在家無怨。'
>
> Zhonggong asked about *ren*.
>
> The Master replied, 'When outdoor, behave as though you are meeting important guests; when employing the common people, behave as though you are overseeing a great sacrifice. What you do not desire for yourself, do not impose upon others. [In this way], you will have no ill will in public, and no ill will at home.'

Here we see a perfect balance between *li* and *ren*. Normative behaviours are aligned with their corresponding attitudes and values when one internalizes and demonstrates respect, sincerity, reverence, dutifulness and empathy. In this case, *ren* motivates and directs the person to think, feel and do what is right, while *li* guides and regulates her to think, feel and do what is right *in the right way*.

Having clarified and expounded the relationship between *li* and *ren*, I shall further explicate the concept of *ren* for the rest of this chapter. For a start, it is important to note that there are two senses of *ren* used in the *Analects*: general and specific.

Two senses of *ren*: General and specific

Up to this point, I have been using *ren* as a broad and higher-order term that encompasses other desirable qualities. In the *Analects*, however, Confucius also uses *ren* in a more specific and restricted sense. Take the following two verses on *ren*:

4.1 子曰：'里仁爲美。擇不處仁，焉得知？'

The Master said, 'It is beautiful to live where *ren* is. If a person does not choose to live with *ren*, how can he be wise?'

9.29 子曰：'知者不惑，仁者不憂，勇者不懼。'

The Master said, 'A wise person is not confused, a *ren* person is not anxious, a courageous person is not afraid.'

In the first verse (4.1), *ren* is used as a general term that includes the quality of wisdom; a person can be wise *only if* she cultivates *ren* in her life (i.e. 'beautiful to live where *ren* is') (also see 14.4, 13.27 and 17.6 where *ren* is used as an all-encompassing and higher-order concept).[12] I have utilized this general sense of *ren* in my earlier discussion on the relationship between *ren* and *li*. Returning to 3.3, 12.1 and 12.2, Confucius is saying that the realization of *ren* as a universal concept is intricately tied to the observance of *li*. In the second verse (9.29), however, *ren* is used as a specific term that exists side by side with other desirable qualities such as wisdom, courage and reverence (also see 12.22, 14.28

and 15.33 where *ren* is used as a first-order and one-among-many concept).

The two senses of *ren* are not contradictory because *ren* is a multifaceted concept that defies a straightforward definition. The two senses exist as Confucius chooses to highlight different aspects of *ren* based on the issue at hand, the profile of the one asking the question, and the context in which the topic was raised.[13] Having clarified the two senses of *ren*, we shall examine the importance and key characteristics of *ren*.

The importance of *ren*

The importance Confucius places on *ren* is seen in his assertion that 'the common people [need] *ren* more than water and fire' (民之於仁也，甚於水火) (15.35); 'a person who loves *ren* could not be surpassed' (好仁者，無以尚) (4.6); and 'when [it comes to being] *ren*, do not yield even to [your] teacher' (當仁，不讓於師) (15.36). Confucius even commends those who sacrifice their life to achieve *ren*:

> 15.9 子曰：'志士仁人，無求生以害仁，有殺身以成仁。'
>
> The Master said, 'Among purposeful scholar-officials and *ren* persons, none would save their lives by harming *ren*, and they might well give up their lives to become *ren*.'

As in the case for *li*, it is important to not just act according to *ren* but to love *ren*. Confucius laments that he has yet to meet 'people who love *ren*' (好仁者) (4.6). He proclaims that 'it is beautiful to live where *ren* is' (里仁爲美) (4.1), signifying the combined aesthetic and ethical appeal of *ren*. By pointing that 'a *ren* person is content to be *ren*' (仁者安仁) (4.2), Confucius further highlights the state of ease and joy a person experiences when she abides in *ren*.

What is a *ren* person like?

Confucius describes a '*ren* person' (仁者) as 'not anxious' (不憂) (9.29, 14.28). Confucius explains the secret to the *ren* person's lack of anxiety:

'[If you] examine within [and] and [you are] not ashamed, why be anxious [and] why be afraid?' (內省不疚，夫何憂何懼？) (12.4). The reason why a *ren* person has nothing to be ashamed is because '[if you are] set on *ren*, [you will be] free from evil' (苟志於仁矣，無惡也) (4.4). Such a person has disciplined herself by observing *li* in her thoughts, feelings and actions (12.1) and consequently faces no ill will in her public or private life (12.2). The reverse is true of a person who has not achieved *ren*. Confucius asserts that 'one who is not *ren* cannot remain long in adversity, nor can [he] remain long in joyful [circumstances]' (不仁者不可以久處約，不可以長處樂) (4.2). Such a person will find adversity unbearable, unlike a *ren* person who finds contentment in all circumstances. For the same reason, a person without *ren* would not remain long in joyful circumstances as she would eventually become discontented and crave for greater things in life.

We therefore find two contrasting portrayals of a *ren* person and a un-*ren* person. One who possesses *ren* is contented, guiltless and at peace with the world and herself because she has achieved harmony. As noted in 1.12, the most important function of *li* is harmony that acts as the guiding standard for all things. A *ren* person, by observing *li*, has achieved internal and external harmony in her thoughts, feelings and actions, and demonstrates her attainment of harmony through *ren* behaviours, attitudes and values.

A *ren* person is an ethical person *and more*. Like *li*, *ren* is not just an ethical concept but is more accurately described as a *spiritual-ethical-aesthetic concept*. Let me briefly explain each of the spiritual, ethical and aesthetic angles. First, the spiritual angle of *ren* stems from heaven as the source of normativity. A *ren* person is like Confucius who is conscious of the presence of heaven, understands the mandate of heaven (2.4), is careful not to offend heaven (3.13), is aware that heaven is the author of virtue in her (7.23) and desires to broaden the Way (15.29). Such a person models herself upon heaven, like what sage-king Yao did (8.19). She strives to fulfil heaven's mandate by broadening the Way through observing *li*.

Second, the ethical angle of *ren* focuses on feeling, thinking and doing what is desirable in one' interactions with and service for others in society. It is concerned with qualities that govern human relationships such as filial piety, reverence, deference, trustworthiness and so on.

As Confucius has much to say about these qualities in the *Analects*, I shall postpone a detailed discussion of these qualities and their relationship to *ren* to a later section.

Finally, the aesthetic angle of *ren* is highlighted in Confucius' rhetorical question, 'What has a person who is not *ren* got to do with music?' (人而不仁，如樂何？) (3.3). We have already learned in the previous chapter that music complements the observance of *li* in harmonizing one's actions with one's attitudes and values. Confucius adds in 13.3 that '[when] matters are not accomplished, *li* and music will not flourish; [when] *li* and music do not flourish, punishments will miss the mark; [when] punishments miss the mark, the people will not know what to do' (事不成，則禮樂不興；禮樂不興，則刑罰不中；刑罰不中，則民無所錯手足). Linking 13.3 to 3.3, the flourishing of music refers to the success of music in regulating human behaviours, attitudes and values towards the achievement of *ren* in accordance with *li*. Integrating the spiritual, ethical and aesthetic angles, a *ren* person may echo with Confucius that she 'understands the mandate of heaven' (知天命) (spiritual dimension), 'can follow [her] heart-mind's desires without overstepping the line' (從心所欲，不踰矩) (ethical dimension), and '[her] ear is attuned' (耳順) and 'set on learning [the arts and humanities]' (志于學) (aesthetic dimension) (2.4).[14]

Ren as loving others

What then is the essence of *ren*? Confucius sums it up with just two words: 'love others' (愛人) (12.22). But that prompts two further questions: What does 'loving others' mean? And how does one love others? The next section answers these two questions.

What does 'loving others' mean?

For a start, 'loving others' does not mean liking everyone unconditionally, nor does it mean that a *ren* person should not or does not dislike anyone. Confucius states that 'only a *ren* person is capable of liking people and disliking people' (唯仁者能好人，能惡人) (4.3), that is, only a *ren* person can truly discriminate between good and evil people. She does so not on the basis of one's own preferences or biases but on the principle of *ren* itself: 'If you are set on *ren*, you will be free from evil' (苟志於仁矣，無惡也) (4.4). It follows that a *ren* person is one who only loves those who conduct themselves in accordance with *li* (cf. 12.1, 12.2). A *ren* person's discretion and prudence also deter her from pursuing harmony at all costs. This is because she is aware that 'to know and achieve harmony without being regulated by *li* will not work' (知和而和，不以禮節之，亦不可行也) (1.12). Accordingly, she strives to promote unity among human beings in accordance with *li* where the shared vision is the attainment of *ren* behaviours, attitudes and values.

Just as loving others does not mean liking everyone regardless of the person's character, loving others does not mean trying to get everyone to like you. Confucius highlights this in his reply to his disciple:

13.24 子貢問曰：'鄉人皆好之，何如？'

子曰：'未可也。'

'鄉人皆惡之，何如？'

子曰：'未可也；不如鄉人之善者好之，其不善者惡之。'

Zigong asked, 'All the villagers like him. How about that?'

The Master said, 'It is not enough.'

'All the villagers hate him. How about that?'

The Master said, 'It is not enough. It would be better for the good villagers to like him, and those who are not good to hate him.'

Confucius' point is that a person's ethical character is revealed in the contrasting receptions she gets from different people around her. A *ren* person, for example, would be received with love by people who similarly embrace *ren*. Concomitantly, those who reject *ren* would condemn a *ren* person. Loving others, therefore, is not about being popular and compromising your beliefs and principles in order to please others.

What then does loving others entail? Confucius addresses this question below:

6.30 '夫仁者，己欲立而立人，己欲達而達人。能近取譬，可謂仁之方也已。'

'A *ren* person, in desiring to [take a] stand, helps others to [take their] stand; in desiring to reach [a goal], helps others to reach [their goal]. Taking what is near as an analogy can be said to be the method of *ren*.'

I have already briefly touched on this verse in the previous chapter on *li*. The phrase 'taking what is near as an analogy' refers to extending 'what is near', that is, extending one's personal interests to further the interests of others. In other words, a *ren* person loves others by wishing for others what she wishes for herself, and demonstrates such a desire by enabling others to take a stand, that is, observe *li*, even as she observes *li* herself (cf. 8.8, 14.41). Loving others therefore entails 'helping people to become good, not helping people to become evil' (成人之美，不成人之惡) (12.16).[15] Confucius' concept of 'loving others' is therefore underpinned by the principle of co-humanity, as connoted by the character '仁' (*ren*); our interests are necessarily and inextricably intertwined with the interests of others in the community. It also brings us back to the concept of harmony where loving others will result in mutual trust, care and cooperation (1.12). This harmony – where there is diversity, rather than homogeneity, in unity – can only be achieved when we observe *li*. We are reminded once again of the symbiotic relationship between *ren* and *li* where the *only way* to observe *li* correctly is to possess and manifest *ren* behaviours, values and attitudes.

How does one love others?

But how does one love others in practical terms? Loving others basically means relating to people around us according to a set of desirable qualities such as courage (勇 *yong*) (14.4), strength (剛 *gang*), decisiveness (毅 *yi*), simplicity (木 *mu*) and deliberateness in speech (訥 *ne*) (13.27). Among the many qualities mentioned by Confucius, four qualities stand out as particularly instrumental in guiding us to love others:

- *zhi* (知 wisdom)
- *shu* (恕 empathy and reciprocity)

- *zhengming* (正名 rectification of names)
- *xiao* (孝 filial piety).

Let us look at the qualities in turn. First, ***zhi*** (知) refers to wisdom. Although *zhi* is also used in the *Analects* to refer to knowledge or understanding (e.g. see 1.1, 6.20, 15.19), Confucius intends *zhi* to be more than a cognitive awareness or intellectual process, as shall be explained shortly. *Zhi* is closely related to *ren* as Confucius asserts that '[if a person] does not choose to live with *ren*, how can [he] obtain wisdom?' (擇不處仁，焉得知) (4.1). 'A wise person follows *ren* to profit [from it]' (知者利仁) (4.2). Just as a *ren* person is 'not anxious' (不憂), a wise person is 'not confused' (不惑) (9.29, 14.28). We can understand the close relationship between *zhi* and loving others by revisiting the passage where Confucius interprets *ren* as loving others:

12.22 樊遲問仁。

子曰：'愛人。'

問知。

子曰：'知人。'

樊遲未達。

子曰：'舉直錯諸枉，能使枉者直。'

樊遲退，見子夏曰：'鄉也吾見於夫子而問知，子曰，"舉直錯諸枉，能使枉者直"，何謂也？'

子夏曰：'富哉言乎！舜有天下，選於眾，舉皋陶，不仁者遠矣。湯有天下，選於眾，舉伊尹，不仁者遠矣。'

Fan Chi asked about *ren*.

The Master said, 'Love others.'

He asked about *zhi*.

The Master said, 'Be wise towards others.'

Fan Chi did not understand the meaning.

The Master said, 'By raising the straight above the crooked, you are able to make the crooked straight.'

Fan Chi left, saw Zixia and asked, 'I went to see the Master and asked about wisdom. He said, "By raising the straight above the crooked, you are able to make the crooked straight." What does he mean?'

Zixia said, 'How rich is the meaning of these words! When Shun ruled the world, he selected and raised Gao Yao up from among the multitude, and those who were not *ren* kept their distance. When Tang ruled the world, he raised up Yi Yin from among the multitude, and those who were not *ren* kept their distance.'

Confucius' reply to Fan Chi's question about the meaning of *zhi* is '知人' (*zhiren*) which can be translated variously as 'know others', 'understand others' or 'be wise towards others'. The first two translations are not plausible as the passage itself explains to us that Confucius was not merely referring to knowing or understanding others intellectually. We are informed about Confucius' meaning of *zhi* from Zixia's example of sage-kings Shun and Tang. These kings promoted officials Gao Yao and Yi Yin respectively to high positions, as they knew these officials to be virtuous ministers. By acknowledging the admirable qualities of these officials and creating the opportunity for them to make use of their qualities, the sage-kings demonstrated the quality of *zhi* or 'wisdom' – they *put into practice what they know of people around them.*[16]

It is not a coincidence that 'loving others' and 'being wise towards others' are mentioned in the same passage. The actions of Shun and Tang to ensure that only virtuous ministers were promoted manifested their love for the masses; their actions reflected not their selfish interest to perpetuate their own power but their altruistic desire to benefit the people. Their aim to restrain those who are not *ren* dovetailed with their goal to promote *ren* among the people. Both wisdom and *ren*, therefore, worked hand-in-hand in the sage-kings' action. Yang (1980) explains that '"raise the straight up above the crooked so that the crooked will be made straight" reflects *ren*, while knowing who is "straight" and promote such a person to leadership reflects wisdom' (p. 139). The sage-kings therefore exemplify wise persons who 'follow *ren* to profit from it' (知者利仁) (4.2).

How then is wisdom related to *li*? Recall that 'a *ren* person, in desiring to [take a] stand, helps others to [take their] stand; in desiring to reach [a goal], helps others to reach [their goal]' (6.30). A *ren* person therefore is a wise person, as she loves others by 'taking a stand' or observing *li* in her interactions with others. A ruler for good government, as explained by Confucius, needs all the three qualities of wisdom, *ren* and *li*.

> 15.33 子曰：'知及之，仁不能守之；雖得之，必失之。知及之，仁能守之。不莊以涖之，則民不敬。知及之，仁能守之，莊以涖之，動之不以禮，未善也。'
>
> The Master said. 'If a person is wise to attain [it], but is not *ren* enough to protect [it], he will lose [it] even though he has attained [it]. If a person is wise to attain [it], and is *ren* enough to protect [it], but does not guide [the people] with solemnity, the common people will not be respectful. If a person is wise to attain it, is *ren* enough to protect [it], and guide [the people] with solemnity, [but] does not act in accordance with *li*, [the situation is] still not ideal.'[17]

Although the verse does not specify what 'it' refers to, it is definitely something that is good, and is likely to refer to the Way (*dao*) (c.f. 15.29, 15.32, 18.6).[18] Following this interpretation, Confucius' point is that we need to be wise enough to realize the Way, and *ren* enough to protect and manifest the Way by observing *li*.[19]

The next quality that is closely related to Confucius' injunction of loving others is **shu (恕 empathy and reciprocity)**. The following passage helps to illuminate the meaning of *shu* (see also 12.2):

> 15.24 子貢問曰：'有一言而可以終身行之者乎？'
>
> 子曰：'其恕乎！己所不欲，勿施於人。'
>
> Zigong asked, 'Is there one word that can guide a person's entire life?'
>
> The Master replied, 'It is *shu*! Do not impose on others what you yourself do not desire.'

At first glance, the concept of *shu* appears to be about passive action since it is phrased negatively ('do not …'). It appears to stand in contrast to the 'Golden Rule' in the Bible that stresses positive action: '*Do* unto others what you would desire others to do unto you'. However, I do not think that *shu* is only confined to what we should not do unto others; the principle of not doing to others what one does not desire for oneself *presupposes* that the person knows and does unto others what she desires for herself. Rather than seeing *shu* as strictly about what we ought not to do, Confucius' point is that a sensitive and thoughtful consideration of the needs and interests of others, whether passive or active, should guide all our actions.[20] In other words, *shu* is essentially about empathy and reciprocity. Concurring that *shu* denotes both passive and active actions, various translators have translated *shu* as 'using oneself as a measure to gauge the likes and dislikes of others' (Lau), 'putting oneself in the other's place' (Ames and Rosemont) and 'understanding' (Slingerland).[21]

Another passage further clarifies the notion of *shu*:

4.15 子曰：'參乎！吾道一以貫之。'

曾子曰：'唯。'

子出，門人問曰：'何謂也？'

曾子曰：'夫子之道，忠恕而已矣。'

The Master said, 'Zeng! My way is bound together in a single thread.'

Master Zeng replied, 'Yes.'

After the Master left, the disciples asked, 'What did he mean?'

Master Zeng said, 'The Master's way, only *zhong* and *shu*.'

The concept of *zhong* (忠) refers to performing one's duties to the best of one's abilities. It is mentioned alongside *shu* as it conveys the idea of helping others as wholeheartedly as you would when helping yourself (6.30).[22] By stressing the need for putting yourself in the other person's shoes (empathy) and rendering mutual help (reciprocity), *shu* directs us to cultivate *ren* in our thoughts, feelings and actions. The mention of one's way being 'bounded together in a single thread' suggests that we should seek to achieve *shu* coupled with *zhong* in everything that we do.

How then is *shu* related to loving others? *Shu* is intricately linked to *ren* as 'loving others' because the former is a concrete manifestation of loving others through our ability to share the feelings of others (empathy) and constant acts of mutual help and cooperation (reciprocity). Some readers may have observed that *shu* is mentioned alongside *ren* in 12.2, a passage that was cited at the start of the chapter. In elaborating on the meaning of *ren*, Confucius teaches that '[when] outdoor, [behave] as though [you are] meeting important guests; [when] employing the common people, [behave] as though [you are] overseeing a great sacrifice. What you do not desire for yourself, do not impose upon others. [In this way, you will have] no ill will in public, [and] no ill will at home.' (出門如見大賓，使民如承大祭。己所不欲，勿施於人。在邦無怨，在家無怨). It is not a coincidence that Confucius lists *shu* ('What you do not desire for yourself, do not impose upon others') as among the actions, attitudes and values that reflect *ren*. It is also not a coincidence for Confucius to highlight the need to demonstrate *ren* by relating to others as if we are 'meeting important guests' (見大賓) and 'overseeing a great sacrifice' (承大祭). The idea here is to treat everyone the way you wish to be treated – as 'important guests' and honoured participants of a 'great sacrifice' (12.2). Therefore, 12.2 is a key passage that explains how *ren*, *shu* and other desirable qualities are related to one another. Another pertinent example is as follows:

17.6 子張問仁於孔子。

孔子曰：'能行五者於天下為仁矣。'

'請問之。'

曰：'恭，寬，信，敏，惠。恭則不侮，寬則得眾，信則人任焉，敏則有功，惠則足以使人。'

Zizhang asked Confucius about *ren*.

Confucius said, 'A person who is able to put into practice five [attitudes] in the world can be considered *ren*.'

'May I ask what they are?'

He replied, 'Reverence, tolerance, trustworthiness, diligence and generosity. A person who is reverent will not be insulted, a person who is tolerant will win the multitude, a person who is trustworthy will be entrusted with responsibility, a person who is diligent will achieve results, and a person who is generous will be able to get others to do his bidding.'

It is noteworthy that the above-mentioned qualities are based on *shu* – treating others in the same way you wish to be treated, with reverence, tolerance, trustworthiness, diligence and generosity. This relates to Confucius' description of a *ren* person: one who possesses the qualities of courage (勇) (14.4), as well as strength, decisiveness, simplicity and deliberateness in speech (剛、毅、木、訥) (13.27). A *ren* person is courageous, strong and decisive enough to exercise empathy and reciprocity (*shu*) in her actions and words.

Exercising *shu*, however, does not mean that we love everyone *in the same way and to the same extent*. Confucius advocates a form of love that is based on different and differentiated social roles and relationships. To understand this point, we need to look at another quality highlighted by Confucius: ***zhengming*** (正名 **rectification of names**). A central passage to explicate the meaning of *zhengming* is as follows:

12.11 齊景公問政於孔子。

孔子對曰：'君君，臣臣，父父，子子。'

公曰：'善哉！信如君不君，臣不臣，父不父，子不子，雖有粟，吾得而食諸？'

Duke Jing of Qi asked Confucius about governing.

Confucius replied, 'Ruler ruler, minister minister, father father, son son.'

The Duke said, 'Good! If the ruler be not a ruler, the subject not a subject, the father not a father, the son not a son, then even if there were grain, would I get to eat it?'[23]

Confucius' reply of 'ruler ruler, minister minister, father father, son son' may appear nonsensical to us but the Duke's reply showed that he clearly understood him. To understand what Confucius is saying, we need to cross-reference this passage with another passage where Confucius speaks of *zhengming*:

13.3 子路曰：'衛君待子而爲政，子將奚先？'

子曰：'必也正名乎！'

子路曰：'有是哉，子之迂也！奚其正？'

子曰：'野哉，由也! 君子於其所不知，蓋闕如也。名不正，則言不順；言不順，則事不成；事不成，則禮樂不興；禮樂不興，則刑罰不中；刑罰不中，則民無所錯手足。故君子名之必可言也，言之必可行也。君子於其言，無所苟而已矣。'

Zilu said, 'If the Duke of Wei waits for you to administer his state, what would you do first?'

The Master said, 'It is definitely *zhengming*.'

Zilu said, 'Is that so? How could you be so pedantic! Why *zhengming*?'

Confucius: 'How uncouth you are! A *junzi* should remain silent on matters he does not understand. When names are not correct, what is said will not be used effectively; when what is said is not used effectively, matters will not be accomplished; when matters are not accomplished, *li* and music will not flourish; when *li* and music do not flourish, punishments will miss the mark; when punishments miss the mark, the people will not know what to do with themselves. Thus the *junzi* uses names that certainly can be spoken, and what is said certainly can be acted upon. A *junzi* is never careless where speech is concerned.'[24]

I shall set aside the discussion of *junzi* for the time being and focus on the connection between names and good government. The central idea here is that names are not just words for referents; they possess an intrinsic normative force. One who is given a title ought to live up to the expectations commensurate with the title. When titles are incorrectly and indiscriminately bestowed, people would fail to perform the social roles and responsibilities associated with the title. Hence, the phrase 'what is said is not used effectively' means that words or titles have lost their meanings and efficacy. The flourishing of *li* and music requires a state of order where both the ruler and the people are able to perform their assigned tasks smoothly. The social order and trust will give everyone the peace of mind to focus on observing *li* and finding joy in music.[25] Furthermore, the observance of *li* has the salutary effect of educating the people in certain desirable dispositions and conduct; Confucius reiterates this point in another verse: 'keep them in line through *li*, and they will have a sense of shame and order themselves' (齊之以禮，有恥且格) (2.3).

On the other hand, when people fail to live up to their names, that is, fulfil the responsibilities that come with their titles, there will be a gradual breakdown of social order, where punishments are incorrectly meted out. People would then become unruly and confused. Social breakdown also leaves the people bereft of ethical guidance through *li* and music, which then propagates the vicious cycle of poor government. It is important to clarify here that Confucius does not object to the existence of laws and punishment; as evident in 13.3, his focus is not on punishment *qua* punishment but 'punishments that miss the mark' (刑罰不中). In particular, what he disapproves of are the *excessive* punitive measures used by political leaders of his time for their personal gains and power. Their selfish actions led inevitably to a neglect of the cultivation of *ren* and the inappropriate observance of *li*. In contrast to excessive punitive measures, Confucius believes that a correct understanding, internalization and practice of *li* are the prerequisites for an appropriate conception, interpretation and implementation of laws for a society.[26]

We are now in a position to understand 12.11. When Confucius uttered, 'ruler ruler, minister minister, father father, son son', he was advising the Duke to ensure that everyone in his state – be he/she a ruler, minister, father, mother, son, daughter etc. – lived up to the roles and responsibilities associated with their names or titles. Failure to do so would result in social chaos and disorderly masses who 'will not know what to do [with themselves]'. The Duke understood and agreed with the normative force of Confucius' argument; he responded that without *zhengming*, he knew he would not be able to eat the grain, that is, his state would be unable to enjoy material prosperity and social stability.

The concept of *zhengming* reinforces Confucius' emphasis on the importance of learning the *Book of Songs*. He points out that 'if you do not learn the *Songs*, you will be without words' (不學《詩》，無以言) (16.13) and 'to become a person and not study the *Zhounan* and *Shaonan* is like a person who stands with his face to the wall' (人而不爲《周南》,《召南》, 其猶正牆面而立也與) (17.10). To Confucius, language and literature are not just the means of linguistic expression and narration of the human condition; they guide us to achieve *ren* by observing *li*. Confucius stresses the need for us not to be careless or frivolous in our speech as he is cognizant that words have ethical significance. He observes that 'it is rare for *ren* to be accompanied by a glib tongue and ingratiating appearance' (巧言令色，鮮矣仁) (1.3). A *ren* person should be one who is 'slow to speak' (其言也訒) because she is aware that aligning one's action with one's words is 'difficult to achieve' (爲之難) (12.3). Against the backdrop of *zhengming*, the advice to be slow to speak and align one's action with one's words is needful since these would ensure that one fulfils one's names or titles by 'walking the talk'.[27]

The teaching of *zhengming* also helps us to understand why Confucius disapproves of a boy's behaviour in the following episode:[28]

> 14.44 闕黨童子將命。或問之曰：'益者與？'
>
> 子曰：'吾見其居於位也。見其與先生並行也。非求益者也，欲速成者也。'
>
> A boy from Que Dang brought a message [for Confucius]. Someone asked Confucius, 'Is he likely to make any progress [in learning]?'
>
> The Master said, 'I have seen him sitting at the seat [of adults and] walking alongside his elders. He is not looking to make progress but desiring quick results.'

Confucius' critique is that the boy is not acting according to his age, but instead is too anxious to grow up and be treated as an adult. The boy's actions of sitting with and walking alongside his elders are evidence of violations of *li*; the custom then was for children to sit at a specific position, face a certain direction and walk slightly behind the adults.[29] His actions therefore reflect his incorrect understanding of and flippant disregard for his social role.

Returning to the topic of *shu*, it follows that performing one's social roles properly entails that we show empathy and reciprocity according to our social roles in relation to others. Loving others, as encapsulated in *ren*, means that we love everyone in a socially differentiated manner based on our assigned roles. A ruler, for example, is expected to love his subjects in ways that befit his position as a ruler. A ruler who lives up to his name is one who, among other things, promotes virtuous officials so as to keep immoral persons at bay (12.22), achieves the Way through wisdom, *ren* and *li* (15.33), wins the hearts of the multitude, and is able to get others to do his bidding by modelling qualities of reverence, tolerance, trustworthiness, diligence and generosity (17.6). That is what

Confucius means when he advises a lord: 'A person who governs a state needs to be correct (正 *zheng*). If you lead by being correct, who would dare to be incorrect?' (政者，正也。子帥以正，孰敢不正) (12.17). The end result of *zhengming* is social harmony where a community of like-minded people perform their different but complementary roles and collectively broaden the Way.

Among the various social roles, Confucius singles out that of a child towards one's parents. The desirable quality that a child should have is **xiao (孝 filial piety)**, the fourth quality that is closely associated with *ren*. Confucius, in his comment on the *junzi* (the exemplary or noble person), teaches that 'when the *junzi* is sincerely committed to his parents, the masses will be inspired towards *ren*' (君子篤於親，則民興於仁) (8.2). This verse identifies a direct relationship between filial piety and *ren*: filial piety is an effective motivation for the pursuit of *ren*.[30] Further elucidating the relationship is the following verse by a disciple of Confucius:

1.2 有子曰：'其爲人也孝弟，而好犯上者，鮮矣；不好犯上，而好作亂者，未之有也。君子務本，本立而道生。孝弟也者，其爲仁之本與！'

Master You said, 'It is rare for a person who is filial and respectful to his elders to transgress against his superiors. It is also unheard of for a person who is not inclined to transgress against his superiors to be inclined to start a rebellion. A *junzi* devotes his efforts to the root, for once the root is established, the Way will grow. Being filial and respectful to one's elders could be said to be the root of *ren*!'

Describing filial piety as the root of *ren* suggests that the cultivation of *ren* should start with one being filial to one's parents and elders. Being filial, as noted in the chapter on *li*, does not just mean providing material needs for one's parents; it also entails behaving in a way that does not make one's parents anxious (2.6), showing respect to one's parents (2.7), matching one's actions with the appropriate and genuine countenance (2.8), and being affectionately committed to one's parents (8.2). Being filial, in short, is to relate to one's parents through *ren* behaviours, attitudes and values in accordance with *li*, as pointed out by Confucius: 'While your parents are alive, serve them according to *li*; when they are dead, bury them according to *li*, and offer sacrifice to them according to *li*' (生，事之以禮；死，葬之以禮，祭之以禮) (2.5). Filial piety, that is, observing *li* in one's relationship with one's parents, is the first step in cultivating *ren*.

The reason why filial piety is of great importance to Confucius is that he is mindful of the natural, spontaneous and deep bond between parents and children. That is why Confucius criticizes his disciple Zaiwo (also known as Yu) for being 'not *ren*' when the latter told Confucius that he did not see the need to mourn the death of his parents for three years, as was customary in those days:

17.21 子曰：'予之不仁也！子生三年，然後免於父母之懷。夫三年之喪，天下之通喪也，予也有三年之愛於其父母乎！'

The Master said, 'Yu is really not *ren*! A child is free from his parents' bosom only after three years of care. The practice of three years of mourning is observed throughout the empire. Surely Yu has received three years of love from his parents!'

Through showing affection and love towards one's parents, a person gradually learns to do likewise to other people around her. In other words, performing one's role as a child and a sibling in a family enables that person to similarly perform other social roles such as being a friend, a colleague and a subject in society. This progression of loving one's parents through filial piety to loving people outside one's family is noted by Confucius:

1.6 子曰：'弟子入則孝，出則悌，謹而信，汎愛眾，而親仁。行有餘力，則以學文。'

The Master said, 'A young man should be filial at home, and respectful towards his elders in public, be cautious in speech and trustworthy, love the multitude broadly and be close to those who are *ren*. If there is energy left after doing the above, use it to study culture.'

From the above, we can identify four categories of people mentioned: one's parents, one's peers (those who are *ren*), elders in public and the general populace. The quality of *ren* is expressed through filial piety, friendship, respect and love. We are encouraged to demonstrate *ren* in our speech ('be cautious in speech'), actions ('be trustworthy'), and choice of company ('be close to those who are ren'). Education in culture (文 *wen*) contributes to one's observance of *li* too; as previously pointed out in the chapter on *li*, 'culture' refers to all the manifestations of Zhou *li*, including its knowledge base, values, beliefs, systems and practices that have been passed down through the generations and expressed in various forms such as traditional texts and the exemplary conduct of virtuous rulers (cf. 7.25, 9.5, 19.22, see chapter 6 for further discussion of culture). However, the studying of culture, although important, is secondary to the internalization and demonstration of *ren* in one's daily life through filial piety and other virtues.

So important is filial piety as the root of *ren* that Confucius, when asked why he was not involved in governing, replied: 'The *Book of Documents* says, "Filial – by being filial and friendly to one's brothers, a person is executing the work of governing." Doing [this] is being involved in governing. Why must one be "involved in government"?' (書》云：'孝乎惟孝，友于兄弟，施於有政。'是亦爲政，奚其爲爲政？) (2.21). We learn from the above verse that filial piety is the starting point for one to demonstrate *ren* and extend *ren* to society at large; the ensuing social order and harmony allow one to 'govern' or regulate society. Confucius believes that good government stems from filial piety and necessarily involves ethical leadership through the observance of *li*. A good ruler is therefore one who believes that '[the ruler should set an example] first before [he expects his people to] work hard' (先之勞之) (13.1).

That filial piety is the root of *ren* helps us to understand a difficult passage in the *Analects*:

13.18 葉公語孔子曰：'吾黨有直躬者，其父攘羊，而子證之。'

孔子曰：'吾黨之直者異於是：父爲子隱，子爲父隱。直在其中矣。'

The Governor of She said to Confucius, 'In our village there is a straight person. His father stole a sheep, and his son testified against him.'

Confucius said, 'In our village those who are straight are different: fathers cover up for sons, and sons cover up for fathers. Being straight is to be found in this.'

At first glance, it appears that Confucius is condoning theft, going to the extent of praising a person who covers such an act as being 'straight' or upright. However, this interpretation is not tenable as it contradicts Confucius' other teachings in the *Analects*, such as the need to be trustworthy and reverent in one's dealing with others (17.6), not doing unto others what you do not wish others to do unto you (12.2, 4.15), cultivates *ren* through friendship (12.24) and loving others (12.22). Furthermore, tolerating and approving the act of stealing goes against Confucius' own claim that a *ren* person is not anxious because she has nothing to be ashamed of (9.29, 14.28, 12.4); surely one would feel guilty after taking something that she knows does not belong to her? Overall, a state that is comprised of parents who have no qualms about stealing and children who have no remorse about covering up for them cannot be a society where the Way prevails and is broadened.

An alternative and more plausible interpretation is to understand Confucius as not condoning the father's thievery in the verse, but as approving of the son's act of *not* reporting his father's misdemeanour to the authorities. Publicly testifying against one's parent threatens to destroy the filial bond between parents and children, and *a fortiori*, undermines the root of *ren*. Not giving one's parent over to the authorities, however, does not mean that the child should do nothing or condone his parent's wrongdoing. Elsewhere, Confucius advises children to articulate their disagreements with their parents appropriately as follows:

4.18 子曰：'事父母幾諫，見志不從，又敬不違，勞而不怨。'

The Master said, 'In serving your father and mother, remonstrate with them. If you see that they do not comply [with your suggestion], be respectful and do not disobey them. You may be distressed but do not complain.'

Given that Confucius advocates achieving the Way through the observance of *li* rather than by the rule of law, it is not surprising that he

The Concept of Ren 99

prefers to rely on moral suasion (gentle remonstration with one's parents) rather than punishment (reporting one's parents to the authorities). Of course, one could still question whether gently remonstrating with one's parents is sufficient to deter them from stealing, and whether it is always wrong for a child to report his parent's misdemeanour to the authorities. While one may fault Confucius' leniency with erring parents, I think we need to see that his stance stems largely from his desire to preserve the precious parent–child bond, since filial piety is the foundation of *ren*. It is arguable that Confucius is hoping that everyone, including errant parents, would gradually order himself or herself, stop committing unloving acts such as stealing, and start loving others through the observance of *li*.[31]

The preceding sections have discussed the concept of *ren* as loving others and its relationship with other desirable qualities underscored by Confucius. Premised on *ren*, one learns to love others, be they one's parents, elders, friends or the general populace, in accordance with *li*.[32] The virtue of loving others is expressed through the qualities of *zhi* (wisdom), *shu* (empathy and reciprocity), *zhengming* (rectification of names) and *xiao* (filial piety).[33] Coupling this with our understanding of *li* and *ren* thus far, we can summarize Confucius' key teachings through a Confucian framework as follows (Figure 4.1):

The Confucian worldview consists of several concentric circles.[34] At the heart of Confucius' teaching is *li* that comprises the harmonization of

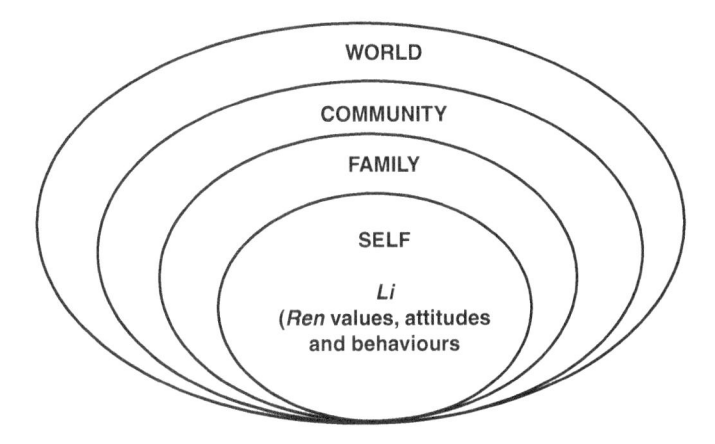

Figure 4.1 A Confucian framework

ren values, attitudes and behaviours that cover all aspects of one's life. The innermost circle represents the self where one's observance of *li* begins with self-cultivation. The Confucian self is not atomistic or solitary; it is intricately tied to one's social relationships and interactions with other human beings from one's family, community and the world. One learns to progressively observe *li* in one's thoughts, feelings and actions, beginning with one's family through filial piety, before moving on to people in the community (peers, juniors, and elders) and the world.

Conclusion

We have explored the concept of *ren* by first understanding its relationship with *li* as well as the two senses of *ren* (general and specific) as used in the *Analects*. We have also looked at the essence of *ren* as 'loving others' and examined the relationship between *ren* and other related qualities, namely *zhi* (wisdom), *shu* (empathy and reciprocity), *zhengming* (rectification of names) and *xiao* (filial piety). In manifesting the above qualities, Confucius emphasizes the need for us to harmonize our thoughts, feelings and actions by observing *li*.

Having discussed Confucius' teachings on *ren*, it is timely to make three concluding observations about *ren*. First, Confucius' ethical philosophy has been described as belonging to the tradition of *Virtue Ethics*. In the Western traditions, the three main moral/ethical theories are Consequentialism, Deontology and Virtue Ethics.

Consequentialism basically states that the goodness of one's moral action is determined by the consequences of one's actions as guided by one or more moral rules. An example of a consequentialist rule-based ethical theory is *Utilitarianism* that is derived from the writings of philosophers such as Jeremy Bentham and J. S. Mill. Briefly, utilitarians believe that what is good is what will bring the maximum happiness to the maximum number of people. This principle of utility serves as the rule to adjudicate all cases. In contrast to Consequentialism, *Deontology* basically states that the rightness of one's moral action is determined by absolute moral duties that are independent of consequences. An example of a deontological ethical theory is *Kantianism* that originated from Immanuel Kant. Kantians essentially believe that what is right is that which stems from doing one's duty. Kant bases his criterion for doing one's moral duty on what he calls 'Categorical Imperative' that states: 'Act only according to that maxim whereby you can at the same time will that it should become a universal law.'

Confucius' ethical thought falls under *Virtue Ethics* as it defines the goodness of persons not in terms of the consequences of their moral actions, moral rules or absolute moral duties. Rather, Confucius focuses on the *character* of the person performing the moral act and highlights the virtues or character traits that constitute human excellence and promote human flourishing. The ideal human being that exemplifies the excellent ethical character is the *junzi* – the topic for the next chapter. Confucius propagates a return to and the observance of *li* as the totality of normative human behaviours that are accompanied by corresponding attitudes and values in all aspects of one's life. Rather than a strict set of moral rules or duties, *li* is a pattern or discourse to guide and regulate people in their everyday conduct.[35] A person is virtuous, according to Confucius, when she internalizes and manifests *ren* behaviours, attitudes and values that empower her to autonomously act in and react to situations ethically.[36]

The second observation about *ren* is that Confucius intends for *everyone* – from the ruler to the common people – to strive to achieve *ren*. He stresses that the common people need *ren* more than daily necessities such as water and fire (15.35). Lest we think that only certain people are capable of achieving *ren*, Confucius maintains that 'being *ren* comes from oneself, how could it come from other people?' (爲仁由己，而由人乎哉？) (12.1). He also remarks: 'Is *ren* really so far away? No sooner do I desire it than it is here' (仁遠乎哉？ 我欲仁，斯仁至矣) (7.30). If *ren* is not attainable by everyone, Confucius would not have urged one and all to 'overcome the self and return to *li*' (克己復禮爲仁) (12.1).

Of course, the claim that *ren* is achievable does not mean that *ren* will be achieved by everyone. Neither is Confucius claiming that one can immediately and magically attain *ren* just by desiring it. Given that *ren* means loving others and that it encompasses other qualities such as wisdom, empathy and reciprocity, giving one's best, and filial piety, *ren* cannot simply be realized instantaneously or over a short period. Instead, *ren* and associated attributes such as wisdom and empathy require a long process of self-cultivation. The correct of interpretation of 7.30 is to understand Confucius as positing that anyone can begin to cultivate *ren* anytime because it is within that person's ability to do so. This is another way of saying that 'being *ren* comes from oneself, how could it come from [other] people?' (12.1). The faith and responsibility that Confucius places on human beings (rather than on some supernatural being) for one's success and fulfilment in life explain why Confucianism has been described as a humanistic ideology, where the focus is on the needs, interests and capabilities of human beings.

The third and related observation about *ren* is that the attainment of *ren*, like the observance of *li*, is not an all-or-nothing affair. Different human beings may achieve *ren* to varying degrees, as taught by Confucius:

4.7 子曰：'人之過也，各於其黨。觀過，斯知仁矣。'

The Master said, 'The errors of people belong to different categories. By observing their errors, you will know [the degree to which they are] *ren*.'

Elsewhere, Confucius also commends his disciple Yanhui for 'not violating *ren* for three months in his heart' (其心三月不違仁), unlike 'the rest of the disciples who merely do so only on [certain] days and months' (其餘則日月至焉而已矣) (6.7). To use the analogy of a professional musician, achieving *ren* is not about a person who qualifies as a professional musician once she obtains a music degree from a prestigious music academy. Rather, the achievement of *ren* is more akin to a musician who painstakingly improves her musical expertise through lifelong learning and regular performance.[37] Such a person is like a craftsman who conscientiously 'sharpens [her] tools' (利其器) because she 'desires to be good in her work' (工欲善其事) (15.10).[38] In conclusion, the process of attaining *ren* involves dedication, passion and diligence; Confucius reminds us that 'the *ren* person obtains success only after facing hardships' (仁者先難而後獲) (6.22).

If everyone is potentially capable of attaining *ren* but not everyone will succeed in doing so, who are those who succeed in or come close to attaining *ren*? What are their attitudes, values and actions that set them apart from the rest? The next chapter is devoted to this special group of people, known as *junzi*.

Chapter 5
The Concept of *Junzi*

Figure 5.1 The Chinese character on the right reads *xiao* (filial piety) while on the character on the left reads *yi* (appropriateness)

The two Chinese characters in the photo (Figure 5.1) represent two cardinal virtues in the Confucian tradition. Confucius stresses the attributes of *xiao* (filial piety) and *yi* (appropriateness) in the *Analects*, and associates them with a special type of person known as the *junzi*. The significance of *junzi* is seen in this word being mentioned over 100 times in the *Analects*.[1] *Junzi* (君子) literally means 'son of a lord' and referred to aristocrats during Confucius' time.[2] Confucius used this term, like what he did for *li* and *ren*, but introduced two new and radical elements to it. First, he went beyond the descriptive function of *junzi* to attribute a prescriptive and evaluative dimension to it. A *junzi*, according to Confucius, is what human beings *ought* to aspire to become. Second, Confucius adopted a broader and more inclusive definition of *junzi* – one that is based on merit rather than by birth. *Everyone*, not just the aristocrats, may succeed in becoming a *junzi* if he/she cultivates himself/herself in accordance to Confucius' teachings.[3] Underpinning Confucius' ideal of a *junzi* is his presupposition that nurture is more important than nature. As he puts it, 'Human beings are similar in their nature, but differ as a result of their practice' (性相近也，習相遠也) (17.2).[4]

Before we examine the characteristics of a *junzi* in this chapter, it is necessary to make three clarifications at the outset. First, as in the case for *li* and *ren*, Confucius does not give a straightforward and strict definition of *junzi*. Rather, he chooses to highlight different aspects of the term in his dialogues with different people in various contexts. *Junzi* has been translated by scholars as 'gentleman', 'exemplary person', 'virtuous man', 'superior man', 'paradigmatic man' and 'noble person' etc. Despite the variations, scholars agree that Confucius' concept of *junzi* is the model that human beings should endeavour to achieve. Given that *junzi* is a multi-faceted term that defies a one-word translation, I shall leave this term un-translated. I shall also use *junzi* both as a singular noun and a plural noun, in accordance with the Chinese usage in the original text where no such distinction is made. The specific context in which the word is used will inform the readers whether *junzi* refers to one or more persons.

The second clarification concerns whether the concept of *junzi* is gender-specific. The etymology of the term *junzi* ('son of a lord') has a masculine connotation. It is probable that Confucius, as a man of his time where women typically could not receive an education or hold political office, had men rather than women in mind when he discussed *junzi*, especially *junzi* who are political leaders (what I call '*junzi*-ruler'). Nevertheless, there is no evidence from the teachings of Confucius in the *Analects* that only males can be *junzi*. It is also instructive that the original meaning of a *junzi* – a member of the aristocratic society – included both the male and female offspring of an aristocrat (Li, 2009–10, p. 56). Given that there is no compelling evidence for *junzi* to be confined to only men, I shall use the term *junzi* to include both genders in my translation, exposition and application.[5]

The third clarification, as mentioned earlier, is that a number of passages in the *Analects* refer not just to *junzi* per se but specifically to *junzi* who are rulers or '*junzi*-ruler'. In these verses, Confucius' objective is to exhort rulers to be good political leaders by possessing and demonstrating the qualities of a *junzi*. I believe these verses on *junzi*-rulers are applicable to *all junzi* – whether they are rulers or not – as far as they concern a *junzi*'s character. In other words, all *junzi* are expected to internalize and manifest *ren* behaviours, attitudes and values, and be driven by a desire to fulfil heaven's mandate by broadening the Way (I shall elaborate on this later). The crucial difference between a *junzi* who is not a ruler and a *junzi*-ruler is that the former would not have the same authority and power to do good for the masses (such as promoting virtuous ministers so as to bring peace to the people, cf. 12.22, 14.42) and probably enjoy a relatively smaller sphere of ethical influence on people around them. The rest of the chapter explores the concept of *junzi*, beginning with the meaning of 'the name of *junzi*'.

More than just a name: The concept of *junzi*

Confucius states that 'a *junzi* detests not leaving a name behind after his death' (君子疾沒世而名不稱焉) (15.20). What does 'leaving a name behind' mean? One possible explanation is that it means being publicly recognized as someone great or famous. But this explanation is unacceptable because it conflicts with the preceding verse: 'The *junzi* is concerned with his own lack of ability, not by the failure of others to know him' (君子病無能焉，不病人之不己知也) (15.19). The word '知' (*zhi*) here suggests the idea of knowing or understanding someone appreciatively. That a *junzi* is not concerned with making a name for himself is also noted by Confucius in another remark: 'Not understood by others and yet is not resentful – is this not a *junzi*?' (人不知，而不慍，不亦君子乎) (1.1).

A more plausible explanation for 15.20 is that a *junzi* is upset at *not living up to the standard of a junzi*. This explanation coheres with the concept of *zhengming* (正名 rectification of names) that was discussed in the previous chapter. Briefly, Confucius instructs that a name is more than just a term of address; it connotes a social role with specific responsibilities and expectations commensurate with that name (cf. 4.5, 13.3). Confucius adds that a *junzi* is careful about using and applying names: 'The *junzi* uses names that certainly can be spoken, and what is said certainly can be acted upon. A *junzi* is never careless where speech is concerned' (故君子名之必可言也，言之必可行也。君子於其言，無所苟而已矣) (13.3).

What then is implied in the name of *junzi*, according to Confucius? How should a *junzi* think, feel and act? In particular, with reference to 15.20, what does 'leaving a name behind' entail? We shall answer these questions by relating the ideal of the *junzi* to four Confucian concepts discussed earlier: harmony (和 *he*), *li* (禮), the Way (道 *dao*) and *ren* (仁).

Junzi, harmony (*he*), *li*, the Way (*dao*) and *ren*

A *junzi* is someone who desires and seeks to achieve harmony: Confucius states that 'a *junzi* [pursues] harmony' (君子和) (13.23). We have established that harmony is obtained when a person enjoys peace, delight and concord within herself, and with heaven, other people and her surroundings. Harmony is evident when a *junzi* observes *li* not in a self-conscious and obligatory manner, but spontaneously and joyfully.[6] We have also learned that observing *li* entails not just manifesting *ren* behaviours but also ensuring that these behaviours stem from *ren* attitudes and values.[7]

Outlining the defining characteristics of a *junzi*, Confucius notes that a *junzi* 'acts in accordance with *li*' (禮以行之) (15.18), and 'detests those who are courageous but lack *li*' (惡勇而無禮者) (17.24). To Confucius, courage, as well as all other desirable qualities, is useless unless it is interpreted, internalized and acted out based on *li*; 'courage without *li* is rowdiness' (勇而無禮則亂) (8.2). A *junzi* is one who demonstrates qualities such as courage, deference, caution and candour appropriately, because she is able to look, listen, speak and move without violating *li*. A *junzi* even observes *li* when taking part in sports, as exemplified in the game of archery:

3.7 子曰：'君子無所爭。必也射乎！揖讓而升，下而飲。其爭也君子。'

The Master said, '*Junzi* are not competitive. If they must compete, it is in archery. They bow and make way for each other before ascending [the hall], they offer up toasts after descending [the hall]. They are *junzi* even in competition.'

On the relationship between harmony and *li*, we have already learned in a previous chapter that 'among the functions of *li*, harmony is the most valuable' (禮之用，和爲貴) (1.12). The *internal harmony* of a *junzi* comes about because she not only knows the Way, but also loves and finds joy in it (6.20). The joy that a *junzi* experiences accounts for her being 'calm and relaxed' (坦蕩蕩) (7.37), 'at ease and not arrogant' (泰而不驕) (13.26) and 'free from anxieties and fears' (不憂不懼) (12.4). Besides internal harmony, a *junzi* achieves *external harmony* by promoting peace and cooperation with people through her *ren* behaviours, values and attitudes. Such a person relates to and interacts with people around her based on different and differentiated social roles. In the chapter on *ren*, I have described a Confucian worldview as one consisting of several concentric circles. Starting with self-cultivation in the innermost circle (representing the self), a *junzi* demonstrates filial piety (*xiao*) at home according to *li*, before extending her love to her community (one's peers, juniors and elders) and the world (general society).[8]

A *junzi* is motivated to achieve internal and external harmony because she believes in heaven and 'is in awe of the mandate of heaven' (畏天命) (16.8). So important is a *junzi*'s relationship with heaven that Confucius maintains that 'one who does not understand the mandate has no way of becoming a *junzi*' (不知命，無以爲君子也) (20.3). Understanding heaven's mandate means realizing that 'it is human beings who are able to broaden the Way, not the Way that broadens human beings' (人能弘道，非道弘人) (15.29). A *junzi* is consequently 'anxious about [attaining] the Way' (君子憂道) (15.32) and 'studies in order to reach that Way' (君子學以致其道) (19.7). That is why a *junzi* is prepared to hold an official position in a state, highly coveted it may be, *only if* doing so promotes the Way. An example is Qu Bo-yu who was praised by Confucius as a *junzi* because he was 'willing to hold an office [only] when the Way prevailed in a state' (邦有道，則仕) (15.7).

To realize the Way, a *junzi* channels her energies to establish the root of *ren* – filial piety (孝 *xiao*). A *junzi* is aware that the Way will flourish once the root is established (君子務本，本立而道生) (1.2). To further promote the Way, she chooses to be 'with [people who possess] the Way in order to be corrected by them' (就有道而正焉) (1.14). Conversely, she is 'displeased with [anyone who tries to please her in] ways that are not in accordance with the Way' (說之不以道，不說也) (13.25). In short, a *junzi* is a possessor of harmony who seeks to realize the Way by observing *li* through *ren* behaviours, attitudes and values.

Junzi and *yi* (appropriateness or rightness)

A distinguishing feature of a *junzi* is the quality of *yi*, as highlighted by Confucius:

4.10 子曰：'君子之於天下也，無適也，無莫也，義之與比。'

The Master said, 'The *junzi*, in [dealing with people and matters in] the world, is not for or against anything; he goes with what is *yi*.'

Yi (義 appropriateness or rightness) refers to thinking, feeling and doing what is appropriate or right by exercising one's individual discernment and discretion.[9] The exercise of *yi* presupposes independent thinking and rational autonomy for one to arrive at an acceptable judgement or decision in a particular situation.[10] Confucius states that a *junzi* is 'proper but not inflexible' (貞而不諒) (15.37), and 'is not inflexible in his learning' (學則不固) (1.8).

The quality of appropriateness is intricately tied to the concept of *li*. We have already learned that *li* covers every aspect of a human life, including looking, listening, speaking and moving (cf. 12.1). I have also pointed out that *li* encompasses a wide spectrum of behaviours, ranging from activities of relatively narrow scope and rigid structure such as ceremonial rites, to activities of relatively broad scope and flexible structure, such as making small talk. The ubiquity of *li* means that it is impossible for anyone to observe *li* by simply relying on a manual of strict rules, even assuming that such a manual exists. What is crucial, if we wish to observe *li* accurately and intelligently, is to acquire the wherewithal to do what is appropriate without violating *li*. That is why the possession of the quality of appropriateness is important.[11]

The relationship between appropriateness and *li* is further spelt out in the next verse:

15.18 子曰：'君子義以爲質，禮以行之，孫以出之，信以成之。君子哉！'

The Master said, 'A *junzi* takes appropriateness as his basic quality (*zhi*), puts it into practice by observing *li*, expresses it with modesty, and completes it by being trustworthy. Such is a *junzi* indeed!'[12]

The verse identifies appropriateness as the 'basic quality' (質 *zhi*) guiding a *junzi* in observing *li*. The concept of basic quality is also mentioned in 3.8 – a passage cited earlier in chapter 3. In that passage, a disciple of Confucius infers that one's basic quality should come before the observance of *li*, just like in painting where one needs to have a plain canvas before colours can be painted on. Read in conjunction with 15.18, the basic quality in the above passage refers to the quality of appropriateness that provides the *junzi* with the discernment and discretion to observe *li* properly, so that she knows how and when to look, listen, speak and move (cf. 12.1). A person who observes *li* correctly will be modest and trustworthy – expressions that reflect the quality of appropriateness.[13] The indispensable presence of appropriateness when one observes *li* reinforces Confucius' caution that *li* should not be observed in a perfunctory, dogmatic and superficial fashion, like what the political leaders of his time did. Rather, *li* should be observed in a whole-hearted, flexible and reflective manner, mediated by individual judgement and decision, so that the *junzi*'s every moment is saturated with *ren*.[14]

Besides possessing and demonstrating the quality of appropriateness, a *junzi* also stands out from the masses in her love for appropriateness. Highlighting the need to 'love appropriateness' (好義) (12.20, 13.4), Confucius outlines the relationship between *junzi* and appropriateness:

17.23 子路曰：'君子尚勇乎？'

子曰：'君子義以爲上，君子有勇而無義爲亂，小人有勇而無義爲盜。'

Zilu asked, 'Does the *junzi* regard courage as supreme?'

The Master said, 'The *junzi* regards appropriateness as above all. A *junzi* who has courage but lacks appropriateness is disorderly; the *xiaoren* who has courage but lacks appropriateness is a thief.'[15]

The term *xiaoren* (小人) literally means 'small person', but Confucius uses it in a normative sense to refer to a 'petty person' or 'inferior person' – a type of person that is the opposite of a *junzi*. Confucius regards appropriateness as the quality that is of utmost importance as it is the mediating principle that guides a *junzi* to know when and how to manifest desirable attributes. In the verse above, appropriateness is essential for a *junzi* to rein in her courage so that she does not overreact or act rashly, and end up causing nuisance and disorder in society. In contrast, a petty person who is bold but lacks appropriateness has no self-control and is emboldened to commit unethical acts.

It is noteworthy that Confucius himself demonstrates the attribute of appropriateness by giving customized answers to questions, depending on the needs of the target audience and contexts. For example, we have seen in the chapter on *li* how Confucius offered two conflicting answers to two disciples who asked the same question (11.22) because of their contrasting personality traits and needs.[16] Confucius 'does not speculate, does not insist on certainty, is not inflexible, and is not self-centred' (毋意，毋必，毋固，毋我) (9.4). An example is Confucius agreeing to go with the majority by wearing linen ceremonial cap instead of one that was made of silk, but taking a minority position by prostrating himself before ascending the stairs (9.3). The *Analects* also informs us that Confucius is skilful in behaving appropriately in different social contexts. For instance, we are told that he is 'deferential and seemingly at a loss of words' (恂恂如也，似不能言者) in his home village but 'eloquent yet respectful in speech' (便便言，唯謹爾) in the ancestral temple and at court (10.1). Another verse records that Confucius consciously adjusts his demeanour in alignment with the person whom he is speaking to, be he a junior official, senior official or a lord (10.2).

It is helpful to further cite two instances in which Confucius did what was appropriate for the occasion, although his decisions were unconventional at that time (and possibly even now). The first example is when Confucius gave his daughter in marriage to a man despite knowing that the latter had a criminal record:

5.1 子謂公冶長，'可妻也。雖在縲絏之中，非其罪也。' 以其子妻之。

The Master said of Gongye Chang, 'He will be a suitable choice for a husband. Although he was imprisoned, he was not guilty of any crime.' He then gave him his daughter in marriage.

One would expect a father to reject or at least hesitate having a son-in-law who had been sentenced to jail. In making such a bold decision that defies societal norms and expectations, Confucius exemplifies his fairness and sense of justice by judging Gongye Chang purely on his ethical character.[17] The second example is recorded in 7.29 where Confucius graciously received a boy from Huxiang. The people of Huxiang had a bad reputation of 'being difficult to talk to' (難與言) and Confucius' disciples were reluctant to grant the Huxiang boy an audience with Confucius. Confucius, however, welcomed the boy and said to his disciples: 'Why be so extreme? He has improved by purifying himself. We should approve of his purification and not hold on to the past' (唯何其？人潔己以進，與其潔也，不保其往也) (7.29). This again illustrates Confucius' refusal to blindly follow popular opinions and prejudices, as well as his accent on exercising one's rational autonomy to do what is appropriate according to *li*.

We may draw three conclusions about the quality of appropriateness from our discussion thus far. First, the quality of appropriateness does not justify wantonness by permitting a person to do *anything* she desires. Confucius stipulates two main criteria to guide one's exercise of appropriateness. First, a *junzi*'s appropriate actions are circumscribed by the bounds of *li* with a focus on doing what is normative. Confucius maintains that a *junzi* models appropriateness by observing *li* with modesty and trustworthiness (15.18). Confucius also avers that appropriateness is at odds with personal gain (利) (cf. 4.16, 14.12, 19.1).

Related to the first point is the second observation that appropriateness is about being trustworthy and keeping one's word. Confucius teaches that 'trustworthiness is close to appropriateness, because one's word can be repeated' (信近於義，言可復也) (1.13). He adds that 'to exalt virtue is to focus on giving your best and be trustworthy, and move towards what is appropriate' (主忠信，徙義，崇德也) (12.10). A *junzi*'s words can be counted upon precisely because these words are consistent with what is appropriate.

Third, the application of appropriateness should be role specific, in line with the idea of *zhengming* (正名 rectification of names) discussed in the chapter on *ren* (cf. 12.11, 13.3). *Zhengming* requires us to understand that our names or titles – as a ruler, minister, father, son and so on – come with specific roles and responsibilities that we are expected to fulfil. We should therefore exercise our discretion and judgement by doing what is appropriate for one another based on our respective social roles and as demanded by the occasion.[18]

The capability of a *junzi* to do what is appropriate may be summed up in this succinct expression by Confucius: 'The *junzi* is not a vessel' (君子不器) (2.12). The word 'vessel' (器 *qi*) here refers to the receptacle used in ceremonial rituals that was designed for specific functions and occasions. Confucius views a *junzi* as being unlike a vessel that can only perform a specific designated function. A *junzi* is not a vessel in the sense that she is able to accomplish varied ends by making her own judgements to respond appropriately to a range of situations. The quality of appropriateness of the *junzi* is what enables her to experience harmony, both within herself and with others, thereby broadening the Way. To return to the verses quoted at the start of this chapter, we now understand why a *junzi* is 'calm and relaxed' (坦蕩蕩) (7.37), 'at ease and not arrogant' (泰而不驕) (13.26) and 'free from anxieties and fears' (不憂不懼) (12.4).[19]

Junzi and *ren*

Besides the quality of appropriateness, another defining characteristic of a *junzi* is *ren*. Confucius highlights the importance of *ren* for a *junzi*:

4.5 '君子去仁，惡乎成名？君子無終食之間違仁，造次必於是，顛沛必於是。'

How could a *junzi* who abandons *ren* merit that name? A *junzi* does not violate *ren* even for as long as it takes to eat a meal. He is certain to be with *ren* even if he is in a hurry or distress.

Here, we are reminded again of a *junzi*'s desire to live in a manner that befits the title of a *junzi*. A *junzi*, as mentioned earlier, is one who 'detests not leaving a name behind after his death' (15.20). Confucius' point in 4.5 is that anyone who is called a *junzi* must possess *ren* constantly. So essential is *ren* for a *junzi* that she does not even leave *ren* for as long as it takes to eat a meal. We have already learned in the previous chapter that *ren* is about loving others through exhibiting wisdom, empathy and reciprocity, rectification of name, and filial piety. Going back to the idea of a *junzi* as not being a vessel, Confucius' message is that a *junzi* is able to flexibly adapt and respond appropriately to diverse situations because her thoughts, feelings and actions reflect the quality of *ren*.

However, not abandoning *ren* does not mean that a *junzi* has perfectly attained *ren*. Recognizing the fallibility of *junzi*, Confucius observes: '[There have been occasions on which a] *junzi* fails to act in a *ren* manner' (君子而不仁者有矣夫) (14.6).[20] Confucius further distinguishes a *junzi* from a sage (聖 *sheng*); he describes a sage as follows:

6.30 子貢曰：'如有博施於民而能濟衆，何如？可謂仁乎？'

子曰：'何事於仁！必也聖乎！'

Zigong said, 'What about a person who gives extensively to the common people and helps the masses? Could he be called *ren*?'

The Master said, 'Why stop at *ren*? This is certainly a sage.'

Although Confucius elsewhere also describes a *junzi* as one who brings peace and security to the people (cf. 14.42), he asserts that it is much harder for a person to become a sage as compared to becoming a *junzi*. The term 'sage' applies only to sage-kings such as Yao and Shun in the *Analects*, and Confucius does not even regard himself as a sage (7.34). The primary focus of Confucius and his disciples, as evidenced in the *Analects*, is the ideal of a *junzi* who is potentially attainable by anyone.[21]

It is also important to reiterate that a *junzi* has not perfected *ren* because *ren* is not a quality that one possesses in an all-or-nothing fashion. Rather, it is a virtue that one progressively acquires through a lifelong process of self-cultivation. A *junzi* possesses *ren* in the sense that she has set her heart-mind on attaining it, and has succeeded in internalizing and manifesting *ren* attitudes, values and behaviours *to a large degree*. An analogy would be that of an Olympic gold medalist. Her medal attests to her high level of competency in her sport, but this does not mean that she is perfect and unbeatable. There remains a possibility that she may not win another gold medal in the next Olympic games due to a lapse in performance, or due to the relatively higher standards of her competitors, as is common in the sporting world. The uncertainty of winning a gold medal the second time means she needs to keep up her training and not rest on her laurels. In the same vein, the self-cultivation of *ren* is not a one-off achievement but a lifelong journey sprinkled with successes and failures.

How then does a *junzi* abide in *ren* and manifest *ren* behaviours, attitudes and values? In line with my Confucian framework that comprises the two main components of the self and others, I shall answer the above question from two inter-related and overlapping angles: the *junzi*'s self-cultivation and her relationships with others.

The *junzi*'s self-cultivation in *ren*

A *junzi* cultivates herself in *ren* behaviours, attitudes and values because she treasures *ren* and is motivated to attain it. The motivation to attain *ren* is premised on her belief that *ren* is potentially attainable by everyone. As Confucius puts it: 'Being *ren* comes from oneself, how could it come from others?' (爲仁由己，而由人乎哉？) (12.1). Confucius declares that 'a *junzi* makes demands on himself' (君子求諸己) rather than on others (求諸人) (15.21). The behaviour of a *junzi* is contrasted with that of a 'petty person who makes demands on others' (小人求諸人) (15.21).[22] Confucius sums up the difference between a *junzi* and a petty person as follows:

14.23 子曰：'君子上達，小人下達。'

The Master said, 'A *junzi* gets through to what is high; a petty person gets through to what is low.'

The adjectives 'high' and 'low' represent the antipodal values, ideals and goals held by a *junzi* and a petty person respectively. The explanation of 'high' and 'low' is given in another verse:

4.11 子曰：'君子懷德，小人懷土；君子懷刑，小人懷惠。'

The Master said, 'The *junzi* cherishes virtue, the petty person cherishes the land; the *junzi* cherishes the law, the petty person cherishes favour.'

This verse distinguishes the *junzi* from the petty person through their opposing priorities in life. The *junzi* values 'high' ideals such as virtue and the principles of fairness and order that underpin the law; the petty person values what is 'low' – the accumulation of material possessions such as land, and personal gain at the expense of the law.[23]

That the *junzi* places a premium on *ren* is further noted in another verse:

17.24 子貢曰：'君子亦有惡乎？'

子曰：'有惡：惡稱人之惡者，惡居下流而訕上者，惡勇而無禮者，惡果敢而窒者。'

Zigong said, 'Does a *junzi* detest anything?'

The Master said, 'He does. A *junzi* detests those who proclaim what is evil in others; detests those in low positions who slander their superiors; detests those who are courageous and lack *li*; detests those who are resolute and stubborn in getting what they want.'

We see here that a *junzi* generally despises attitudes, values and behaviours that disregard the welfare of others and violate *li*. Rather than exploiting others and seeking personal interests, a *junzi* can be 'entrusted with great responsibilities' (可大受) (15.34) and 'persists even in the face of adversity' (固窮) (15.2), unlike 'a petty person who will be overwhelmed by it' (小人窮，斯濫矣) (15.2).

Driven by the goal of attaining *ren*, a *junzi* is careful about her speech and actions. Confucius describes a *junzi* as one who 'desires to be slow to speak yet quick to act' (欲訥於言而敏於行) (4.24). Such a person is 'cautious in speech' (慎於言) (1.14), as she knows that her words directly reflect her character and affect the name of a *junzi*. 'A *junzi* detests one who finds an excuse to argue for what he has earlier rejected' (君子疾夫舍曰欲之而必爲之辭) (16.1) – this refers to someone who is inconsistent, insincere and pretentious in speech. In contrast, a *junzi* is cautious and sincere in speech because of her desire to fulfil what she has said. That is why a *junzi* 'feels ashamed when her words exceed her actions' (君子恥其言而過其行) (14.27). A *junzi* is so mindful of the performative nature of words that she rather 'says something only after she has acted upon the words' (先行其言而後從之) (2.13).[24]

A *junzi*'s caution in speech and stress on action extend to her assessment of people and situations. Confucius points out that 'a *junzi* does not promote someone [merely] based on what the person says, nor does she reject what is said based on the [background of the] speaker' (君子不以言舉人，不以人廢言) (15.23). The first part of the verse means that the *junzi* does not regard a person highly just because of the person's words; she would take her time to observe if the speaker follows up with concrete action. The second part of the verse means that a *junzi* does not dismiss an idea just because it originates from a dubious or undesirable source; she is fair-minded enough to evaluate the idea itself objectively.

The *junzi*'s self-cultivation to achieve *ren* necessitates a devotion to learning. Confucius asserts that a *junzi* 'loves learning' (好學) (1.14) and 'learns culture broadly' (博學於文) (6.27). A *junzi* loves and proactively engages in learning because such a process enhances her observance of *li* and cultivation of *ren*. Learning, according to Confucius, does not mean textual memorization and accumulation of knowledge. He distinguishes between two types of learned persons:

6.13 子謂子夏曰：'女爲君子儒！無爲小人儒！'

The Master said to Zixia, 'Be a *junzi ru*, not a *xiaoren* (petty person) *ru*.'

The word *ru* (儒) refers to 'specialists concerned with transmitting and teaching the traditional rituals and texts of the Zhou' (Slingerland, 2003, p. 57). Confucius' point is that having knowledge of the rituals and classics does not automatically make one a *junzi*. While the acquisition and teaching of traditional rituals and texts of the

Zhou are essential, a scholar and transmitter of Zhou culture must first and foremost be a *junzi*. Otherwise, the studying and transmission will remain just academic pursuits, and will not lead to the realization of the Way. Such a specialist, although learned, will remain a petty person. I shall postpone a detailed discussion of Confucius' concepts of learning and culture to a subsequent chapter. It suffices to note, for now, that learning, for Confucius, is not to be carried out by rote nor should it be an uncritical process. Rather, learning should be active, reflective, action-oriented and driven by a love of learning.

The *junzi*'s relationships with others

The *junzi* does not cultivate herself in isolation. A *junzi* is unable to acquire and demonstrate *ren* behaviours, attitudes and values without living in a community, and interacting with people around her. The following passage outlines the connection between self-cultivation and benefitting others:

14.42 子路問君子。

子曰：'修己以敬。'

曰：'如斯而已乎？'

曰：'修己以安人。'

曰：'如斯而已乎？'

曰：'修己以安百姓。修己以安百姓，堯 舜其猶病諸？'

Zilu asked about *junzi*.

The Master said, 'He cultivates himself in order to be respectful.'

'Is that all?'

'He cultivates himself in order to bring peace to others.'

'Is that all?'

'He cultivates himself in order to bring peace to the multitude. Even Yao and Shun would have found such an endeavour daunting.'[25]

Confucius' comment about cultivating oneself, being respectful and bringing peace to others in 14.42 corroborates what he teaches elsewhere about *ren*. As noted, Confucius describes a *ren* person as one who 'in desiring to [take a] stand, helps others to [take their] stand; in desiring to reach [a goal], helps others to reach [their goal]' (己欲立而立人，己欲達而達人) (6.30). In 12.22, Confucius explains that *ren* involves loving and knowing others by 'raising up the straight above the crooked so that the crooked will be made straight'. This act refers to recognizing and appointing virtuous ministers in order to keep evil people at bay. 14.42 informs us that the goal of a *junzi* is to bring peace to the people by promoting ethical leadership and eradicating immorality. By being respectful and bringing peace to others, 'the *junzi* helps others to become their best, not their worst' (君子成人之美，不成人之惡) (12.16).[26]

How then does a *junzi* relate to others in a manner that reflects and promotes *ren* attitudes, values and behaviours? First, a *junzi* devotes her effort to the root of *ren* that is filial piety (1.2), by being 'sincerely committed to her parents' (篤於親) (8.2). She observes filial piety not superficially but whole-heartedly, as described by Confucius about a *junzi* who mourns for her deceased parents: 'The *junzi* in mourning finds no relish in good food, no joy in listening to music, and no comfort in the place of dwelling' (夫君子之居喪，食旨不甘，聞樂不樂，居處不安) (17.21).

Besides being a filial child, a *junzi* relates to others in the spirit of sincerity, cordiality, deference, dutifulness, respect, humility, prudence and appropriateness. Confucius notes this as follows:

16.10 孔子曰：'君子有九思：視思明，聽思聰，色思溫，貌思恭，言思忠，事思敬，疑思問，忿思難，見得思義。'

Confucius said, 'The *junzi* has nine considerations: when looking, he thinks about seeing clearly; when hearing, he thinks about hearing acutely; regarding countenance, he thinks about appearing cordial; regarding demeanour, he thinks about looking deferential; in speech, he thinks about giving his best; when conducting affairs, he thinks about respect; when facing doubt, he thinks about asking [for advice]; when angry, he thinks about repercussions; when confronted with potential gain, he thinks about appropriateness.'

An example of a *junzi* who exemplifies the above characteristics is Zichan, as observed by Confucius:

5.16 子謂子產，'有君子之道四焉：其行己也恭，其事上也敬，其養民也惠，其使民也義。'

The Master said of Zichan, 'He has the way of the *junzi* in four respects: he was reverential in the way he conducted himself, respectful in serving his superiors, generous in caring for the common people, and appropriate in employing the services of the common people.'

On the specific qualities needed for government service, Confucius outlines five virtues of a *junzi*-ruler: 'The *junzi* is generous but not wasteful, works [the people] hard without their complaints, has desires but is not covetous, is at ease but not arrogant, and is awe-inspiring but not fierce' (君子惠而不費，勞而不怨，欲而不貪，泰而不驕，威而不猛) (20.2).

Another mark of a *junzi*'s relationships with others is her positive influence on people around her. Focusing on the *junzi*-ruler, Confucius teaches that 'the common people will be inspired to *ren*' (則民興於仁) and 'not be cold towards one another' (則民不偷) when the *junzi* is 'sincerely committed to his parents' (篤於親) and 'do not forget his old friends' (故舊不遺) (8.2). By observing and being inspired by *junzi*, people will know what to do (such as practising filial piety) and what not to do (such as being cold towards one another). When advising a ruler on effective government, Confucius avers: 'The virtue of the *junzi* is like the wind, the virtue of the petty person is like the grass. When the wind blows, the grass is sure to bend' (君子之德風，小人之德草。草上之風，必偃) (12.19). Confucius posits that a ruler should be a *junzi*-ruler who governs through virtue rather than punitive legal measures so as to influence the common people through his positive influence. Confucius states that a ruler should 'lead [the common people] with virtue and keep them in line through *li*, and they will have a sense of shame, and order themselves' (道之以德，齊之以禮，有恥且格) (2.3). By ruling through virtue and *li*, a ruler would instil in the people a sense of right and wrong in accordance with *li* and a personal conviction to follow *ren*. What Confucius has in mind is essentially a form of enculturation where the masses learn about, internalize, and observe *li* based on the example of the *junzi*-ruler.[27]

So confident is Confucius of the positive and powerful influence of the *junzi* that he believes that *junzi* are able to transform even the 'barbarians':[28]

9.14 子欲居九夷。

或曰：'陋，如之何？'

子曰：'君子居之，何陋之有？'

The Master desires to live among the Nine Barbarian Tribes.

Someone said, 'How could you bear their uncouthness?'

The Master said, 'When a *junzi* dwells there, where is the uncouthness?'

Here we see Confucius' confidence that a *junzi* is able to transform the attitudes, values and behaviours of 'barbarians' – non-Chinese tribes who were perceived by ancient Chinese as crude and uncivilized.[29] The idea here is the potential of *every* human being – regardless of ethnicity, language, locality and other human differences – to be inspired by a *junzi* towards *ren* by observing *li*.

Conclusion

We can now return to the question posed at the start of the chapter. With reference to 15.20, the *junzi*'s desire to 'leave a name behind' refers to living up to the standard expected of a *junzi*. A *junzi* is one who dwells in harmony by setting her heart-mind to realize the Way, observes *li* through the quality of appropriateness and abides in *ren* through self-cultivation and helping others. By doing the above, the *junzi* joins hands with other *junzi* in broadening the Way (cf. 15.29).

It should be pointed out that being a *junzi* is not about homogeneity and eradication of all individual differences. In other words, being a *junzi* is not about sacrificing one's individual identity, personality and aspirations in life so as to fit into the mould prescribed by Confucius. After all, as asserted by Confucius: 'A *junzi* [pursues] harmony and not sameness' (君子和而不同) (13.23). What unites the *junzi* is their shared goal of broadening the Way by observing *li* and abiding in *ren*. The emphasis is on *ren* behaviours, attitudes and values rather than a list of do's and don't's (recall *the prevailing li* mentioned in the chapter on *li*). Far from stifling or suppressing one's individuality, *li* empowers the *junzi* to exercise the quality of appropriateness and achieve harmony with *ren* in her thoughts, feelings and actions.[30]

The end result is a *junzi* who possesses personal autonomy, critical reflection and creativity. Let me elaborate on these characteristics in turn. First, a *junzi* demonstrates personal autonomy by setting her heart-mind to fulfil heaven's mandate and choosing to live a life of *ren* in accordance with *li*. Her aspiration to attain *ren* by loving others, coupled with her exercise of appropriateness, requires her to engage in ethical consideration, evaluation and judgement, none of which is possible without autonomy and agency.[31]

Second, a *junzi* demonstrates critical reflection when she exercises her personal autonomy. The etymology of the word 'critical' can be traced to two Greek roots: *kriticos* (meaning 'discerning judgement') and *kriterion* (meaning 'standards'). Being critical is about exercising one's judgement not arbitrarily but based on certain standards; critical reflection is about careful consideration that leads to a reasoned judgement (Tan, 2013). The qualities of *zhi* (wisdom) and *shu* (empathy and reciprocity) are particularly relevant to encourage and empower a *junzi* to be reflective and critical in her daily life. By putting into practice what she has learned, sharing the feelings of others, and rendering mutual benefit, a *junzi* is able to think, feel and act in a contextually sensitive and appropriate manner.[32]

Third, a *junzi* is one who exercises creativity. Here, creativity does not refer to revolutionary or innovative thinking that marks a break from the past. Confucius states that he 'transmits but does not make; trusts in and loves antiquity' (述而不作，信而好古) (7.1). This does not mean that Confucius *merely* transmits the knowledge and practices of antiquity; instead, he adapts and selects practices from sage-kings who love and act in accordance with the Zhou *li*. Furthermore, by re-interpreting familiar terms during his time, such as *li*, *ren* and *junzi*, Confucius creatively presents a new philosophy and way of life not only for China but the rest of the world.[33] An example is Confucius' novel claim that anyone should and can become a *junzi*. His description of a *junzi* as being more than just a vessel (2.12) implies that a *junzi* is versatile, talented and imaginative by going with what is appropriate in his dealings in the world (4.10, also see 1.8, 15.37).[34]

While everyone has the potential and should aspire to be a *junzi*, not everyone will succeed in becoming one. The attainment of such an ideal necessitates a whole-hearted, arduous and lifelong devotion to and application of learning. What this learning entails, as well as other educational issues, is the focus of the next chapter.

Chapter 6
The Concepts of *Xue*, *Wen* and *Si*

Figure 6.1 A statue of Confucius inside the compound of Taiwan Normal University

Introduction

Confucius is probably best known for his contribution as an educator. I was therefore not surprised to find his statue prominently on display inside the compound of Taiwan Normal University (see Figure 6.1 above). Among his progressive educational ideals is his belief that teachers should 'teach without discrimination' (有教無類 *youjiao wulei*, literally 'teach without category') (see the inscription in the photo above). The word 'category' (類 *lei*) here refers to all kinds of human categories such as one's family background, financial status, social position, individual ability etc.[1] Confucius essentially advocates that a teacher should not reject any student based on his or her personal background, but provide equal learning opportunity for all. But how should teaching and learning be carried out, according to Confucius? This chapter expounds on Confucius' concepts of *xue* (learning), *wen* (culture) and *si* (thinking).

Some preliminary comments about Confucius' notion of education are in order. More than knowledge transmission and spoon-feeding, the Chinese term for 'education' is *jiaoyu* (教育) that comprises 'instruction' (教 *jiao*) and 'nurture' (育 *yu*). Interestingly, this dual emphasis on instruction and nurture in education is also implied in the English word 'educate'. This word is derived from the Latin *educatus* that suggests both the act of 'bringing up' (from the word *educare*) that corresponds broadly to *jiao* (教 instruction), and 'leading forth' (from the word *educere*) that corresponds broadly to *yu* (育 nurture). Combining the etymology of 'education' in both Chinese and English, I propose the following definition of education to guide us in exploring Confucius' ideas:

> Education refers to bringing up (or instructing) and leading forth (or nurturing) a person in one's thoughts, feelings and actions through providing a totality of human experiences.

The above definition of education entails that education is more than just schooling or *formal education*. There is also *non-formal education* where learning takes place at sites outside schools, such as community centres and religious institutions. Adding to formal and non-formal education is *informal education* that occurs through a person's daily interactions with other people and the surroundings.

What then is the relationship between education and *li*? Recall that *li* refers to the totality of normative human behaviours that are accompanied by corresponding attitudes and values in all aspects of one's life. We may then modify our above definition of education as follows:

Education refers to bringing up and leading forth a person in one's thoughts, feelings and actions *in accordance with li* through providing a totality of human experiences.

The above definition requires further unpacking through an explanation of the key words. First, the expression 'in accordance with *li*' refers to the alignment of one's thoughts, feelings and actions with Zhou *li*. All the normative attitudes, values and behaviours in *li* are encapsulated in the general and higher-order quality of *ren*. An educated person, in other words, is one whose thoughts, feelings and actions are marked by *ren* in all aspects of life. Such a person, according to Confucius, is a *junzi* – an exemplary person who abides in *ren* and observes *li* joyfully in order to broaden the Way and fulfil heaven's mandate. Next, the expression 'bringing up' or 'instructing' refers to inculcating *li* in the student through *xue* (學 learning) and *wen* (文 culture) – two major concepts emphasized by Confucius. The expression 'leading forth' or 'nurturing', on the other hand, refers to encouraging the student to engage in *si* (思 thinking) – another central concept in Confucius' philosophy. Finally, 'providing a totality of human experiences' underlines the fact that education is not just cognitive development but an integration of a student's thoughts, feelings and actions through applying what one has learned. The idea of 'totality' highlights the reality that education occurs not just within the four walls of a school but in a variety of social contexts.

Having discussed the key words, we shall examine Confucius' concepts of learning (*xue*), culture (*wen*) and thinking (*si*) based on the above-mentioned inter-dependent and mutually reinforcing components of education: 'bringing up', 'leading forth' and 'providing a totality of human experiences'.

Education as 'bringing up': Learning (*xue*) and culture (*wen*)

Confucius underscores the concept of *xue* (學 learning or study) when he exhorts all to 'learn as if you cannot catch up, and as if you fear losing it' (學如不及，猶恐失之) (8.17). Confucius himself is an example of one who recognizes the priority of learning. He tells his disciples that he was 'set on learning at fifty' (十有五而志于學) (2.4), and that he 'quietly stores up what is learnt and is insatiable in learning' (默而識之，學而不厭) (7.2, also see 7.17). He shares his learning experience: 'I once went without food the whole day and without sleep the whole night by focusing on thinking; that was not beneficial and it is better to spend the time learning' (吾嘗終日不食，終夜不寢，以思，無益，不如學也) (15.31). The significance of learning arises from its relationship with *ren*, as explained by a disciple of Confucius:

19.6 子夏曰：'博學而篤志，切問而近思，仁在其中矣。'

Zixia said, 'Learn extensively and hold fast to your aspiration, inquire earnestly and reflect on present [issues] – *ren* is to be found in this.'

This verse informs us that one achieves *ren* by learning in a broad-based, focused, sincere and contemplative manner. Engaging in and loving learning are therefore necessary in one's lifelong quest to acquire *ren* in order to broaden the Way. The long-drawn process of learning, as implied in the expression 'learn extensively', requires much human effort and self-cultivation. That human beings respond differently towards learning and consequently obtain contrasting results leads Confucius to conclude that human beings are 'similar in nature but differ as a result of practice' (性相近也，習相遠也) (17.2).

The motivation for learning: Holding fast to the Way (*dao*)

Given the primacy of learning, what should be our motivation to learn? For one, the purpose of learning is not for selfish gains. Confucius observes that most people found it 'not easy to learn for three years without thinking of an official salary' (三年學，不至於穀，不易得也) (8.12). He praises those ancient scholars who learned 'for their own sake' (爲己) and disapproves of scholars of his time who learn 'for the sake of others' (爲人) (14.24). To learn 'for the sake of others' is to study for the purpose of receiving praises and rewards from others.

In contrast, learning for one's own sake entails two things. First, it is about *deriving joy in learning* rather than gaining personal material rewards from such learning. Confucius stresses the need for a love of learning: 'Be firmly committed to love learning' (篤信好學) (8.13). The value of delighting in learning is in alignment with Confucius' declaration that 'a person who loves is better than a person who [simply] knows' (知之者不如好之者) (6.20). Confucius elaborates on the consequences of *not* loving learning:

17.8 '好仁不好學，其蔽也愚；好知不好學，其蔽也蕩；好信不好學，其蔽也賊；好直不好學，其蔽也絞；好勇不好學，其蔽也亂；好剛不好學，其蔽也狂。'

To love *ren* without loving learning will result in foolishness; to love wisdom without loving learning will result in a lack of self-restraint; to love trustworthiness without loving learning will result in harm; to love frankness without loving learning will result in acrimony; to love courage without loving learning will result in unruliness; to love firmness without loving learning will result in recklessness.

The verse above informs us that the love of learning is key to a person's love of other virtues; without the former, such a person would be incapable of appropriately expressing her love of the latter in her life.

Besides deriving joy in learning, learning for one's own sake also entails learning for a higher purpose – to *fulfil the mandate of heaven* by broadening the Way (*dao*). Confucius remarks that 'the *junzi* learns for the sake of the Way' (君子學以致其道) (19.7).[2] Confucius elaborates on the connection between learning and the Way:

8.13 子曰：'篤信好學，守死善道。危邦不入，亂邦不居。天下有道則見，無道則隱。邦有道，貧且賤焉，恥也；邦無道，富且貴焉，恥也。'

The Master said, 'Be firmly committed to love learning, hold fast to the good Way till death. Do not enter a state that is in crisis, and do not dwell in a state that is disordered. Make yourself available when the Way prevails in the world, but remain hidden when it does not. It is a disgrace to be poor and lowly when the Way prevails in the state, and it is a disgrace to be rich and noble when it does not.'

Given that the focus of this passage is the Way, it is arguable that the 'learning' mentioned at the start of the passage refers to learning *for the sake of the Way*. Confucius exhorts his disciples to promote the Way by holding fast to it till one's death. He further advises his disciples to promote the Way by taking up official appointments in a state (as expressed in 'make yourself available'). However, Confucius' disciples should not take up office indiscriminately but do so only if they could play a significant role in broadening the Way. Also, when assuming office in a state, they should ensure that the state is one where the Way is valued and adhered to, as evident in the prevalence of stability and order. The last sentence in the passage reiterates the need to render one's service only in states where the Way prevails: to remain poor and lowly in a state that promotes the Way indicates that one is not doing one's part to realize the Way by taking up high official positions in that state. Conversely, to be rich and hold a high rank in a state that does not promote the Way is wrong as it implies that one is more concerned with enriching oneself and not doing one's part to realize the Way. In such a case, the only option to promote the Way is to leave that state.

It should be added here that although Confucius counsels his disciples not to enter a state that is in crisis and to remain hidden when the Way does not prevail, he also teaches that they should speak up when they find a ruler saying something that is not right. When asked by Duke Ding if there is a saying that can ruin a state, Confucius replied, 'If what [the ruler] says is not good and no one opposes him, is this not almost a case of a saying that can ruin a state?' (如不善而莫之違也，不幾乎一言而喪邦乎？) (13.15). But it should be clarified that this does not mean that one should criticize a ruler in an aggressive and confrontational way. Keeping in mind 12.1 about being guided by *li* in what and how we think, feel and do, Confucius is saying that one should speak up against a ruler *in accordance with li*. Again, we can turn to Confucius as a model of civil engagement that is guided by *li*. On the one hand, he does not shy away from articulating his disapproval of the conduct of the political leaders (cf. 3.1, 3.2, 3.10, 3.26 etc.). On the other hand, he does not stage a public protest or start a revolution, but expresses his disagreements in a respectful manner and does not impose his views on any state. History also informs us that Confucius, in seeking political office and dissemination of his ideas in various states, chose to leave a state when he faced rejection or disappointment from the political leaders, rather than staying on to launch a coup d'état.

To summarize this section, to 'learn for one's own sake' (14.24) is to love learning and study to fulfil heaven's mandate by broadening the Way.[3] Confucius sums up the above when he exclaims that '[a *junzi*] chooses to be close to [people who possess] the Way in order to be corrected [by them]; [such a person] can be said to love learning' (就有道而正焉, 可謂好學也已) (1.14).

The content of learning: Culture (*wen*)

Having established the importance of and motivation for learning, what then is the *content* of learning? The *Analects* informs us of the four loci of Confucius' teachings, namely, *Culture* (文 *wen*), *Conduct* (行 *xing*), *Dutifulness* (忠 *zhong*) and *Trustworthiness* (信 *xin*) (7.25). *Conduct* focuses on *ren* behaviours that are in accordance with *li*. Such behaviours are necessarily accompanied by *ren* attitudes and values, given that *ren* is not just about one's actions but involves the harmonization of one's actions, thought and feelings. *Dutifulness* and *Trustworthiness* complement *Conduct* by emphasizing the need for a person to do her best and be consistent in her *ren* behaviours, attitudes and values. What has not been discussed thus far is the first locus, *Culture* (文 *wen*), which is the topic for this section.

Confucius highlights the significance of culture as follows:

9.5 子畏於匡, 曰: '文王既没, 文不在兹乎? 天之將喪斯文也, 後死者不得與於斯文也; 天之未喪斯文也, 匡人其如予何?'

When the Master was surrounded in Kuang, he said, 'With King Wen dead, does not culture reside here [in me]? If heaven is going to destroy culture, those who come after me would not be able to have it. If heaven is not going to destroy culture, what can the people of Kuang do [to me]?'

In the above verse, Confucius expresses his confidence that the culture of King Wen has not been lost and still remains with him. King Wen is a sage-king known for his virtuous rule in accordance with Zhou *li*. King Wen is also mentioned in another verse: 'The Way of Kings Wen and Wu has not yet fallen to the ground but lives in the people' (文武之道，未墜於地，在人) (19.22). Informed by 19.22, we can infer that the 'culture' in 9.5 is the culture of the sage-kings that directs human beings to the Way of heaven. This culture covers all the manifestations of Zhou *li*, including its knowledge base, values, beliefs, systems and practices that have been passed down through the generations and expressed in various forms such as traditional texts and the exemplary conduct of virtuous rulers.[4]

Some readers may wonder whether 7.25 (about Confucius teaching and promoting culture) contradicts 1.6 where he appears to downplay the learning of culture:

1.6 子曰：'弟子入則孝，出則悌，謹而信，汎愛眾，而親仁。行有餘力，則以學文。'

The Master said, 'A young man should be filial at home, and respectful towards his elders in public, be cautious in speech and trustworthy, love the multitude broadly and be close to those who are *ren*. If there is energy left after doing the above, use it to study culture.'

At first glance, 1.6 seems to suggest that the learning of culture is optional and secondary. But this interpretation contradicts not just 7.25 but also other verses such as 9.5 where Confucius expresses gladness that the culture of King Wen still resides in him; 9.11 where Confucius broadens his disciple with culture; and 6.27 where a *junzi* is described as one who is well-versed in culture. Hence, the correct interpretation of 1.6 is to see Confucius as valuing the learning of culture, not for its own sake, but for one's inculcation of filial piety (which is the root of *ren*) and other desirable qualities (such as doing one's best and loving the multitude). Put otherwise, culture should be studied only if doing so enables the learner to acquire *ren*.

Four key characteristics of culture

Although the *Analects* does not systematically outline Confucius' curriculum for culture, it has provided sufficient information for us to identify four key characteristics of culture. First, culture consists of a **broad-based curriculum** that serves to expand the horizon of the learner, enabling her to be well informed. Confucius himself is described as being 'broad in learning' (博學) (9.2) and a disciple of Confucius testifies that Confucius 'broadens me with culture' (博我以文) (9.11).

Second, the learning of culture involves the learning of '**the arts**' (藝 *yi*), as encouraged by Confucius:

7.6 子曰：'志於道，據於德，依於仁，遊於藝。'

The Master said, 'Set your aspiration on the Way, base yourself on virtue, lean upon *ren*, and journey in the arts.'

The 'arts' refers to the 'six arts' (六藝 *liuyi*) – a set of subjects or domains typically learned by students in ancient China. They are *li* (禮 *li*), music (樂 *yue*), archery (射 *she*), charioteering (御 *yu*), calligraphy or writing (書 *shu*) and mathematics (數 *shu*). The expression 'journey in the arts' paints a picture of a traveller who roams far and wide to seek out and appreciate the various 'arts'. Let us briefly look at each of the 'six arts'.

Not much is known of charioteering and mathematics from the *Analects*. Charioteering is mentioned only briefly in 9.2, where Confucius wonders, perhaps half-heartedly, if he should specialize in it. As for the other four arts (*li*, archery, music and writing), Confucius has dwelled on them at some length in various portions of the *Analects*.

The first 'art' is *li*. We have already examined *li* in earlier chapters so I shall not rehearse the discussion here. Suffice to say that the *li* Confucius has in mind is not *the prevailing li* that he has criticized as deficient, but the Zhou *li* that was demonstrated by the sage-kings. In the context of *xue* (learning), studying *li* means being acquainted with and practising the various types, purposes and appropriate ways of observing *li*. For example, a child needs to be taught how to observe ceremonial rituals, greet her parents and teachers, and ask the right questions in accordance with *li*. This enculturation process requires formal, informal and non-formal education where she observes and learns from her parents, siblings and other people in her community.

The next 'art', *archery*, is mentioned in the *Analects* when Confucius emphasizes the proper way of shooting: 'There is no need to pierce the leather target as the strength varies from archer to archer; such is the ancient Way' (射不主皮，爲力不同科，古之道也) (3.16). The purpose of archery in this context is recreational rather than training for warfare. Confucius' point is that we should be sensitive to the differing physical strength of the archers, and not aim to outdo each other by piercing the leather target. Confucius' reference to the 'ancient Way' suggests that the observance of *li* based on the ways of the sage-kings extends even to the sports. The reminder to be empathetic and gracious to one another in archery is noted in another verse where Confucius praises the *junzi* for 'bowing and making way for each other before ascending [the hall], and offering up toasts after descending [the hall]' (揖讓而升，下而飲) (3.7). Here we see that archery, as well as charioteering, illustrates Confucius' injunction about 'not moving if it is not in accordance with *li*' (非禮勿動) (12.1). Through a person's participation in sports, she learns to coordinate her bodily movements in such a way that her *ren* thoughts, feelings and actions are harmonized to observe *li*.[5]

Like *li*, the 'art' of *music* has already been discussed in chapter 3 so I shall not repeat the discussion here (for relevant verses, see 3.23, 7.14, 13.3, 16.5). The 'art' of *writing or calligraphy* is presumably part of the learning of languages and humanities. I have already discussed the significance of language (words) in chapter 3 (on the aesthetic facet of *li*) and chapter 4 (on *zhengming*, rectification of names). The mastery of writing is likely to be accompanied by the proper pronunciation of words in classical works such as the *Book of Songs* and *Book of Documents*. Confucius himself provides a model of using the correct pronunciation when reading these two texts (7.18). The 'art' of writing might also include extrapolating lessons from the *Book of History* (e.g. see 14.40) and historical events (e.g. see 14.5, for other relevant verses on language and poetry, see 1.15, 3.8, 12.11, 13.3, 16.13, 17.9, 17.10).[6]

The connection of archery, music and writing (and probably charioteering and mathematics) to *li* demonstrates that the various 'arts' are neither discrete subjects, nor should they be taught in isolation. They should therefore not be viewed as stand-alone school subjects found in modern schools where a tendency is to prepare students for high-stakes exams. Rather, the 'arts' are interrelated and valued for jointly guiding a student to achieve *ren* by observing *li* holistically. Such a person not only becomes knowledgeable, confident, well mannered and refined, but also is able to achieve spiritual-ethical-aesthetic harmony by integrating her mind and body.[7]

Third, the learning of culture is essential for a person to achieve **a balance between culture or more precisely cultural refinement (文 *wen*) and one's basic quality (質 *zhi*)**. Confucius explains as follows:

6.18 子曰：'質勝文則野，文勝質則史。文質彬彬，然後君子。'

The Master said, 'When one's basic quality overwhelms cultural refinement, the result is crudeness; when one's cultural refinement overwhelms basic quality, the result is pedantry. When there is a balance of basic quality and cultural refinement, the result is a *junzi*.'[8]

I have already explained the meaning of 'basic quality' in Chapter 5. By examining another verse where the same word is used (15.18), we can infer that it refers to *yi* (義 appropriateness):[9]

15.18 子曰：'君子義以爲質，禮以行之，孫以出之，信以成之。君子哉！'

The Master said, 'A *junzi* takes appropriateness as one's basic quality, puts it into practice by observing *li*, expresses it with modesty, and completes it by being trustworthy. Such is a *junzi* indeed!'

We have already learned in the chapter on *junzi* that the quality of appropriateness involves the exercise of individual discretion and judgement in specific contexts. Returning to 6.18, Confucius' point is that cultural refinement that stems from the learning of culture is necessary but insufficient if it is not balanced with appropriateness. This is because a person who knows the right thing to do but lacks cultural refinement would not be able to conduct herself in a gracious and socially acceptable manner. Instead, she may come across as unlearned, coarse and ill mannered. The reverse is also true: A person who is culturally refined but lacks a sense of appropriateness is ill equipped to do the right thing. Such a person is likely to come across as overly intellectual, snobbish and domineering. That is why Confucius stresses that cultural refinement alone does not make one a *junzi*: 'When there is a balance of basic quality and cultural refinement, the result is *junzi*' (6.18). Confucius even deprecatingly refers to himself as an example of a person who lacks such a balance: 'In cultural refinement, I can be compared with others. In living the life of a *junzi*, I have yet to achieve that' (文，莫吾猶人也。躬行君子，則吾未之有得) (7.33).

Another passage elaborates on how one's basic quality and cultural refinement are equally important:

12.8 棘子成曰：'君子質而已矣，何以文爲？'

子貢曰：'惜乎，夫子之説君子也！駟不及舌。文猶質也，質猶文也。虎豹之鞹猶犬羊之鞹。'

Ji Zicheng said, 'Being a *junzi* is only about his basic quality; what does he need cultural refinement for?'

Zigong said, 'It is a pity for you, sir, to say that of *junzi*! A team of horses cannot catch up with one's tongue. Cultural refinement is no different from basic quality; basic quality is no different from cultural refinement. The skin of a tiger or a leopard, when shorn of hair, is no different from the dog or sheep.'

Ji Zicheng is only partially correct to recognize that a *junzi* needs the basic quality of appropriateness. In response, Zigong reiterates the need for a person to have both the quality of appropriateness (basic quality) and cultural refinement. The learning of culture is necessary to supplement appropriateness because the former is the external package, analogous to an animal's fur, which makes one animal both distinguished and distinguishable from another.

How then can a person strike a balance between appropriateness and cultural refinement? This brings us to the fourth and final characteristic of culture – **cultural refinement needs to be restrained by *li***. The *Analects* records the following two verses that illuminate the connection between the learning of culture and the observance of *li*:

6.27 子曰：'君子博學於文，約之以禮，亦可以弗畔矣夫！'

The Master said, 'A *junzi* who learns culture broadly and is restrained by *li* is able to not deviate [from what is right].'

9.11 夫子循循然善誘人，博我以文，約我以禮，欲罷不能。

The Master is good at leading me on step by step; he broadens me with culture and restrains me with *li*; I could not give up even if I wanted to.

We see in the above verses a contrast between the *broadening* function of culture and the *restraining* function of *li*. The word *yue* (約 restrain) has the idea of restricting or disciplining a person so as to prevent her from going astray. Cultural refinement alone is insufficient to prevent a person from deviating from what is right; a culturally refined person may be scholarly but pedantic and insensitive to the needs of others – actions that violate *li*. Such a person therefore needs to be restrained or disciplined by *li* so as to know how to look, listen, speak and move appropriately. By doing so, she will be kept in line and not go astray. The importance of the restraining function of *li* prompts Confucius to advise a ruler to 'keep [the masses] in line through *li*, and they will have a sense of shame and order themselves' (齊之以禮，有恥且格) (2.3).

To conclude this section on learning, we see that Confucius underscores 'learning for one's own sake' by learning with love and joy in order to broaden the Way. He particularly favours a cultural education that is anchored on the 'six arts' and revolves around the cultivation of *ren* in accordance with *li*. The mastery of culture results in cultural refinement that needs to be balanced with appropriateness in one's observance of *li*. The outcome is the educational ideal of a *junzi* – someone who seeks to fulfil heaven's mandate by realizing the Way through abiding in *ren* and observing *li*.

It is noteworthy that Confucius' conception of learning is integrative in three ways. First, by stressing the need to not just learn but also love and apply learning, Confucius highlights the harmonization of one's thoughts, feelings and actions. Second, the 'six arts', as mentioned, are distinct but inter-dependent to direct the learner to observe *li* in all areas of her life. Third, Confucius combines theory with practice by requiring the learner to observe *li* in real life, be it in archery or doing what is appropriate for an occasion. Such learning requires the learner's active participation, personal engagement and constant application. It is what we would term today as a 'student-centred education', as opposed to a 'teacher-centred education' where the teacher relies predominantly on a didactic and transmission mode of teaching. This does not mean, however, that didactic and transmission mode of teaching is bad or irrelevant for students; lecture-style teaching and memorization are still required, especially in the learning of the fine details of ceremonial rituals or the precise meanings of the poems in the *Book of Songs*. What Confucius does not endorse is pure spoon-feeding, rote learning and regurgitation without understanding, personal appropriation and application.[10] Having examined the concept of learning, we shall proceed to explore another key educational concept of Confucius.

Education as 'leading forth': Thinking (*si*)

Closely related to the concept of learning is the concept of *si* (思 thinking). *Si* does not just mean 'thinking' in the sense of any mental activity performed by an individual. Rather, it is a broad term that encompasses a range of thought processes, from relatively simpler processes such as remembering, to more advanced processes such as reflection, analysis, synthesis, evaluation, making connections, drawing analogies, making inferences, and forming judgements. In other words, *si* includes what we would call 'higher-order thinking' today.[11] To avoid confusing 'thinking' as *si* with 'thinking' as any mental activity, I shall refer to the former as *si* in the rest of the book.

Si goes in tandem with learning, as stated by Confucius:

2.15 子曰：'學而不思則罔，思而不學則殆。'

The Master said, 'Learning without *si* leads to bewilderment; *si* without learning leads to perilousness.'

Confucius believes that a person who learns without *si* will be perplexed as she has not sufficiently understood and pondered on what she has learned. Conversely, a person who thinks a lot but does not have sufficiently broad knowledge will be imperilled, as her actions are not adequately informed and guided by a knowledge base. *Si* therefore serves to educate or lead a person forth by enabling her to reflect, internalize and appropriate what she has learned.

Si – or more accurately, *si* that goes with learning – is critical because it is the prerequisite for one to observe *li*. Given that *li* covers all normative behaviours as well as corresponding attitudes and values, we need to personally reflect on what we learn to make sense of our environments and respond appropriately. The need for active reflection that guides one's exercise of discretion and judgement explains why a *junzi* is praised for 'not being inflexible in learning' (學則不固) (1.8), and for 'going with what is appropriate' (之於天下也，無適也，無莫也，義之與比) (4.10).[12]

Three key characteristics of *si*

Given the importance of *si*, what does it entail? There are three key characteristics, the first one being that *si* involves a process of inquiry where **one actively reflects, asks and seeks answers to questions**. Confucius himself displays this process of inquiry in one incident recorded in the *Analects*:

3.15 子入太廟, 每事問。

或曰：'孰謂鄹人之子知禮乎？入太廟, 每事問。'

子聞之, 曰：'是禮也。'

When the Master entered the Grand Ancestral Hall, he asked questions about everything.

Someone said, 'Who said that this son of man from Zou village knows *li*? On entering the Grand Ancestral Hall, he asked questions about everything.'

When the Master heard of this, he said, 'The asking of questions is *li*.'

It is obvious that Confucius' asking of questions was not the usual practice of people during his time, nor was such a behaviour positively construed as observing *li*.[13] Confucius was instead labelled by an observer as being ignorant of *li*. By responding that the asking of questions is itself *li*, Confucius is pointing out the need for *si* where we actively reflect, ask and seek answers to questions.[14]

The significance of asking questions leads Confucius to express his disappointment with his disciple Yanhui for not raising any questions to Confucius' teaching. Confucius laments that 'Yanhui is of no help to me;

he does not dislike anything I say' (回也非助我者也，於吾言無所不說) (11.4).¹⁵ Besides exhibiting the characteristic of *si* by conscientiously asking questions, Confucius also models the quality of *si* by looking for the answers himself. He describes his passion and persistence in pursuing a satisfactory answer: 'A peasant asked me something and [my mind] was empty; I attacked [the question] from both ends until I got everything out of it' (有鄙夫問於我，空空如也。我叩其兩端而竭焉) (9.8).

The second characteristic of *si* is that it involves **extending one's learning through higher-order thinking.** This may be achieved in three main ways: building upon what one has learned; drawing inferences; and forming personal judgements about people and things. Let us explore each of the ways. First, Confucius emphasizes the need to extend one's learning by *building upon what one has learned*. He asserts the need to 'be aware of what one lacks daily, and do not forget what one has acquired monthly' (日知其所亡，月無忘其所能) (19.5). Confucius himself 'listens widely, selects what is good and follows it' (多聞，擇其善者而從之) (7.28). The 'selection of what is good' presupposes an ability to understand, analyse, evaluate and synthesize what one has learned. All these activities require active and higher-order thinking on the learner's part. In another passage, Confucius explains how he extends his own learning by building on what he has learned:

15.3 子曰：'賜也，女以予為多學而識之者與？'

對曰：'然，非與？'

曰：'非也，予一以貫之。'

The Master said, 'Zigong, do you think I am the kind of person who has learnt widely and remembered it all?'

Zigong said, 'Yes. Is it not so?'

The Master said, 'No. I bind it all together with one thread.'

The 'one thread' mentioned in the passage is explicated in another passage (4.15); it refers to doing one's best (忠 *zhong*) as well as showing empathy and reciprocity (恕 *shu*). What Confucius means is that he has processed what he has learned and organized them into a coherent whole through personal reflection.

It is therefore not surprising that Confucius expects his disciples to do likewise by extending their thinking based on what they have learned.[16] This is achieved, first of all, by relating what one has learned to real life. Confucius encourages his students to learn poems from the *Book of Songs* because 'the *Songs* can give you inspiration, observation [skill], [ability to] live with others, and [means to express] grievances' (《詩》, 可以興, 可以觀, 可以羣, 可以怨) (17.9). I have already explained the meaning of this verse in Chapter 3. With regards to *si*, Confucius is encouraging the young people to go beyond rote learning to reflect on the implication and application of the poems to their daily lives. Contemplating on the literary beauty of the poems and drawing ethical lessons from them will inspire a person to appreciate life, co-exist harmoniously with others, and communicate effectively. All the above outcomes are possible *only if* the learner *si* or reflects critically on the poems.

The second way to extend one's learning is by *drawing inferences from what one has learned*. Confucius highlights this:

7.8 子曰：'不憤不啓, 不悱不發。舉一隅不以三隅反, 則不復也。'

The Master said, 'I do not enlighten a person who is not striving [to understand]; I do not provide [the words to a person] who is not already struggling to speak. If I have raised one [corner] and the person does not come back with the other three [corners], I will not [teach that person] again.'

In the above verse, Confucius stresses the importance of self-motivation in learning. He expects his students to strive to understand what they learn and express themselves with the right words. Rather than spoon-feeding, a teacher should only provide the initial point of learning and prompt the student to draw their own conclusions subsequently. I shall give two examples of inferential thinking manifested by Confucius' disciples. The first example is an exchange between Zigong and Confucius on *li* and the Way:

1.15 子貢曰：'貧而無諂, 富而無驕, 何如？'
子曰：'可也；未若貧而樂, 富而好禮者也。'

子貢曰：'《詩》云："如切如磋，如琢如磨" 其斯之謂與？'

子曰：'賜也，始可與言《詩》已矣，告諸往而知來者。'

Zigong said, '"Poor without being ostentatious, wealthy without being arrogant". What do you think of this saying?'

The Master said, 'It is acceptable, but not as good as "Poor yet enjoy the Way, wealthy yet love *li*".'

Zigong said, 'The *Song* says, "Like bone carved and polished, like jade cut and ground". Is this not what you have in mind?'

The Master said, 'Zigong, only with someone like you can one discuss the *Songs*; you know what is to come based on what has been said.'

Upon learning from Confucius the need to enjoy the Way and love *li*, Zigong was able to relate this teaching to a line from the *Book of Songs* regarding bone and jade. Just as the carving and polishing of bone as well as the cutting and grounding of jade are laborious, enjoying the Way and loving *li* require a long drawn process of self-cultivation. Confucius' compliment to Zigong that he 'knows what is to come based on what has been said' confirms that Zigong possesses *si* or inferential thinking.

The second example involves another disciple, Zixia, who demonstrated his ability to draw an analogy based on another line from the *Songs*:

3.8 子夏問曰：'"巧笑倩兮，美目盼兮，素以爲絢兮。" 何謂也？'

子曰：'繪事後素。'

曰：'禮後乎？'

子曰：'起予者商也！始可與言《詩》已矣。'

Zixia asked, '"Entrancing smile with dimples, beautiful eyes so clear, colours upon the unadorned base". What is the meaning?'

The Master said, 'The plain base comes first, then the colours are applied.'

Zixia said, 'Just like *li* that comes after?'

The Master said, 'It is you who have illuminated me! It is only with someone like you that one can discuss the *Songs*.'

Upon learning from Confucius about the meaning of a line from the *Book of Songs*, Zixia correctly infers that *li* (represented by the colours) comes after *yi* (appropriateness) (represented by the plain base) (for an exposition of the quality of appropriateness, see Chapter 5). Like Zigong, Zixia's effort is met with Confucius' praise for his ability in inferential thinking. We see that both Zigong and Zixia are able to build upon what they have learned, thereby extending their learning. They are examples of learners who are able to deduce the other 'three corners' based on the 'one corner' given by the teacher (7.8).

The third way to extend one's learning is by *forming personal judgements about people and things:*

15.28 子曰：'眾惡之，必察焉；眾好之，必察焉。'

The Master said, 'When the multitude hates a person, you must examine the matter; when the multitude loves a person, you must examine the matter.'

Confucius' point here is that we should not form our judgement of a person by purely relying on what other people say about that person. Rather, we should investigate the matter ourselves and draw our own conclusions from available evidence. Not to do so and to simply go with the majority is to commit the fallacy of *ad populum*. This ability in independent thinking is intricately linked to the quality of appropriateness that characterizes a *junzi*. We have learned in the previous chapter that a *junzi*, 'in his dealings in the world, is not for or against anything; he goes with what is appropriate' (之於天下也，無適也，無莫也，義之與比) (4.10). Doing what is appropriate is about exercising one's discernment and discretion so that one knows how to carry oneself and make acceptable responses in a particular context. This would not be possible if the person merely learns *li* by rote and is unable to think for oneself.

Forming one's own judgements extends to the observance of *li* where we need to reflect on the relevance of specific practices of *li* and modify them if necessary. We see this in Confucius in the following passage that was cited earlier in the chapter on *li*:

9.3 子曰：'麻冕，禮也；今也純，儉，吾從眾。拜下，禮也；今拜乎上，泰也。雖違眾，吾從下。'

The Master said, 'A linen ceremonial cap is prescribed by *li*. Nowadays, a silk cap is used instead; this is frugal and I follow the majority on this. To prostrate oneself before ascending [the steps to the hall] is prescribed by *li*. Nowadays, one prostrates oneself [only] after ascending [the steps to the hall]; this is arrogant. Although this goes against the majority, I prostrate myself before ascending [the steps to the hall].'

Here we see an example of how Confucius exercises his judgement in two contrasting ways. In the first instance, he supports modifying a practice of *li* – substituting ceremonial cap made of linen with that made of silk. In another instance, however, he opposes a prevailing practice and insists on adhering to the traditional practice of *li* by prostrating oneself before ascending the steps to the hall. It is instructive that Confucius' judgement is not made arbitrarily or influenced by his personal preferences. Rather, he bases his claims on the ethical standards of frugality (in the first instance) and reverence (in the second instance). These ethical standards reflect the general quality of *ren* that defines the normativity of *li* (see the chapter on *ren* for an exposition of this concept and its relationship with *li*).

The third characteristic of *si* is that it involves **self-examination**. This characteristic follows logically from the other two: a learner should actively reflect, question and extend her learning so as to lead to self-improvement. That the observance of *li* involves not just one's behaviours but also one's attitudes and values implies that we need to constantly examine our own thoughts, feelings and actions.[17] Confucius exhorts all to self-examine: 'When you meet someone who is worthy, consider being his equal; when you meet someone who is not worthy, look inward and examine yourself' (見賢思齊焉，見不賢而內自省也) (4.17). A disciple of Confucius heeds his advice by doing the following:

1.4 曾子曰：'吾日三省吾身： 爲人謀而不忠乎？與朋友交而不信乎？傳不習乎？'

Master Zeng said: 'Every day I examine myself on three counts: Have I done my best in my undertakings on behalf of others? Have I been trustworthy in my interactions with friends? Have I failed to put into practice what was passed to me?'

By examining oneself whole-heartedly, one is motivated and reminded to correct one's shortcomings and observe *li* more faithfully. Such a person is not anxious or fearful, as she has nothing to be ashamed of, as noted by Confucius in his portrait of a *junzi*:

12.4 司馬牛問君子。

子曰：'君子不憂不懼。'

曰：'不憂不懼，斯謂之君子已乎？'

子曰：'內省不疚，夫何憂何懼？'

Sima Niu asked about the *junzi*.

Confucius said, 'The *junzi* is not anxious or fearful.'

'Does being a *junzi* just mean not being anxious or fearful?'

The Master said, 'If you examine yourself and find nothing to be ashamed of, why should you be worried or fearful?'

Three observations of Confucius' concept of *si*

Overall, we have noted that *si* demands the learner's utmost attention and devotion to continuous study and self-improvement. I would like to make three further observations about Confucius' concept of *si*. First, although the English word 'thinking' tends to be associated with the cognitive rather than affective faculty in the Western tradition, it has no such meaning or connotation in the Confucian tradition. 'Thinking' in the sense of *si*, for Confucius, necessarily involves both the heart and the mind where *rationality and emotion are integrated*.[18] Highlighting the need to engage one's heart-mind (心 *xin*,) Confucius encourages all to 'set your heart-mind on the Way' (志於道) (7.6); he claims that he could follow his 'heart-mind's desires without overstepping the line' (從心所欲，不踰矩) (2.4).

Second, *si*, according to Confucius, should involve thinking *about something*. Confucius shares that 'I once went without food the whole day and without sleep the whole night by focusing on *si* that was not beneficial; it is better to spend the time learning [the content]' (吾嘗終日不食，終夜不寢，以思，無益，不如學也) (15.31). Confucius' point is that *si* cannot occur in a vacuum and needs to be based on a specific content. To borrow the analogy from 3.8, one needs to have a plain base (specific content) to which the colours (*si*) can be applied. Confucius' disciples had to learn the *Songs* first before they could draw inferences from them and connect the *Songs* to their experiences (cf. 1.15 and 3.8).

Some readers may wonder whether 15.31 contradicts another verse in the *Analects* where Confucius talks about the *concurrent* practice of learning and *si*. I have reproduced the two verses below to facilitate our comparison:

15.31: 'I once went without food the whole day and without sleep the whole night by focusing on *si*; that was not beneficial; it is better to spend the time learning.' (吾嘗終日不食，終夜不寢，以思，無益，不如學也)

2.15: 'Learning without *si* leads to bewilderment; thinking without learning leads to perilousness.' (學而不思則罔，思而不學則殆)

The key to reconciling the two verses is to clarify the different senses of *si* involved in learning. Recall that *si* is a broad term that encompasses a range of thought processes, from relatively simpler processes such as remembering, to more advanced processes such as reflection, analysis, synthesis, evaluation, making connections, drawing analogies, making inferences, and forming judgements. The first sense of *si* refers to the process of understanding or making sense of what one is learning. This is what Confucius has in mind when he asserts that learning without *si* will lead to bewilderment, since one is unable to comprehend the very thing one is learning (2.15). The second sense of *si* refers to more advanced thought processes such as analysis, synthesis, evaluation, drawing analogy, making inferences, and forming judgements. *Si* in this sense is meaningful for a learner *only after* she has sufficiently acquired a basic foundational knowledge (15.31). As the saying goes, 'a little knowledge is a dangerous thing': a person who hastily critiques an issue without first understanding it may end up misrepresenting or distorting the issue.[19] Whether we are referring to the first or second sense of *si*, what is clear is that *si* and learning work hand in hand to lead forth a person in the process of education.

The third observation about *si* is that Confucius underscores *contexualized thinking* that involves reflecting on one's own cultural heritage. Confucius describes how he treasures ancient Chinese tradition: 'I transmit but do not make; I trust in and love antiquity' (述而不作，信而好古) (7.1). As noted in earlier chapters, this does not mean that Confucius advocates a blind adherence to tradition. We have seen how Confucius, while favouring Zhou *li*, also selectively promotes following the calendar of the Xia, riding on the carriage of the Yin, wearing the ceremonial cap of the Zhou and playing the *shao* and *wu* (cf. 15.11). We have also learned how he was prepared to question and modify certain practices of *li* (cf. 9.3). I propose describing Confucius as a 'conservative innovator' in the sense that he teaches his students to embrace the best of the Chinese tradition while prodding them to think critically about the tradition at the same time.

Education as 'providing a totality of human experiences'

The final aspect of education concerns the provision of a totality of human experiences for students. The 'totality of human experiences' comes from three main channels: applying what one has learned; interacting with one's teacher; and learning from role models and other people.

Experience derived from personal application

Confucius stresses the need for a learner to apply what she has learned in her life. He states that he expects his students to be action-oriented: 'I do not know what to do with a person who does not say, "What should I do? What should I do?"' (不曰 '如之何，如之何' 者，吾末如之何也已矣) (15.16). It is no coincidence that the *Analects* begins with this verse that extols the virtue of a theory-practice nexus: 'To learn and practise [what you have learned] from time to time, is it not a pleasure?' (學而時習之，不亦說乎) (1.1). The word 'pleasure' reiterates Confucius' teaching about the need to find joy in something, and not simply to know and love it (cf. 6.20). In the context of 1.1, Confucius is emphasizing the joy one derives from harmonizing one's actions ('practise what you have learned') with one's knowledge ('to learn'). Another way of putting it is that Confucius underlines application and not simply academic learning. His philosophy is highlighted in the following passage:

13.5 子曰：'誦《詩》三百，授之以政，不達；使於四方，不能專對；雖多，亦奚以爲？'

The Master said, 'If a person can recite three hundred *Songs*, but is unable to perform an official duty entrusted to him and exercise his initiative when sent abroad, what good are the many *Songs* to him?'

Here Confucius is not asserting that memorizing the *Songs* is useless; such an interpretation would contradict other verses where he encourages his students to learn the *Songs* (cf. 16.13, 17.9, 17.10). His point, rather, is that one should learn the *Songs* with the objective to draw ethical lessons that can be applied to one's life. As already explained, Confucius' point about 'without words' in 'if you do not learn the *Songs*, you will be without words' (不學《詩》，無以言) (16.13) is that such a person is unable to communicate well with others. Linking 16.13 to 13.5, what Confucius means is that effective communication through learning the *Songs* is a prerequisite for anyone who wishes to fulfil his official duties or exercise his initiative as an overseas ambassador. A person ignorant of the *Songs* is 'like a person who stands with his face to the wall' (其猶正牆面而立也與) (17.10) – unable to interact well with others in accordance with *li*.

The need for personal application extends beyond language and literature to the 'arts' of archery and music: one learns archery not theoretically but by engaging in the sport in accordance with *li* (cf. 3.7). Similarly, one learns music not for the sake of pure listening pleasure but to put into practice the ethical lessons one has learned from different musical pieces (cf. 16.5, 8.8). The inseparability of learning and practice explains why Confucius includes *Conduct* as one of the four loci of teaching in 7.25 (see the earlier section on culture). In short, all learning should culminate in application where the student integrates her thoughts, feelings and actions in accordance with *li*.

What, then, is the relationship between learning, *si* and practice? I have earlier noted that learning provides a foundation upon which one reflects on what one has learned (cf. 15.31). After acquiring some basic knowledge, one should proceed to reflect on the learning points (2.15). *Si* not only enables a person to acquire a deeper understanding of what one has learned, but also facilitates self-examination and the application of knowledge to one's life. In other words, one puts into practice what one has learned *through reflective thinking*.[20]

The centrality of personal application prompts Confucius to conclude that we can tell a person's true character, not based on how much she knows or claims to know, but on how she behaves:

2.10 子曰：'視其所以，觀其所由，察其所安。人焉廋哉？人焉廋哉？'

The Master said, 'Look at a person's means [to achieve an end], observe his motive [for achieving that end], and examine his source of contentment. How then would that person be able to hide [his character]?'

Confucius also teaches that it is through people's conduct that we can differentiate them: '[People are] close together by nature, but far apart through practice' (性相近也，習相遠也) (17.2). In one account, Confucius shares how he retracts his negative assessment of a disciple upon further observation of the latter's actions:

2.9 子曰：'吾與回言終日，不違，如愚。退而省其私，亦足以發，回也不愚。'

The Master said, 'I speak with Yanhui the whole day, but he never disagrees with me and seems stupid. When he leaves and I examine what he does in private, I find that he is able to illustrate [what I have said], Yanhui is not stupid at all.'

Just as we can know a person's virtue and the extent to which she has applied her learning through her actions, we can know a person's faults in the same way. Confucius maintains: 'The errors of people belong to different categories. By observing their errors, you will know [the degree to which they are] *ren*' (人之過也，各於其黨。觀過，斯知仁矣) (4.7).

The premium Confucius places on personal application helps us to understand why he characterizes a *junzi* as one who 'says something only after one has acted upon the words' (先行其言而後從之) (2.13) and 'feels ashamed when one's words exceed one's actions' (君子恥其言而過其行) (14.27). Confucius' emphasis on acting upon what one has learned might have rubbed off on his disciple Zilu; it is recorded in the *Analects* that 'Zilu's only fear, when he has heard something and has yet to act upon it, is that he would hear [more things]' (子路有聞，未之能行，唯恐有聞) (5.14).

Experience from interacting with one's teacher

Besides personal application, one also gains experiences by interacting with one's teacher. We can identify four distinguishing features of a teacher as outlined by Confucius.[21] First, a teacher is one who is *enthusiastic about teaching*. Confucius himself 'instructs others without growing weary' (誨人不倦) (7.2, also see 7.34), and is 'so zealous that he forgets to eat, "[so] joyful that he forgets about worry, and does not know that old age has befallen him"' (發憤忘食，樂以忘憂，不知老之將至云爾) (7.19). Prepared to give his all to his disciples, he says: 'I do not hide anything from you; I do not do anything that is not shared with you' (吾無隱乎爾。吾無行而不與二三子者) (7.24).

Second, a teacher is *a learner*. Such a person is adept at connecting the old with the new. Confucius points out that a person 'is worthy to being a teacher [when she] keeps alive the old in order to know the new' (溫故而知新，可以爲師矣) (2.11). Seeking self-improvement, she is able to constantly learn and discover new ideas by revising and building on what she has learned. Confucius models this as he 'listens widely, selects what is good and follows it' (多聞，擇其善者而從之) (7.28).

Third, a teacher *does not discriminate in terms of whom she should teach*. Confucius' philosophy to 'teach without category' (有教無類) (15.39), mentioned at the start of the chapter, is that a teacher should teach all students regardless of their family background, social class, financial status, aptitude and other contingent differences. Such a non-prejudicial and meritocratic belief in teaching was radical during Confucius' time, as only those from aristocratic families could enjoy the privilege of formal education.[22] We know from the *Analects* and historical records that Confucius' students came from a cross-section of social backgrounds, including those of humble birth such as Zhonggong and Zizhang.[23] Confucius was prepared to teach anyone who was willing to learn from him. He states that 'to anyone who, on his own accord, gives me [as little as] a gift of dried meat, I have never denied instruction to such a person' (自行束脩以上，吾未嘗無誨焉) (7.7). In the context of ancient China, the gift of dried meat is a meagre gift given to someone whom one is meeting for the first time (Yang, 1980, p. 72).[24] Confucius' point is that even if a person were so poor that he can only afford to give the teacher a token gift, Confucius would still be willing to take him as a student.

Fourth, a teacher *tailors her teaching to suit the specific needs of her students*. This principle has since been encapsulated in a well-known Chinese proverb, '因材施教' (*yincai shijiao*, literally 'teach according to aptitude') which means 'customized teaching'. The classic passage in the *Analects* that illustrates customized teaching is 11.22 (see chapter 2 for a discussion of this passage). In that passage, Confucius gives two opposing answers to two disciples (Zilu and Ranyou) who asked the same question. Confucius' objective was to guide them to observe *li* based on their individual personalities and developmental needs.[25] This passage also reminds us that a good teacher is one who exhibits appropriateness by exercising her discretion and wisdom by helping her students realize their potential, and empathy and reciprocity by treating her students with sensitivity and loving care.[26]

Experience from learning from role models and other people

Besides learning from one's teacher, a student also receives an education when she interacts with different strata of people in society. Confucius highlights the benefits of learning from role models, especially from the sage-kings and *junzi*. Confucius exhorts his students to 'be intimate with [those who are] *ren*' (親仁) (1.6) and 'make friends with scholars who are *ren*' (友其士之仁者) (15.10).[27] We have already noted the transformational influence of *junzi* on people around them in the previous chapter (cf. 9.14, 12.19). In stressing the need to learn from role models, Confucius is not instructing us to mimic their movements and observe *li* in a mechanical or superficial way. Rather, we learn from role models by being inspired by them through their life goals, personal qualities and achievements so that we may likewise observe *li* whole-heartedly. In other words, role models serve as spiritual-ethical-aesthetic exemplars to guide and motivate us to join them in broadening the Way.

Role models are not the only people that we should learn from; Confucius avers that we could and should learn from *anyone*:

7.22 子曰: '三人行, 必有我師焉: 擇其善者而從之, 其不善者而改之。'

The Master said, 'When walking with two other persons, I am bound to find a teacher among them: I choose to follow the good person, and correct myself when I am with a person who is not good.'

It is evident that one needs humility to learn from everyone, especially those whom we perceive to be beneath us in status or qualification. Confucius explains that Kong Wenzi was given the title of 'cultured' (文 *wen*) because he was 'diligent and loved learning, and not ashamed of asking [advice from] those below him' (敏而好學，不恥下問) (5.15). The possibility of learning from everyone – be they good examples to emulate, or bad examples whose shortcomings we are to avoid – reminds us once again that learning, for Confucius, is an active, lifelong and life-wide process that is intimately linked to real-life application.

Conclusion

We have learned that education, according to Confucius, is about instruction and nurture. It entails bringing up and leading forth a person in accordance with *li* by providing a totality of human experiences. Despite giving everyone the opportunity to learn, Confucius is realistic enough to know that different people will attain different educational outcomes:

9.30子曰：'可與共學，未可與適道；可與適道，未可與立；可與立，未可與權。'

The Master said, 'You can learn with someone and not walk the same Way together; you can walk the same Way together and not take a stand with him; you can take a stand together and not exercise discretion in the same way.'

The above verse sums up Confucius' conception of the educational process: it involves one's quest in learning (*xue*), walking in the Way (*dao*) and taking a stand (*li*). The verse also succinctly points out the different levels of success human beings will obtain from learning. Having examined the key concepts of Confucius, we shall apply his educational thought to the twenty-first century in the next chapter.

Notes

Chapter 2

1 According to Zhu (2009, pp. 35–6), *li* is mentioned 71 times in the *Analects*.
2 For a good discussion on the conceptual evolution of *li* in ancient China, see Cua (2002).
3 Slingerland (2001) observes that Confucius is 'disgusted by the prospect of form unaccompanied by emotional substance' (p. 28).
4 Other writers interpret this verse differently. Chong (1998), referring to Lau (1979)'s translation of '諂' (*chan*) as 'obsequious', claims that 'Confucius also warns against obsequiousness in performing the rites [*li*] (3.18)' (p. 75). Lai (2006) reads it as Confucius 'mak[ing] light of those who are over-zealous in their adherence to *li*' (p. 71). Slingerland (2003), on the other hand, interprets it to mean that '[r]itual practice [*li*] had so degenerated by Confucius' age that a proper ritual practitioner was viewed with suspicion or disdain' (p. 24). *Pace* Chong, Lau and Lai, I support Slingerland's interpretation as the word 'jinli' (盡禮) literally means 'completely or thoroughly *li*' with no negative connotation in the context.
5 The literal translation is 'The Master replied, "Without *li*, do not look; without *li*, do not listen; without *li*, do not speak; without *li*, do not move"'. But such a translation, although accurate, is awkward and does not fully bring out Confucius' point.
6 The character '非' (*fei*) literally means 'not'. Sun and Fu translate '非禮'(*feili*) as 'do not . . . when it is not in accordance with *li*' (不符合禮的話不 . . .), Yang translates it as 'do not . . . when [you are] not supposed to do so' (不該. . . 不要去 . . .), and Ames and Rosemont translate the expression slightly differently, as 'anything that violates'. Lau and Slingerland translate *feili* positively as 'unless it is in accordance with *li*'.
7 My definition is similar to Yu (1998)'s definition of *li* as 'the totality of socially acceptable behaviour patterns and lifestyles, including both moral and non-moral norms' (p. 326). But a key difference is that I have included 'corresponding attitudes and values' as part of the definition, to highlight the integration of one's thoughts, feelings and actions.
8 Ames and Rosemont (1998) underscore the pervasive nature of *li*. They reject the translation of *li* as 'ritual' on the basis that the latter is 'almost

always pejorative, suggesting as it often does compliance with hollow and hence meaningless social conventions' (p. 52). They explain their understanding of *li* as follows: 'The compass is broad: all formal conduct, from table manners to patterns of greeting and leave-taking, to graduations, weddings, funerals, from gestures of deference to ancestral sacrifices – all of these, and more, are *li*. They are a social grammar that provides each member with a defined place and status within the family, community, and polity. *Li* are life forms transmitted from generation to generation as repositories of meaning, enabling the youth to appropriate persisting values and to make them appropriate to their own situations' (p. 51).

9 Hagen (2010) distinguishes *li* in terms of whether it is fixed and external or flexible and internal. He proposes three definitions of *li*: 'Definition [1] suggests that *li* is a privileged and determinate external code. Definition [2] still seems to imply that *li* are external standards of some kind, but it emphasises their malleability. However, since *li* not only cover a very broad range, but are thought to be evolving, and culturally contingent, and since *li* are at least in part dependent upon values and interpretation, *li* cannot be, on this view, entirely external. An exemplary exercise of *li* involves the integration of tradition and personal adaptation. However, this does not go as far as description [3], which treats *li* more fundamentally internal. *Li* is here treated as a set of virtues, rather than a set of rules of action. While most treatments of *li* seem to place it somewhere in the range between [1] and [2], I will argue that Confucius's *li*, at least for the more cultivated, is better conceived as spanning [2] and [3]' (p. 5). Unlike Hagen, I do not see *li* (i.e. Confucius' *li*) in terms of whether it is external or internal. In my view, *li* is both internal (in terms of appropriate attitudes and values) and external (in terms of the normative behaviours that follow logically from the attitudes and values). My continuum focuses on the different categories of *li* in terms of their scope, structure and degree of individual improvisation allowed. But I agree with Hagen's observation that 'most explanations [of *li*] fail to sufficiently emphasise or elaborate upon the internal dimension of *li*' (p. 5), what he terms a 'sense of ritual propriety'.

10 Commenting on the scope of *li*, Shun (1993) observes as follows: 'The actual examples of *li* found in the *Analects* have to do largely with ceremonious behaviour (3.4, 3.15, 3.17, 9.3, 17.11), but it remains unclear how broad the scope of *li* is when the text makes such general observations as that one has to learn *li* to take a stand (8.8, 16.13, 20.3) or that *li* is the ideal basis for government (2.3, 4.13)' (p. 458). My view is that *li* is *both* narrow and broad, depending on the category of *li* in question. In other words, *li* comprises a range that varies from narrow to broad, as represented by the continuum.

11 Wilson (1995) asserts that for 'all its insistence upon the personal investment of each individual participant, then, Confucian ritual practice is still

more fruitfully compared to classical orchestral music than to jazz improvisation' (p. 274). However, I think his comment applies only to certain categories of *li*. As noted in the text, I have used both classical orchestral music and jazz music as analogies for the two extreme categories of *li*.

12 Slingerland (2001) explains how Book 10 of the *Analects* serves to illustrate Confucius' observance of *li* in his everyday life: 'Indeed, the entirety of book 10 of the *Analects* – an extended account of Confucius's ritual behaviour – can be seen as a model of how the true sage flexibly adapts the principles of ritual to concrete situations. Although this book is often skipped over in embarrassment by Western scholars sympathetic to Confucianism but nonetheless appalled by the seemingly pointless detail and apparent rigidity of behaviour, this discomfort is based upon a fundamental misunderstanding. While the scope and detail of Confucian ritual certainly (and quite rightly) seems alien to a modern Westerner, it is important to understand that what is being emphasised in this chapter is the ease and grace with which the Master embodied the spirit of the rites in every aspect of his life (no matter how trivial) and accorded with this spirit in adapting the rites to new and necessarily unforeseeable circumstances' (p. 103).

13 Grange (2004) aptly describes *li* as a 'pattern of unending gestures' – '*Li* is the social grammar used by communities to convey their most important values. It is a pattern of unending gestures that communicate meaning and value to a community's members. They are unending because genuine gestures have a symbolic depth that is more or less inexhaustible' (p. 51).

14 This does not mean that *li* is limited to the ethical dimension. As I shall argue in subsequent chapters, it is more accurate to describe *li* as containing a spiritual-ethical-aesthetic dimension.

15 Chan (2000) elaborates on the importance of ethical considerations in 9.3: 'These examples suggest that ethical judgment follows directly from the Confucian claim that *li* performance must be informed by the right attitudes and motivations. They do not exhaust the meaning of ethical judgment, but highlight how the Confucian conservative approach to tradition, in its advocacy of *li*, harbours a "built-in" critical component. . . . In the practice of *li*, one should certainly aim at both perfect ritual form and full ethical content (compare 6.18, 12.8)' (p. 251).

16 Commenting on 8.8 on learning to stand by observing *li*, Slingerland (2003) claims: 'The point is that the cultivation of the self should start with the study of the Odes. Taking one's place through ritual [*li*] involves, as discussed in 2.4, taking one's role as an adult among other adults in society; something that requires a mastery of the rituals governing social interactions. Steps one and two thus represent, respectively, cognitive shaping through learning and behavioural shaping through ritual training' (p. 80). While I agree with Slingerland's interpretation of 8.8, I do not think that

li training (or what he calls 'ritual training') is just about behavioural shaping; it should include cognitive and affective shaping as well.
17 Lai (1995) uses the idea of participation in a ceremony to explain the function of *li*: 'Acting according to *li* within the social sphere allows one to participate in social "ceremony": one becomes socially competent and interacts with others – understanding what is required by various roles within various relationships – with seeming effortlessness' (p. 255).
18 Recognizing the flexible nature of *li*, Lai (1995) notes that *li* 'can be modified and, indeed, are varied and variable and manifest differently as they pertain to each different situation and to each particular relationship, although they may provide general guidelines for each kind of relationship' (pp. 255–6).
19 Ames and Rosemont (1998) rightly point out that observing *li* is 'a process of internalisation of the roles and relationships that locate one within community' and that '[f]ull participation in a ritually-constituted community requires the personalisation of prevailing customs, institutions, and values' (pp. 50–1). But they go a step further and argue that Confucius advocates that we need to make the tradition our own through 'creative personalization'. In their words, '[P]ersonal refinement is only possible through the discipline provided by formalised roles and behaviours. Form without creative personalisation is coercive and dehumanising law; creative personal expression without form is randomness at best, and license at worse. It is only with appropriate combination of form and personalisation that community can be self-regulating and refined' (p. 52). This position has led some writers such as Yu (1998) to counter that Ames and Rosemont have overemphasized the place for individual creative effort. My stand is that Ames and Rosemont are correct insofar as they are referring to instances of *li* that are relatively broad in scope as well as fluid and flexible (on the right side of the continuum), therefore necessitating individual judgement and modifications. It is unlikely, however, that Confucius would support the idea that we should creatively personalize ceremonial *li*, given how he reprimanded the rulers of his time for being too 'creative' in appropriating rituals that rightfully belonged to the emperor. In summary, the personalization of *li* in the sense of involving our personal attitudes and values when we observe *li* is necessary for all cases of *li*, but creative personalization in the sense of modifying the practices of *li* is applicable only to some instances of *li*.
20 Different writers have placed different emphases on the characteristics of *li*. Writers such as Fingarette (1972), Ivanhoe (1991b) and Yu (1998) have highlighted the relatively rigid, and tradition-based performance of *li*. On the other hand, writers such as Ames and Rosemont (1998), Jones and Culliney (1998) and Hagen (2010) have underscored personal creativity in the observance of *li*. My stand is that the question of whether we should emphasize tradition or personal creativity in the observance of *li* depends

on which category of *li* we are talking about. For a useful discussion and critique of Fingarette's views, see Fu (1978); Wilson (1995); Chong (1998); Ivanhoe (2007); and Hagen (2010). For a useful discussion and critique of Ames and Rosemont's views, see Chong (1998); Yu (1998); and Elliott and Tsai (2008).

21 On the importance of attitudes, Cua (2005) points out that the observance of *li* 'express[es] the actor's trait, and, if it has moral import, it is an expression of a cultivated attitude or virtuous disposition which may uniquely reveal the actor's character' (p. 52, as cited in Hagen, 2010, p. 5).

22 Luo (2010) links *li* to conformity with moral rules: 'If *li* refers to a collection of practices and norms that dictate propriety in all aspects of social life, then *li*-basing is essentially rule-basing according to which moral norms along are the ultimate criteria for all ethical evaluations. For instance, a righteous person is someone whose behaviour is in conformity with moral rules' (p. 128). In my view, Luo is right about *li* being essentially about conformity to moral rules if we accept the definition of *li* as 'a collection of practices and norms'. But this definition of *li* is unsatisfactory as it ignores the values and attitudes that should accompany the practices and norms. That is why it is important to stress the beliefs, dispositions and outlook that direct one's behaviour: without these, it is easy for *li* to degenerate into a set of do's and don'ts, which was what happened during Confucius' time.

23 A modern day analogy, although an imperfect one, is the common albeit ungrammatical expression – 'free gift'. This inclusion of the word 'free' is redundant, since the word 'gift' already implies that the item is free of charge. But the deliberate addition of the word 'free', especially in advertisements, serves to emphasize the fact that the gift is given without any need for payment. Likewise, when Confucius talks about the need for a ruler to observe *li* and show deference (4.13), the reference to showing deference is actually redundant since a person who observes *li* will naturally manifest deference. But Confucius chooses to make such a reference to drive home the point that deference goes hand in hand with one's observance of *li*.

24 The two sense of *li* used by Confucius in the *Analects* also applies to his concept of *ren*, as I shall explain later in the chapter on *ren*.

Chapter 3

1 The character '作' (*zuo*) is ambiguous hence is difficult to translate. Ames and Rosemont translate it as 'forge new paths', Lau and Slingerland translate it as 'innovate' and Yang translates it as 'create' (創作). I have adopted the literal translation of '作' as 'making' to convey the point that Confucius did not create the norm. The choice of the word 'making' instead of 'innovating' also means that I am setting aside the controversial debate on

the extent to which Confucius was an innovator. I shall address this question in a subsequent discussion. The character '信' (*xin*) is also ambiguous. Ames and Rosemont translate it as 'confidence' (信心) while Lau interprets it as '[being] truthful in what I say' (信赖). I follow Slingerland in translating it as 'trust in' (信靠), as the context is about Confucius having faith in antiquity.

2   Wilson (1995) explains the meaning of the 'Way of the Sage Kings of Old': 'This expression refers to a Golden Age in which the basic features of civilised human life were thought to have been discovered and instantiated in a perfect social, political, and ethical order. Yao, Shun, and Yu are the paradigmatic examples of these sage kings, the Golden Age being thought to have occurred during their respective reigns (2357–2198 BCE)' (p. 270).

3   For more information on the Duke of Zhou, King Wen and other characters mentioned in the *Analects*, see Cai (1996).

4   Ames and Rosemont render '二代' (*erdai*) as 'Xia and Shang' while Lau translates it as 'two previous dynasties'. I prefer the more literal translation of 'two Ages'. Despite the different choice of words, translators concur that the subjects in question were the Xia and Shang dynasties.

5   Ivanhoe (1990) maintains that Confucius' approach can be described as 'refined traditionalism': 'He did not invent the *li* nor did he derive them from some set of underlying moral principles. Questions about what constituted the right or the good were, for him, already answered. He never questioned the legitimacy of the traditional rituals. He regarded the culture of the Chou [Zhou] – the culture described by the traditional rituals which he followed – as both inspired and protected by Heaven' (p. 28). But I do not think that Confucius' approach should be described as 'refined traditionalism' because verses such as 2.23 and 15.11 suggest that Confucius does not promote an indiscriminate adoption of *li* from earlier dynasties but a judicious selection of what he believes to be the norm adhered to by the sage-kings. Also see the next note on this topic.

6   Referring to 15.11, Hagen (2011) argues that Confucius advocates 'selective traditionalism': 'Yan Hui is advised to borrow eclectically from the best parts of the tradition, a stance that can be called "selective traditionalism." Although it is undoubtedly conservative, the fact remains that choosing which elements are to be conserved is necessarily an interpretive project and the resulting mix will always be novel. These considerations militate against the idea that Confucius is trying to return to a particular way that existed in the past' (p. 9). While I agree with Hagen's point about Confucius' 'selective traditionalism', I wish to add that Confucius *is* trying to return to a particular way that existed in the past. Confucius' selective traditionalism is not arbitrary or subjective, but is based on the Way as adhered to by the sage-kings from the previous dynasties. Confucius promotes a return to the lost Golden Age insofar as the practices of the previous dynasties were in accordance with the Way.

7 Commenting on the relationship between normative tradition and the Way in ancient China, Chan (2000) writes that 'a sense of normative tradition emerges' that 'contributed significantly to the formation of Confucian ideals, subsumed conceptually in the *Lunyu* [*Analects*] under the general rubric of the "Dao" or "Way"' (p. 246).

8 Explaining the mandate of heaven, Wong (2008) notes: 'Since the Chou [Zhou] dynasty, the spiritual force was replaced by the Mandate of Heaven. This is a moral law whose constant factor is virtue. In this light, humanity's destiny is linked to his own good words and deeds. It is not based on the existence of a soul, nor on the whim of a spiritual force, as in Greek tradition' (p. 119).

9 Wilson (1995), citing Ivanhoe (1993), points out that the concept of virtue (德 *de*) was mentioned as early as the Shang Dynasty (around the twelfth century BCE) to convey a kind of power which accrued to and resided within a person who had acted favourably towards a spirit or another person (p. 276). Slingerland (2001) adds that Confucius teaches that heaven bestows virtue on anyone who genuinely embraces the Way, which will enable the person to attract people in a non-coercive manner through her moral charisma (p. 242).

10 Ames and Rosemont translate '命' (*ming*) as 'circumstances', Lau translates it as 'Destiny' and Slingerland uses the word 'fate'. I have translated it as 'mandate' in line with my translation for '命' in 2.4 where Confucius professed that he 'understood the mandate of heaven at the age of fifty' (五十而知天命) (2.4).

11 I support Lau's more literal translation of 'the Way is to be found' for '天下有道', instead of Ames and Rosemont's 'the way (*dao*) prevailed' or Slingerland's 'the Way were realised'.

12 Ames and Rosemont (1998) point out that to 'broaden the Way' is 'to experience, to interpret, and to influence the world in such a way as to reinforce and extend the way of life inherited from one's cultural predecessors' (p. 45). Agreeing with Ames and Rosemont, Kim (2004) asserts that 15.29 'implies that people make and remake appropriate ways of living: There is no predetermined, transcendental way of living for Confucius. Appropriateness and propriety of human living is created by persons' conscious efforts' (p. 123). Chan (2000) adds that '[h]istory in this sense is not a mere chronicle of past events but testifies to the *Dao*'s unfolding, as human beings take their place in the development of tradition' (p. 247).

13 A case can be made that Confucius' belief in human beings' ability to broaden the Way is linked to the ancient Chinese belief that 'truth' is not an objective fact but a way of being. Li (2006) explains: 'The Chinese typically do not see truth as correspondence with an objective fact in the world; rather they understand truth more as a way of being, namely being a good person, a good father, or a good son. For them there is no objective truth

carved in stone, and consequently there is not an ultimate fixed order in the world according to which things must operate. The Confucian *Dao* consists of the process of generating an actual order in the world rather than an already fixed order. Without a predetermined truth, human beings have to set boundaries for themselves and for other things as they move forward in the world' (p. 594).

14 Rather than locating knowledge in a transcendental and other-worldly realm, Confucius situates knowledge in the human world. Hall and Ames (1987) observe: 'For Confucius, knowledge is grounded in the language, customs, and institutions that comprise culture. Culture is the given world. Thinking is cultural articulation that renders this givenness effective. There is no knowledge to be gained of a reality which precedes that of culture or transcends its determinations. The "world" is always a human world' (p. 67).

15 Although this verse originates not from Confucius but his disciple, it is reasonable to assume that Confucius would agree with it as the message is consistent with his teaching on promoting peace and order through observing *li*. Chan (2000), commenting on this verse, avers: 'Although these words did not come from Confucius himself but one of his chief disciples, he would no doubt have approved of them' (p. 249).

16 Ames and Rosemont (1998) point out that the word 'harmony' is etymologically related to cooking – the art of bringing together with mutual benefit and enhancement without losing their separate and particular identities (p. 56). Li (2006), on the other hand, traces the root of harmony to music: 'Therefore, we may conclude that the original meaning of *he* as harmony comes from the rhythmic interplay of various sounds, either in nature or between human beings, that is musical to the human ear, and that the prototype of he is found in music. From the notion of he as the harmonious interplay of sounds, it is not difficult to see how this can be expanded, by analogous thinking, to mean harmony in other things and hence harmony in general' (p. 584). Be it in the metaphor of food or music, harmony essentially involves uniting different elements to form an integrated whole, without sacrificing the individuality of the diverse components.

17 Chong (1998) aptly describes a 'harmonious person' as 'one whose motivational attitudes are congruent with the rites [*li*], and gracefully expressed through them, in action' (p. 81).

18 Lau, Yang and Fu translate '好' (*hao*) as 'fond of' (喜爱) while Ames and Rosemont, Slingerland and Yang translate it as 'love' (爱). I have translated it as 'love' as this is consistent with my translation of '好' mentioned in other verses in the *Analects*, such as 1.15 (love *li*) and 1.14 (love learning).

19 Slingerland avers that the object of knowing, loving and enjoying in 6.20 is most likely the Confucian Way (2003, p. 59, also see Slingerland, 2001,

p. 110). For the translation of 1.15, the character '道' (*dao*) does not appear in the expression '貧而樂道' in some texts (e.g. see Lau, 1979; Yang, 1980; and Slingerland, 2003). In other words, the expression in these texts is '貧而樂' with the word '道' (*dao*) omitted. Despite the omission, Lau translates the expression as 'poor yet delighting in the Way'. Likewise, Yang translates it as 'poor yet find joy in the Way' (貧窮却樂於道). Slingerland, however, sticks to the original meaning and translates it as 'poor and yet joyful'. It appears that most translators take the subject in the expression '貧而樂道' to be the Way, despite its omission in some texts.

20 Li (2006) explains that harmony is by its very nature relational: 'It presupposes the coexistence of multiple parties; a single item does not harmonise. As far as harmony is concerned, these parties possess more or less equal significance. Therefore, harmony is always contextual; epistemologically it calls for a holistic approach. A mentality of harmony is a contextual mentality. In other words, persons of harmonious mentality see things, and make judgments on these things, in relation, in context, not in isolation or separation' (p. 589).

21 I coin the expression 'spiritual-ethical-aesthetic dimension' by borrowing the terms 'ethico-aesthetical' from Chong (1998) and 'moral-aesthetic' from Cai (1999). Chong (1998) explains the significance of and relationship between one's aesthetic character and ethical character: 'For Confucius, the aesthetic character is per force, an ethical one. Part of the point of the ethico-aesthetical training is that one's emotions, motivations and attitudes are harmonized with reasons for acting, as spelled out within the rites. As we have seen, the dignified and graceful performance of the rites is, in itself, a thing of beauty' (p. 87). While I agree with Chong, I also wish to highlight the spiritual dimension of *li*. As pointed out earlier, the sage-kings followed the straight Way by modelling themselves upon heaven. Also, the mandate of heaven determines whether the Way will prevail. Without highlighting the spiritual dimension of *li*, Confucius' teaching may be reduced to mere moral rules or human wisdom. Ames and Rosemont assert that for Confucius and ancient China, the aesthetic, ethical and spiritual realms are intertwined, unlike the case in the West: 'Owing to Kierkegaard and others, these three cultural interests [aesthetic, ethical and spiritual] are distinct realms in the West; their interrelatedness would, we maintain, be self-evident to Confucius. Again, the sacred is not *transcendentally* distinct from the secular in China' (p. 61, italics in the original).

22 Hall and Ames (1987) elaborate on the Chinese view of mind and body: 'It is not that the Chinese thinkers were able to reconcile this dichotomy [mind/body problem]; rather, it never emerged as a problem. Because body and mind were not regarded as essentially different kinds of existence, they did not generate different sets of terminologies necessary to describe them'

(p. 20). On 'heart-mind', Ames and Rosemont (1998) maintain that 'to divorce the mind from the heart – the cognitive from the affective – is to reenter the Western metaphysical realm again, most especially via the mind-body dichotomy, and embrace the notion of an ahistorical, acultural seat of pure rationality. To avoid this reference, we render *xin* as "heart-and-mind,"... to remind the reader that there are no altogether disembodied thoughts for Confucius, nor any raw feelings altogether lacking (what in English would be called) "cognitive content"' (p. 56). Gier (2001) points out the significance of the heart-mind in Confucian thought, as opposed to European thought: 'Reason and the passions are united in *xin*, so the dichotomy that has plagued European thought is simply nonexistent. Assuming a thoroughly somatic soul, the Confucius of the *Analects* does not even oppose heart-mind to the senses and appetites, although this dichotomy does appear later in Mencius and Xunzi' (p. 283).

23 Commenting on 2.4, Cai (1999) observes that if 'we recall Confucius' description of his own spiritual progress, we will see that the self or getting spontaneity, the highest form of moral consciousness he achieves at the age of seventy, is akin to, if not entirely identical with, a heightened state of aesthetic experience untainted by specific utilitarian ends or non-purposiveness' (p. 329).

24 Fingerette (1972) highlights the spiritual dimension of *li* by describing it as a sacred phenomenon rooted in a cosmic Way. According to him, *li* has the 'magical' power to shape human beings to become truly human through public formalities such as handshaking and making requests. Commenting on Fingarette (1992), Chan (1984) avers that 'Fingarette has done us a great service by reformulating in a concrete way what the late Professor Charles A. Moore had stated: namely, that "the ethical and the spiritual are one in China"' (p. 429). I agree with Fingerette's interpretation of the spiritual dimension of *li* but I do not agree with all his interpretations of Confucius and the *Analects*. For example, I think that Fingerette may have overemphasized the performative aspect of *li* and overlooked inner attitudes and values. Chong (1999) similarly notes: '[Fingerette's] statement that "The ceremonial act is the primary, irreducible event" seems to endorse the view that the exertion of will, the cultivation of the proper emotions and attitudes, and so forth are either not significant, or less significant, than the return to ceremony. As a result, some of Fingarette's critics have sought to redress what they see as an imbalance through an emphasis on the existence of certain sustained attitudes and an inner life, in relation to *jen* [*ren*]' (p. 35).

25 Chan (2000) highlights the regulative function of the ethical dimension of *li*, noting that it 'helps delineate the matrix of acceptable behaviour, bind the community together, and in so doing give shape to the Confucian conception of culture' (p. 249).

26 The term 'ethical' is more appropriate than 'moral' as the former focuses on character rather than just actions and consequences. Yu (1998) explains that morality is 'characterised as dealing with an agent's actions and their consequences, and as attempting to formulate legalistic moral principles and rules that are universally applicable to all moral actions.... Ethics, on the other hand, is believed to concern, as the word "ethics" itself suggests, an agent's character, or the kind of person an agent is, and treats the agent as culturally and traditionally embedded. Its central notion is "virtue," or the excellence of character, and it takes personal commitment, attachment, and deep convictions into serious consideration. Hence the sphere of ethics is much broader than that of morality' (p. 342).

27 Ames and Rosemont highlight the relational focus of not just Confucius' *Analects* but ancient Chinese texts in general: '[T]he reader should expect to find in classical Chinese texts a more relational focus; not a concern to describe how things are in themselves, but how they stand in relation to something else at particular times' (p. 23).

28 Two comments need to be made about 13.23. First, the context of this verse is about the trait of a *junzi* (noble or exemplary person; see the chapter on *junzi* for details). Nonetheless, it is applicable to all human beings, since Confucius teaches that everyone should strive to be a *junzi*. Second, Bell (2008) rightly points out that this verse originated from the *Zuo Commentary* and originally referred to 'the idea that the ruler should be open to different political views among his advisers' (p. 172). But I think that this does not mean that this verse, as well as other verses on harmony in the *Analects*, *only* has political implications. Just as Confucius borrows familiar terms of the day and expands on their traditional meanings, such as *li* (as well as *ren* and *junzi*, as I shall discuss later), it is reasonable to assume that he has expanded the meaning of harmony beyond that of embracing diverse political views. Li (2006) elaborates on the broad meaning of harmony: 'Harmony, as understood in Confucianism, can occur at various levels. It can take place within the individual. A person can harmonize various parts of his or her body, the mind-heart, and various pursuits in life into a well-functioning, organic whole. Harmony can take place between individuals at the level of the family, the community, the nation, and the world. This may include harmony between societies, harmony within a society with different ethnic groups (or political parties), harmony within the same ethnic group with different kin, and harmony among the same kin. Harmony also can take place between human beings and the natural universe' (p. 588).

29 Fox (1997) interestingly contrasts the 'Western artist' with the 'Confucian artist' as follows: 'The Western artist is often depicted as creating through rebellion; for Confucius, what the artist creates "makes new"' through join-

ing together. Such an artist is less a self-conscious critic than a selfless 'friend of the world' (p. 586).
30 It is instructive that the poetry in the *Book of Songs*, according to Gier (2001), 'was not meant for silent reading and was usually accompanied with music and dance' (p. 293).
31 I have translated this verse literally by not identifying the subject in the sentence 'music was put right and the *Ya* and *Song* were put into proper order'. This translation (that omits the subject) is also adopted by Lau and Slingerland. On the other hand Ames and Rosemont as well as Yang, identify the subject to be Confucius; Ames and Rosemont, for example, translate 9:15 as follows: 'The Master said, "It was only after my return to Lu from Wey that I revised the *Book of Music*, and put the 'Songs of the Kingdom' and the Ceremonial Hymns in proper order."' Also see next note.
32 This is concurred by Gier (2001): '[I]t is said that Confucius, after his return from Wei to Lu, finally put the Book of Odes to music in the proper way, presumably based on a correlation between notes and virtues' (p. 293).
33 For an in-depth discussion of Confucius' views on music, see Jiang (2009).
34 Lai (1996) points out that one of Confucius' insights 'lies in the acknowledgment of the influential forces of tradition and culture in shaping behavioural and moral norms' (p. 72).
35 Cai (1999) elaborates on the relationship between poetry and harmony as follows: 'Confucius holds that good poetry can teach the young how to regulate their inward feelings and bring themselves into harmony with other people. . . . Confucius stresses the evocation of moral consciousness because he believes that in the process one can transform one's emotions into moral sentiments and achieve an inward harmony of feelings and thoughts' (p. 324).
36 Chong (1998) observes that the 'many references to music and the *Odes* [*Songs*] in the *Analects*, in connection with the proper performance of *li*, suggest that the intimate connection between aesthetics and *li* is seen as a motivational tool in character training. . . . Aesthetic discrimination provides a sensitivity to the nuances of balance and harmony, being part and parcel of a "complete person"' (pp. 70, 76). Also see Wong (1998) on Confucius' views on music.
37 Commenting on Zengxi, Chong (1998) points out that he is an example of a person who has harmonized his motivational attitudes and his emotions with *li*: 'Music and the *Odes* [*Songs*] have instilled in him not only knowledge of the rites [*li*], but delight in their form, and this finds expression in his harmonious relation with others' (p. 87).
38 Other writers have different descriptions of the different stages in the observance of *li*. For example, Lai (2006) proposes three continuous and

fluid stages, beginning with the novice stage where the person adheres to the dictates of *li* and is inculcated in the correct forms of behaviour. The next stage is the experimental stage where the learner extracts principles from these behavioural forms through constant practice, and tests out his application of moral principles. The last stage is marked by the deliberations of the mature, cultivated person who recognizes *li* not 'as instruments of rote learning but rather . . . channels for meaningful self-expression' (p. 69). I agree with Lai that one cannot master the observance of *li* from the start but needs to invest much time and effort to learn, think, apply and embody *li*. In that sense, one learns to observe *li* incrementally. However, I disagree with her suggestion of distinguishing the various stages based on, among other criteria, the degree of personal experimentation and self-expression in the observance of *li*. As I have argued in the text, the extent of individual improvisation in one's observance of *li* depends largely on the category of *li*, whether it is relatively narrow in scope, fixed and rigid, or relatively broad in scope, fluid and flexible. Given the wide spectrum of *li*, describing the observance of *li* based on Lai's three stages may not be accurate. Another writer, Hagen (2010), while supporting the idea of incremental ethical development, adds that the various stages are not strictly separated, but may overlap in practice. He writes, 'Rather than a strict code being superseded by the pure improvisation of a virtuoso, the novice and the accomplished follow and improvise at the same time. . . . Even the novice must perform on the real world stage, set with novelty and indeterminacy. The *li* of the novice and that of the exemplary are not entirely different things. The *li* of the *junzi* is just better done, and thus more exemplary' (p. 12). In view of the diverse range of *li*, I think that Hagen's point is more applicable to cases of *li* where there is sufficient room for improvisation, such as during a casual conversation rather than when performing a religious ritual. Depending on the category of *li*, *both* the novice and expert may be expected to adhere strictly to a practice in one instance, and improvise in another instance.

Chapter 4

1 Shun (1993) points out that there are at least two different meanings of *ren*: 'According to one view, the character originally referred to the quality that makes someone a distinctive member of an aristocratic clan. According to another view, it originally had the meaning of love, especially the kindness of rulers to their subjects' (p. 457). Yu (1998) suggests a third possible meaning of *ren*: it is a quality possessed by noble huntsmen, according to the *Book of Songs* (p. 323).

2 The precise relationship between *li* and *ren* in this passage is debatable due to the ambiguity of the character '爲' (*wei*) that could be translated in more than one way. Li (2007) points out that *wei*, besides meaning 'constitutes', could also mean 'can result in, or cause, or enable a person to be' (p. 315). If we were to consider this alternative translation of *wei*, then the expression '克己復禮爲仁' (*keji fuli weiren*) could be translated as 'overcoming the self and returning to *li* result in *ren*'. However, I think there is not enough evidence in the *Analects* for us to attribute a causal relationship between *li* and *ren* (i.e. acting in accordance with *li results in ren*). For the same reason, I prefer not to translate *wei* as 'constitutes' as it is not obvious that a whole-part relationship between *ren* and *li* (i.e. acting in accordance to *li* constitutes *ren*) exists in the *Analects*. I have instead translated *wei* as 'is' – a relatively neutral term that does not imply causation or constitution. It is noteworthy that other Confucian writers have also adopted this translation of *wei*. For example, Tu (1968, p. 30) translates the expression *keji fuli* as 'to conquer yourself and return to propriety is *jen* [*ren*]'; Yang (1980, p. 130) translates it as 'suppressing yourself for all your speech and actions to be aligned to *li*, this is *ren*'; 抑制自己，使言語行動都合於禮，就是仁); Sun (1993, p. 306) translates it as 'restraining yourself and returning to *li* is *ren*' (约束自己而復归于礼就是仁).

3 There is some controversy over the precise meaning of the character '克' (*ke*). As pointed out by Shun (1993), *ke* could mean 'subdue' or 'succeed in'; its meaning also depends on what the object of *ke* is – the self (*ji*) or *li*. This means that the expression *keji fuli* can be translated as 'subduing oneself and returning to the observance of *li*' or 'succeeding in aligning oneself with *li*' (Shun, 1993, p. 465). I believe that *ke* refers to the noun *ji*, thus *keji* should be translated as 'overcoming the self'. This is the interpretation adopted by most translators, including Lau ('overcoming the self'), Ames and Rosemont ('self-discipline'), Slingerland ('restraining yourself'), Yang ('suppress yourself'; 抑制自己), Sun ('restraining yourself'; 约束自己), and Fu ('being able to autonomously carry out the requirements of *li*'; 能够自己做主去实践礼的要求). Despite the variations, all these interpretations converge on the need to observe *li* to achieve *ren*.

4 I have refrained from describing qualities such as tolerance, respect and filial piety as 'moral' or 'ethical' as I think that they contain more than just the ethical aspect. In tandem with Confucius' concept of *li* as containing a spiritual-ethical-aesthetic dimension, all other Confucius' concepts such as *ren*, tolerance, respect and filial piety also possess spiritual-ethical-aesthetic significance.

5 Referring to 12.1, Cheng (2000) argues that 'there are two aspects of the *ren*, the internal aspect of self-transformation of the self and the external aspect of the transformation of others by the self-transformation of the self. It is clear that all Confucian characterisation of *ren* can be identified under these two aspects: To restrain oneself (*keji*) is internal and to restore and practice

proprieties (*fuli*) is external' (p. 37). Another writer who holds a similar view is Tang (1997) who asserts that '*ren* is the basic substance, content, *li* is the form, standard; *ren* is a person's inner cultivation ... while *li* ... reflects the external restraints of society on a person' (仁是本质，内容，礼是形式，准则；仁是人的内心修养 . . . 而礼 . . . 体现了社会对人的外在约束) (p. 137). However, I disagree that 'restraining the self' (*keji*) represents the internal aspect of *ren* and 'returning to *li*' (*fuli*) represents the external aspect of *ren*. Instead of dichotomizing *ren* into internal and external aspects, I would rather think of these two aspects as intergrated; they highlight the need to discipline our entire being (attitudes, values and behaviours) so as to observe *li*. Similarly, the transformation of self and transformation of others are not mutually exclusive but interwoven; we cannot discuss the internal aspect of *ren* without discussing the external aspect of *ren*, and vice versa. Confucius states in 6.30 that 'a *ren* person, in desiring to take a stand, helps others to take their stand; in desiring to reach [a goal], helps others to reach [their goal]'(夫仁者，己欲立而立人，己欲達而達人).

6 Li (2007) interprets 3.3 as follows: 'Confucius holds that *li* may not always result in *ren* and that persons of *ren* may not always follow the rules of *li*. In 3.3 Confucius says that "If a person is un-*ren*, what has one to do with *li*?". This implies that one could follow the rules of *li* without being *ren*' (p. 314). *Pace* Li, I disagree with his interpretation as I think that Confucius is arguing the opposite: Confucius' rhetorical question implies that a person who is not *ren* has nothing to do with *li*.

7 Slingerland (2003)'s translation of *ren* as 'goodness' and Lau (1979)'s translation as 'benevolence' both highlight one's disposition towards doing what is admirable, noble and altruistic. On the other hand, Ames and Rosemont (1998) translate it as 'authoritative conduct' to emphasize *ren* as 'one's entire person: one's cultivated cognitive, aesthetic, moral, and religious sensibilities as they are expressed in one's ritualised roles and relationships' (p. 49). In the same vein, Lai (1995) states that *ren* is 'the substratum, the source, of all human virtue' and 'the manifest characteristic of the human person once s/he has cultivated the virtues and embraced its various aspects in living out life' (p. 254).

8 This does not mean that *ren* is to be understood only in a broad and higher-order sense. It is also used in a more restricted sense in the *Analects*, as I shall explain in a later section.

9 I agree with Chong (1999)'s position that Shun (1993)'s conception of *ren* as a 'cluster of emotional dispositions and attitudes' is too narrow because *ren* encompasses 'a much wider confluence of emotions, attitudes, values, and ultimately a particular ethical orientation that, in the final analysis, would bring about social order' (p. 311; also see Chong, 2007, pp. 19–34). But I would go one step further and argue that *ren* is not just about one's attitudes and values but includes one's actions; *ren* is what makes a thought, feeling and action normative.

10 Commenting on 12.1 and 3.3, Lai (1995) argues that *li* and *ren* were 'linked together inseparably in the *Analects*, and it needs to be noted that there is little or no suggestion that either of the two concepts had fundamental precedence over the other' (p. 256). She therefore objects to Tu's argument that *ren* is a higher-order concept from which *li* derives meaning (p. 257). Tu (1968) has argued that *ren* is an 'inner morality' and 'a higher-order concept which gives meaning to *li*' while *li* is 'an externalisation of *jen* [*ren*] in a specific social context' (p. 34). I agree with Lai that *li* and *ren* are linked, and that it is inaccurate to see *ren* as an inner morality and a higher-order concept that gives meaning to *li*. *Ren* is the inner morality in terms of attitudes and values *as well as* external morality in terms of actions that are in alignment with *li*. Ames and Rosemont note the same point about the inner and outer aspects of *ren*: '*Ren* is not only mental, but physical as well: one's posture and comportment, gestures and bodily communication' (p. 49). I share Ames and Rosemont's argument that we should not think of *ren* only in psychological terms, but recognize that it involves the integration of a person's cognition, affect and behaviour. Nonetheless, I also agree with Tu that *ren* is a higher-order concept; *ren* is the central quality that encompasses all other normative qualities, such as respect, sincerity, and empathy, in our observance of *li*.

11 Chan (2000) makes a similar point when he claims that 'the Confucian formulation of *li* stipulates that it must be informed by *ren*, which at a minimum signifies the presence of certain ethically significant attitudes, emotions and motivations (e.g. respect, conscientiousness, sincerity and care)' (p. 250). I would further argue that *li* must not just be informed by *ren* but also depend on *ren* as the source of normativity. Without *ren*, the observance of *li* will lapse into what I call the 'prevailing *li*' – the type of *li* that Confucius objected to. For more discussion and debate on the relationship between *ren* and *li*, see Cua (1978), Cua (1993); Tu (1979), Tu (1985); Shun (1993), Shun (2002); Chong (1999), Chong (2007); and Li (2007).

12 Another example of *ren* as used in the general sense is 13.19: Fan Chi asked about *ren*. The Master said, 'Be deferential at home, be respectful in handling matters, be ready to give your best in your relationships with others. Even if you were to go and live among the barbarians, you should not abandon these qualities' (樊遲問仁。子曰：'居處恭，執事敬，與人忠。雖之夷狄，不可棄也。') Here, *ren* is reflected in the specific qualities of deference, respect and giving one's best. Conceptualizing *ren* as a general, higher-order tem, Tu (1968) explains: 'It seems that the best way to approach the concept of *jen* [*ren*] is to regard it first of all as the virtue of the highest order in the value system of Confucianism. In other words, *jen* [*ren*] gives "meaning" to all the other ethical norms which perform integrative functions in a Confucian society' (p. 31).

13 Other writers also share my view that *ren* is used in more than one sense. For example, Shun (1993) observes: 'That "jen" [*ren*] is used in both ways is seen from the fact that *jen* is both listed as one desirable quality among others, such as wisdom and courage (9.29, 14.28), and described as something that includes other desirable qualities such as courage (14.4)' (p. 457). Luo (2011) likewise notes, 'These renditions can be classified into two categories reflective of different understandings of *ren*: 1. *ren* as a first-order, particular virtue, in which sense it is one virtue among many. 2. *ren* as the higher-order, general virtue, in which sense it is an umbrella term used to cover a variety of virtues' (p. 427). Li (2007) also maintains that '*ren* can mean either one single quality of affection among other desirable qualities in a person or an all-encompassing ethical ideal that includes all desirable qualities' (pp. 320–1). Likewise, Yu (1998) contrasts *ren* as a complete virtue and *ren* as a particular virtue.

14 Kim (2006) asserts that *ren* is more than just an ethical concept: 'I must stress that this notion of *ren* should be understood not necessarily in ethical terms (whether as the supreme virtue or as the source of all virtues) but more inclusively in terms of the working of the human spirit: that is, not only in ethical but in aesthetic life as well' (p. 118). While I agree with Kim that *ren* is more than ethical, I think it is not just ethical and aesthetic, but spiritual as well. Slingerland (2001) acknowledges the spiritual dimension of *ren*, stating that 'the ideal of becoming a *ren*-person was not conceived to be a merely contingent practice but, rather, was seen as correlating human beings with the will of Heaven' (p. 117).

15 The subject for 12.16 is not the *ren* person but the *junzi*. But it is fair to assume that this verse applies to the *ren* person as well, given that there is an inseparable relationship between *ren* and *junzi*. Confucius proclaims: 'How could a *junzi* who abandons *ren* merit that name? A *junzi* does not violate *ren* even for as long as it takes to eat a meal.' (君子去仁，惡乎成名？君子無終食之間違仁) (4.5). I shall elaborate on this relationship in the chapter on *junzi*.

16 Ames and Rosemont (1998) translate *zhi* as 'realize'. They explain: '"To realize" has the same strong epistemic connotations as "to know" or "knowledge" in English. You may say you believe whatever you like, but you can only *know*, or *realise* something, if that something is indeed the case. In addition, it underscores the performative, perlocutionary meaning of *zhi*: the need to author a situation and "make it real"' (p. 55, italics in the original). Hall and Ames (1987) add that *zhi* is 'a process of articulating and determining the world rather than a passive cognisance of a predetermined reality'; to 'know' is 'to influence the process of existence within the range of one's viable possibilities' (p. 55). Grange (2004) also highlights the unity of feeling, thinking and doing through *zhi*: '*Zhi* names the process whereby we realise both the existence and the value of what is known. By internalising the embodied

intelligence that grasps what is really going on, we take on the character of the reality we claim to know. In this way feeling, thinking and doing unite to uncover the core values embedded in life's situations' (p. 53).

17 In this verse, the subject of the expression 'is still not ideal' (未善也 *weishan ye*) is not defined, thus different translators have identified different subjects for the verse. Ames and Rosemont believe that the subject is the common people ('they are still not good enough at it'); Lau, however, takes it to be the person who fails to observe *li* ('he will fall short of perfection'); Slingerland, on the other hand, interprets the subject as the 'it' that is not attained by the person ('it will never be truly excellent'). My view is that the subject refers to the situation the person is in, that is, the situation is still not ideal (未善也) for the person to attain 'it'. The next note explains the referent of 'it'.

18 The view that 'it' here probably refers to the Way is consistent with Confucius' call for everyone to return to Zhou *li* in order to realize the Way as revealed by heaven. He constantly urges all to attain and broaden the way (15.29), given that the Way has not prevailed on earth (18.6). Interpreting 'it' as the Way is also supported by the previous verse (15.32) where Confucius describes the *junzi* as being anxious to obtain the Way. The view that 'it' refers to the Way is also held by Slingerland (2003), p. 187. Yang (1980), on the other hand, points out that 'it' could refer to an official position (祿位 *lüwei*) or the state (國家 *guojia*).

19 Note here that the concept of *ren* is used in 15.33 in a specific sense, unlike the case in 4.1 and 4.2 where it is used in a general sense.

20 I agree with Mou (2004) that 6.30 may be considered the positive version of *shu*. 6.30 states: 'A *ren* person, in desiring to take a stand, helps others to take their stand; in desiring to reach [a goal], helps others to reach [their goal]. Taking what is near as an analogy can be said to be the method of *ren*' (夫仁者，己欲立而立人，己欲達而達人。能近取譬，可謂仁之方也已). In comparing *shu* with the Golden Rule mentioned in the Bible, Mou (2004) claims that 'the two versions share the same core idea to the effect that one can use one's own desires as a guide to how to treat others' (p. 221).

21 Cua (1992) elaborates on the concept of *shu* as follows: 'The insight of the Confucian notion of reciprocity (*shu*) may be reformulated in this way: "how others feel about our actions towards them should be internally related to our feeling about those actions, and hence their feelings should penetrate our motives." Differently put, human lives within a moral community are possible because there exists a reciprocity of individual wills oriented toward a common *telos*, implying an acknowledgment of a bond. The bond is, so to speak, the intersection of individual lives, an anchorage for both personal and cultural identity. It is this attitude that provides a sense of significance to personal lives. Respect for persons, especially in the

light of *jen* [*ren*], is not just a Kantian respect for persons as ends in themselves, but a respect for individual styles of life, deemed as polymorphous expressions of a common culture' (p. 54).
22 Ivanhoe (1990) explains the relationship between *li*, *zhong* (performing one's duties to the best of one's abilities), and *shu* (empathy and reciprocity): 'Without a firm commitment to *li*, the "kindness" of *shu* can collapse into vague, formless sentimentality and the "loyalty" of *chung* [*zhong*] can degenerate into blind, mechanistic obedience. Neither *chung* [*zhong*] nor *shu* can be understood apart from the *li*, and only in support of each other do they constitute *jen* [*ren*]' (p. 28).
23 I have translated Confucius' words literally in 12.11, which may not make sense to readers at first glance. I shall explain the meaning of this verse in the text. Lau translates it as 'Let the ruler be a ruler, the subject a subject, the father a father, the son a son'; Yang translates it as 'A ruler must behave like a ruler, a minister like a minister, a father like a father, and a son like a son' (君要像个君，臣要像个臣，父亲要像父亲，儿子要像儿子); Ames and Rosemont translate it as 'The ruler must rule, the minister minister, the father father, and the son son'; Slingerland translates it as 'Let the lord be a true lord, the ministers true ministers, the fathers true fathers, and the sons true sons'.
24 Loy (2003) outlines three possible interpretations of 13.3 and argues that 'the overriding concern of the Master in 13.3 is that people speak in some correct manner, more specifically, that they should use names correctly' and that 'the *zhengming* proposal of 13.3 is most likely concerned with the speeches of the political elite' (p. 34). As much as I agree with Loy that *zhengming* includes a correction of what is spoken, I also share Lai (1995)'s view that 13.3, as well as 12.11, goes beyond speech to a correction of behaviour. In Lai's words: '[T]he thrust of this doctrine is that terms used to designate the range of human relationships carry with them not only descriptive content but also evaluative force (*Analects* 13:3.1–5). . . . individuals have to live appropriately according to the titles and names, indicating their ranks and statuses within relationships, by which they are referred to. These terms prescribe how values upholding the various roles are to be realized within the fundamental reality of the lived human world' (pp. 251–2).
25 On the connection between *li* and music, see the discussion on music in the chapter on *li*.
26 Sim (2010) posits that Confucius does not reject the use of laws: 'Despite Confucius' preference for exemplary leadership and *li* for the cultivation of virtue, he might not be entirely averse to the use of laws. This is suggested in his discussion of the proper use of names (*zhengming*) in 13.3 of the *Analects* for proper government (see also 16.2)' (p. 199, also see Sim, 2007). I agree with Sim's view that Confucius may not be entirely averse to the use of laws

but I think Confucius may be too sanguine about the transformational effect of *li*, overlooking the complementary need for law and punishment for a fallible world. I shall revisit this point in the concluding chapter.

27 Ames and Rosemont (1998) note that language was viewed by Confucius and ancient Chinese thinkers not merely as a way of describing the world or of communicating one's beliefs about it, but as a means of guiding actions in the world. In their words: '[L]anguage is both performative and prescriptive; it both does something to the world and recommends how it should be' (p. 31). Arguing along the same line is Lai (1995) who points out that unlike early Western philosophy that assumes that the primary purpose of language is to describe the world and communicate ideas or beliefs about the world, *zhengming* 'operates on the presupposition that the primary function of language is to instill attitudes guiding choice and action. Language use should be manipulated as a means of social control' (p. 252).

28 I was alerted to the episode in 14.44 as an example of the violation of *zhengming* by Lai (1995) who observes: 'This idea of acting appropriately – say, as wife, son, or younger brother – was a theme so deeply entrenched in Confucian philosophy that the *Analects* records an instance when Confucius himself commented that the adult-like abilities of a child were indeed inappropriate' (p. 253).

29 According to Yang (1980) who cited from the *Liji* (禮記 Book of Rites), the boy mentioned in 14.44 sat in the position of the host on the north and faced south, which violated the ritual manner of the time.

30 It should be pointed out that 8.2 refers not just to any *junzi* (exemplary or noble person) but one who holds the position of a ruler. In this sense, when a *junzi*-ruler is committed to his parents, the masses will look up to him and be inspired towards *ren*. A *junzi* with no official position might also influence or inspire others but may not be able to have the same influence or inspiration as a ruler, under normal circumstances. Exceptions would be *junzi* who are not political leaders but celebrities in their own right, such as movie stars, popular singers and even famous bloggers.

31 Yu (1998) explains how filial piety is the root of *ren*: 'Kinship involves a natural hierarchy and through it is established natural authority relations, while its extension/expansion to other social relations naturalises the idea of hierarchy and authority in the wider society. By the same token, the feeling toward one's brothers makes one agreeably altruistic. A family may not be a democratic forum or provide a context for equality, but it is a place one loves to be in' (p. 332).

32 On the relationship between *ren* and performing one's social roles, Slingerland (2001) explains as follows: 'One does not learn to cultivate *ren* in solitude, but rather through fulfilling one's role-specific social duties and

participating in a judgment community of fellow practitioners, under the careful tutelage of one's teacher. Confucian moral excellence is thus firmly grounded in the role-specific duties of an individual located within a specific familial and social context' (p. 105). Ivanhoe (1991) adds: 'On the Confucian view, all human lives are intertwined with one another, and so it is impossible to seek for personal or familial well-being apart from social well-being. This is why ethical thinking has never been divorced from political and social theory in Chinese thought. This also explains why it is so difficult to separate the issues of personal and public well-being. . . . One cannot be a certain type of person – a *ren* individual – unless one works to create a certain kind of family and society. The Confucian virtues are communal to a degree unfamiliar to most Western traditions' (p. 57).

33 Pointing out that *ren* concerns the well-being of humanity, Cua (1992) asserts that *ren* involves 'the difficult task of transforming existing society into a human community of mutual concern or personal relationships' (p. 62).

34 I borrow the idea of human relationships comprising several concentric circles from Tu (1979) and Lai (1995). Lai explains that the Confucian self is 'the centre of relationships, from which concentric circles of influence emanate, moving gradually from the family, as the innermost ring, to the community, country, and world' (p. 267). One could of course question whether human beings really learn or should learn to love others in such a manner, starting with one's family in the inner-most circle before moving to other people in the outer circles. For a good critique of Tu (1979)'s concept of concentric circles, see Ten (2003). I thank Kim-chong Chong for drawing my attention to the article by Ten.

35 In her comparison between Confucius and Kant, Wawrytko (1982) avers that both Kant and Confucius emphasize a non-utilitarian commitment as well as the pivotal element of judgement in respecting the Moral Law (for Kant) or following the Way (for Confucius). Nonetheless, she highlights a key difference between Kant and Confucius: 'Yet the greatest divergences between the theories of Kant and Confucius also occur in these areas, particularly with regard to the Confucian Mean and its flexibility of standards. These stand in sharp contrast to the universal quality and rigidity of Kant's laws. Here, then, Confucian thought makes its most significant contribution to the synthesis, firmly linking theory and practice' (p. 250). Despite citing Wawrytko (1982), I do not agree with all her arguments in the paper. Lai (1995) rightly critiques Wawrytko's paper as follows: 'Although Wawrytko's study is an interesting one, she has dangerously narrowed the Confucian concept of *tao* [*dao*] in rendering it as being analogous to the Kantian Moral Law. While Kant's Moral Law is not unconnected with his views on human nature, it is primarily a moral theory. In Confucian philosophy, one could never successfully

separate, and understand a "moral" portion independent of the larger philosophical context. Implicit in Confucius' teachings is the belief that personhood is not and cannot be compartmentalized: the self is at once social, moral, political, and intellectual. Wawrytko misunderstands the realm of the moral in Confucian thought while at the same time vastly reducing and narrowing the scope and applicability of concepts such as *tao* [*dao*]' (p. 259).

36 Gier (2001) elaborates on Confucius' thought as a form of Virtue Ethics: 'The imperatives of virtue ethics – be patient, be kind, be compassionate, be courageous – better equip an individual to negotiate the obstacles of the moral life. The virtue-ethics approach is not to follow a set of abstract rules, but to develop a unique ensemble of behaviours, dispositions, and qualities that lead to human excellence. Virtue ethics may not have pat answers to specific cases – no ethical theory could offer this – but it does prepare the moral agent for adaptation, innovation, and flexibility' (p. 300). For further readings on Confucianism and virtue ethics, see Yu (1998), Slingerland (2001) and Van Norden (2003).

37 Tu (1968) also cautions against treating *ren* as an objective entity that one either possesses or not at all: 'The problem is not "either-or," for Confucius upholds a varied degree of actualisation of *jen* [*ren*]. Every human being embodies *jen* [*ren*] to a certain extent, but no one in the process of becoming a man who more fully embodies *jen* [*ren*] can reach the perfect stage' (p. 32).

38 In the context of 15.10, Confucius' focus is on sharpening one's tools by serving ministers who are virtuous and befriending scholars who are *ren*. I am applying the same idea of sharpening one's tools to one's cultivation of *ren*.

Chapter 5

1 Zhu (2009, p. 37) informs us that the word *junzi* appears 107 times in the *Analects*. The concept of *junzi* is so central in the *Analects* that Ahn (2005) asserts that '[i]f a subtitle were given to the *Analects*, it would be "Joy of Being a *Junzi*"' (p. 109).

2 Li (2009–10) explains the historical meaning of *junzi* before Confucius' time: 'The original meaning of "a gentleman" [*junzi*] is that he is a member of aristocratic society, which even includes female members. This society is composed on the basis of blood relations. Its members, as long as they have the same surname (it is another matter for aristocracy with different surnames), are all the offspring of the ruler; either they are the children of the deceased ruler, or they are the children of the current ruler, and that is why they are called gentlemen. In the upper reaches of noble society, there are emperors, dukes, and marquises; below that are ministers and knights. Gentlemen is the

general term for this type of people' (p. 56). For further discussion on the use of the term *junzi* before Confucius' time, see Lu (1982) and Lin (1987).
3 This does not mean that Confucius believes that everyone will eventually become a *junzi*. The different outcomes of aspiring *junzi* depend on contingent factors such as different capabilities, motivations and unequal access to resources. What Confucius teaches is that everyone, from the aristocrat to the common person, may and should strive to become *junzi*. It is helpful to note that Confucius himself probably did not belong to the aristocratic clan. I shall return to this point about the potential and actuality of one becoming a *junzi* in the concluding chapter.
4 Ames and Rosemont (1998) point out that Confucius appropriated common terms during his time such as *junzi* and *xiaoren* (literally 'small person') for his own use, 'giving them connotations and denotations that shifted their sense and reference away from position, rank, birth, or function toward what we (not he) would term aesthetic, moral, and spiritual characteristics' (p. 61).
5 Notably, translators such as Lau and Slingerland use the male pronouns for *junzi*, while Ames and Rosemont as well as Chong use gender-neutral expressions.
6 Rosemont (2001) contrasts a *junzi* with a *shi* (士 scholar-official). The latter, who is at the initial stage of ethical development, tends to be precise, formal and perhaps even punctilious, whereas the former's conduct 'is not forced, but rather effortless, spontaneous, creative'; 'The *shi* does, while the *junzi* more nearly is' (Rosemont, 2001, p. 85, cited in Hagen, 2010, p. 11). It would appear that *shi* are still in the first or intermediate stage of knowing or loving *li*, whereas the *junzi* have reached the final stage of finding joy in *li*. See chapter 3 for details of the three stages of observing *li*.
7 Emphasizing the importance of having appropriate corresponding attitudes to accompany one's actions, Cua (1992) notes: 'This attitude of caring is basic in the sense that it renders intelligible a variety of the agent's reactive feelings and actions toward its object, not just in the sense of a fundamental principle, but in the sense of exemplifying that attitude of seriousness toward the objects deemed to have moral import. Similarly, some of the virtues like benevolence (*jen* [*ren*] in the narrow sense of benevolence) or courage cannot be taught without inculcating the attitude of active concern and care for the well-being of every human' (p. 52).
8 Cai (1999) also sees harmony as comprising both inner and outer dimensions. He explains as follows: 'After a gentleman has achieved harmony in temperament, learning, and conduct, Confucius believes, he should be entrusted with the responsibilities of the state. By conducting his private and public life in the spirit of propriety and temperance, he helps bring the entire society into harmony.... In short, his inward harmony will radiate far and wide, reaching from his individual self to the family to the state and to the heavenly *Dao*' (p. 320).

9 Commenting on 4.10, Slingerland (2001) observes that '[t]his sort of situation-centred reasoning resembles Aristotelian *phronesis* and ultimately "what is right" in the ethical realm corresponds to what the gentleman (that is, the good person) would do' (p. 103). The concept of *phronesis* is expounded in Aristotle's *Nicomachean Ethics* and is usually translated as 'practical wisdom' or 'prudence'. On a comparative study of the views of Confucius and Aristotle, see Yu (1998); Gier (2001); Sim (2007); Sim (2010).

10 Cheng (1972) suggests that we may analyse the quality of appropriateness (*yi*) in terms of two components relevant to the process of moral decision-making: 'First, there is understanding or perception of an end on the part of the moral subject. This is the subjective self-knowledge of good truth (or the way). Second, there is a potential state or situation which needs a fitting action to make it a moral state or situation. There is an objective quality in a situation which one must correctly perceive in order to make an appropriate decision and to take a course of action' (p. 272).

11 Yu (1998) challenges the argument of Hall and Ames (1987) that the quality of appropriateness reflects a capacity to import an agent's significance into the world through one's flexibility to interact with and integrate into ever-changing situations. Yu counters that far from being personal, creative and novel, appropriateness is conventional on the basis of Zhou *li* (p. 345). However, I do not think that Hall and Ames are arguing that appropriateness is *all* about the personal and subjective, independent of Zhou *li*. Rather, they are saying that an agent, while adhering to Zhou *li*, is empowered to personalize and modify it if necessary to suit the needs of the occasion. Furthermore, just because Confucius insists on the continuity of the Zhou *li* does not mean that the Zhou *li* is to be practised wholesale without adaption. I have pointed out in chapter 3 that verses such as 2.23 and 15.11 show that Confucius judiciously selects what he believes to be the norm modelled by the sage-kings. Verses such as 9.3, 4.10, 11.22, 5.1, 2.12 and 15.37 also inform us that appropriateness is about demonstrating one's flexibility and exercising one's judgement especially in novel situations. To the extent that appropriateness is about a capacity to import a person's significance into the world in accordance with *li*, I agree with Hall and Ames that appropriateness is particular, creative and responsive. Yu (1998) illustrates this point by likening the prescriptions of *li* – for example, 'what kind of ceremonial cap one should wear, and even when one should prostrate oneself before ascending steps in to see a king (9.3)' – to 'the rule that requires one to wear a black tie to a fellows' dinner at Oxford' (p. 326). To Yu, this dinner appears to be a ceremonial ritual in terms of its prescriptions regarding how one should dress, where one should sit and even how one should hold a spoon – aspects of *li* that are relatively easy to perform. From my experience as a visiting academic, however, the real challenge in

attending a fellows' dinner at Oxford or Cambridge, is the social interactions that take place during the dinner: How does one hold and keep up a conversation? What questions and responses are appropriate for the occasion? How does one appear genuinely interested in what the other person is saying without appearing phony or nosy? Conversation etiquette cannot simply be prescribed by hard and fast rules; rather, they require one to exercise appropriateness to respond in a contextually sensitive way.

12 I have translated *yi* (義) as 'appropriateness' for 15.18 instead of Ames and Rosemont's 'appropriate conduct' as I think that *yi* here is not confined to conduct, but includes corresponding attitudes and values as well. Yang translates *yi* as 'appropriateness' (合宜 *heyi*) for 15.18 and *yi* as 'reasonable and fitting' (合理適當 *heli shidang*) for 4.10. Slingerland translates *yi* as 'rightness' which is close to the meaning of 'appropriateness'. Lau translates *yi* as 'morality' which, in my view, is not accurate as it has a different meaning altogether. The word *zhi* (質) in the same verse is difficult to translate. The literal meaning of *zhi* is 'quality', 'nature' or 'substance'. Lau translates it as 'native substance' (6.18), 'stuff' (12.8) and 'basic stuff' (15.18), which I find unclear. Slingerland translates it as 'native substance' (6.18, 12.8) or 'substance' (15.18) but this suggests innate human nature, which is not evident in the verse. Given that *zhi* literally means quality, and the context of the verse is on what is basic in human beings, I have translated it as 'basic quality'.

13 Chan (2002) highlights the significance of reflective judgement and ethical discretion because of the fluid and non-definitive nature of *li*: 'Human life-situations are varied and complex. Rites as norms of conduct are often too general to give precise guidance in the making of concrete moral decisions. There may be novel situations, borderline cases, and hard cases (where some rites are in conflict with others) that call for reflective judgment and moral discretion. Because of this, Confucians often emphasise weighing and moral discretion (*quan*), flexibility (*wu gu*), and timeliness (*shih*) in making moral decisions in particular circumstances' (p. 288).

14 Chong (1998) explains the relationship between *li* and *yi* (appropriateness): 'Embedded within the *Analects* is an account of *li* which allows for modification, based on a certain spirit in which *li* is to be practiced. This encompasses certain attitudes integral to the concept of *li*, and *yi* may be said to describe the proper expressions of *li*, or the carrying out of *li*, in the right spirit' (p. 69). Cua (1992) adds that observing *li* is compatible with maintaining a flexible and critical stance on issues: 'The attitude to be inculcated is not a blind adherence to customary standards, but one of respect for established practices. This respect is not incompatible with the agents maintaining a critical stance on issues to which existing morality does not provide ready-made solutions' (p. 53).

15 Lau translates *yi* (appropriateness) in 17.23 as 'moral'. While I agree that *yi* is about doing what is morally appropriate or right, the word 'moral', in my view, is too nebulous to capture the essence of *yi*. Furthermore, the word 'moral', in the contemporary English-speaking world, may connote ideas drawn from Western moral theories that may not apply to Confucius' views. Examples of such ideas are linking morality to a law (such as Utilitarianism) or establishing a specific criterion for morality (such as Kantianism). That is why I avoid using the word 'moral' and prefer the term 'ethical' instead.

16 Ahn (2005) explains how Confucius is greatly attuned to the specific situations and problems of his disciples: 'For instance, when people ask Confucius about filial piety, his replies are idiosyncratic to each questioner (*Analects*, 2.5; 2.6; 2.7; 2.8). His flexibility does not result from an ethical relativism. Rather, Confucius wants to help the questioner realise his (or her) specific tasks, though based on the same ideal' (p. 108).

17 Slingerland (2003) points out the significance of Confucius' act from 5.1: 'The social stigma attached to former criminals in early China was enormous and inescapable, since criminals were prominently branded, tattooed, or physically mutilated. In giving his daughter in marriage to a former criminal, Confucius is flouting conventional mores and making a powerful statement concerning the independence of true morality from conventional social judgments' (p. 39).

18 Gier (2001) uses a musical analogy to explain how the quality of appropriateness is circumscribed by our social roles: 'Confucian virtue aesthetics is also role specific just as these examples from the fine arts are. Even though the younger brother may have his own particular style of deferring to his elder brother, he has no freedom not to defer or take on other roles not appropriate to *li*. Similarly, violin players do not switch to the French horn while performing their concertos' (p. 286).

19 On a *junzi*'s cultivated ease, Lai (2006) notes, 'The profundity of the Confucian picture of ethical deliberation lies in a particular cultivated ease due in part to the confidence of the paradigmatic person [*junzi*]. The confidence in turn comes about as a result of his tested ability to deliberate and act successfully in a range of contexts' (p. 78).

20 The literal translation of 14.6 is: 'There are *junzi* who are not *ren*' (君子而不仁者有矣夫). This translation, in my view, is misleading as it suggests that there are *junzi* who do not possess *ren* at all. Such an interpretation is unacceptable as it contradicts 4.5 where Confucius states that 'a *junzi* does not leave *ren* even for the space of one meal' (君子無終食之間違仁). I have therefore interpreted the verse as referring to occasional lapses of a *junzi*, where she fails to demonstrate *ren* behaviour. My stand is that a *junzi* is someone who has achieved *ren* to a large extent but is still not perfect. She may falter at times but these lapses do

not make her devoid of *ren*. My translation for 14.6 is similar to Ames and Rosemont's who translate the verse as follows: 'There have been occasions on which an exemplary person [*junzi*] fails to act in an authoritative manner [*ren*]'.

21 Cua (1992) claims that Confucius believes that only a sage can perfectly epitomize *ren* – he is able to 'establish an ethically enduring, harmonious, social and political order'; unfortunately, sagehood is not a practical aspiration for ordinary ethical agents (p. 56).

22 Commenting on 15.21, Lai (2006) notes as follows: 'The *junzi* is independent of the expectations and norms dictated by popular culture. While he relies on his own judgment, the small man by contrast seeks to be affirmed by others; in this way the latter lacks confidence and is reliant on external support (15:21; see also 15:22)' (p. 75).

23 Brindley (2009) claims that Confucius promotes different Ways for the *junzi* and petty person. She argues as follows: 'Indeed, the text appears to promote different types of moral cultivation for different types of people, a fact that is noticeable even in the passage at hand, when Zi You quotes Confucius as having stated: "The *junzi* learns the Way to cherish the people, *xiao ren* learn the Way so that they might be easily ordered [by their superiors to fulfill a task]" (17.4). So, even in this passage, although the ultimate goal of moral education for everyone is universal, the specific goals of such education correspond to roles set for two particular types of people in the sociopolitical hierarchy: leading versus conforming moral agents' (pp. 53–4). Contrary to Brindley's claim, I think that Confucius is not so much *prescribing* different goals of ethical cultivation for the *junzi* and petty person as *describing* the different goals of the *junzi* and petty person. Just because Confucius is aware that the petty person seeks to learn the Way for selfish reasons does not mean that Confucius approves of such motivations.

24 Ames and Rosemont comment on the action-focused philosophy of Confucius as follows: '[H]is vision was one that had to be felt, experienced, practiced and lived. He was interested in how to make one's way in life, not in discovering the "truth"' (p. 5). Interestingly, Li (2005) suggests that Asian Americans' reticence in class might be due to the Confucian teaching regarding the ethical implication of one's words. He writes, 'It was found that EA [East Asian] students believed more in the causal effect of speaking on thinking and learning than Asian-Americans did. Moreover, speaking did not interfere with EA students' performance, but did interfere with the performance of Asian American students. . . . The Asian belief that speaking interferes with learning may well reflect the essential learning virtue of concentration. It is also likely related to Asians' distrust in speaking on moral grounds: Speaking is viewed by Confucians as an act of committing oneself to one's claim; if one is unable to back one's claim with action, one should remain silent' (p. 192).

25 Slingerland (2003, p. 172) rightly points out that this verse is about ruling a state with the focus not on *junzi* in general but *junzi*-as-ruler or what I call *junzi*-ruler. However, I think that it is still appropriate to apply this verse to *junzi* in general (whether ruler or not), since the principle of self-cultivation in order to be respectful and bring peace to others applies to all *junzi*. Although a *junzi*-ruler would be in a more influential position to bring peace to the multitude as compared to a *junzi* who is not an office-bearer, there is no reason why the latter cannot *also* strive to self-cultivate, be respectful and bring peace to as many people as possible. That ordinary *junzi* may be as influential or even more influential than *junzi*-rulers is especially true in our digital age today where bloggers could attract huge followers through various social media platforms. The tenor of this verse is also in line with Confucius' exhortation for everyone to help others while helping themselves (cf. 6.30).

26 Lai (1995) highlights the difference between Western thought that underscores the individual, and Confucian thought that emphasizes the community: 'Apart from presuppositions made regarding human free will, individualism, and autonomy, "Western" views often construct morality on an individualistic basis whereby more weight is assigned to the character, virtue, or behaviour of the individual moral agent than to the interests and lives of other agents. They focus on what each person, *qua* moral agent, does, rather than on what the community as a whole does together. The latter is one of the primary characteristics of Confucian thought' (p. 249). I agree with Lai that there are broad differences between Western thought and Confucian thought in terms of their views on the community and individual. But I also think we should not overstate the differences. As I have argued elsewhere (Tan & Mokhtar, 2010), communitarians in the West such as Taylor (1985, 1989), Sandel (1981), Arthur (1998) and MacIntyre (1988) reject the view of a self that is detached from society and independent of all concrete encumbrances of moral or political obligations. Instead, they assert that that the self is always constituted through community which exists in shared social and cultural understandings, traditions and practices; the community provides the interpretive framework within which individuals form their values, view their world and conduct their lives. It follows that, for the communitarians, individuals need to fulfil their civic obligations and pursue the 'common good', understood as a collective determination of a set of goals or values for the community.

27 Underscoring Confucius' contribution as being the first teacher to recognize the role of paradigmatic individuals in ethical education, Cua (1992) explains: 'In moral instruction or training, paradigmatic individuals [*junzi*] may quite properly play the role of models for imitation or emulation by providing standards of aspiration or examples of competence to be attained. In the inculcation of *jen* [*ren*] or moral concern, they serve as standards of

inspiration by providing a point of orientation rather than specific targets of achievement.... In "acting like" a paradigmatic individual in a particular situation, the agent is trying to re-enact the spirit in which he or she acts, and this involves imaginatively rethinking the concrete significance of moral concern in the present' (p. 60).

28 Confucius and other ancient Chinese called the non-Chinese of their time 'barbarians' as they thought that only the Chinese possessed the *li* that was passed down from the Zhou dynasty. Li (2007) comments as follows: 'Early Confucians apparently thought that only the *li* of their society and time (the Zhou *li*) was *li*, and other societies were without *li* and therefore were barbarians. These Confucians were wrong about *li* just as linguists in the nineteenth century West were wrong about grammar. Different cultures have different forms of *li*. Understanding other peoples' *li* is necessary for one to understand their culture; learning another culture's *li* is a necessary condition for acting appropriately in that culture' (p. 318). I agree with Li's point that to be culturally sensitive, we need to understand other cultures and their different forms of *li*. But this does not mean that all forms of *li* should be promoted. What Confucius advocates is the Zhou *li* – normative behaviours, attitudes and values that focus on *ren* and aim at spiritual-ethical-aesthetic harmony – that transcends the ancient Chinese culture and exists in other cultures as well.

29 Exerting ethical influence is of course not easy. Cua (1992) notes that ethical education consists 'primarily in the development of competence in accord with the established "grounds of reason" and an inculcation of a concern for membership in moral community.... But the heart of the difficulty in moral education lies in helping the learner to develop a sense of autonomy informed by a concern for *jen* [*ren*] in response to changing situations of human life' (pp. 49–50).

30 Cua (1992) explains, 'The ideal of *jen* [*ren*] allows for diversity of individual life plans as well as styles of life so long as they pay heed to the common form of life within a moral community. It is, so to speak, an ideal of "congeniality of excellences" rather than a universally prescriptive norm for human life' (p. 55).

31 In explicating Confucius' conception of ethical autonomy, Chan (2002) argues that 'voluntary endorsement and reflective engagement, can be found in Confucian ethics, while the last two, self-legislation and radical free expression of the individual's will, are not only foreign to, but incompatible with it' (p. 282). In the same fashion, Brindley (2011) avers as follows: 'Though individuals ultimately conform to Heaven's principles and desires concerning the *Dao*, they must act autonomously in order to be able to understand and fulfill it. At least two levels of autonomy are necessary. First, individuals must acquire the motivation to abide in the *Dao*. This involves realising that they must commit themselves to Heaven's sacred

desires out of a responsibility to both Heaven and the people around them, rather than merely out of personal interest. Second, since the *Dao* is not communicated transparently to humans, individuals must also cultivate themselves so as to be able to understand what the *Dao* is and how one might go about fulfilling it. Both of these objectives require continuous individual input, in the form of self-cultivation, acquisition of knowledge, self-reflection, decision-making, and action. None of these processes involves coercion or prescription from Heaven. Rather, individuals must each ascertain for themselves the meaning and importance of Heaven's authority, and they must satisfy its requirements by embodying it in their own, personalised ways. Such types of individual input contribute to Confucius' notion of "enlarging the *Dao*," or adding value to Heaven's moral authority in the world' (pp. 263–4).

32 Cua (1992) states that the process of self-cultivation for a *junzi* 'involves an acquisition and critical interpretation of an established cultural tradition, seen as an embodiment of a concern for human well-being (*jen*), as well as familiarity with rules of proper conduct (*li*), with due regard to reasoned judgment concerning their relevance to particular circumstances (*yi*)' (p. 49). Chan (2000) adds that the observance of *li* includes what he calls 'critical assessment': 'The Confucian reflection on ritual and performance cannot but leave room for criticism and change.... Whether remembering the past so as to distinguish the kind of ideal community of which one wishes to be a member, or reflecting on contemporary events and personages, critical assessment must constantly be deployed. In introspection as well as socio-political or ethical deliberation, the Confucian gentleman cannot for one moment afford to renege on the responsibility of critical study and reflection' (pp. 251–2).

33 Hall and Ames (1987) observe that in Chinese philosophy, 'the mark of excellence is found in the manner in which the wisdom of the originating thinkers of the past is appropriated and made relevant by extension to one's own place and time' (pp. 23–4).

34 Ahn (2005) argues that a *junzi* is a creative person. He draws upon Kohut (1971)'s definition of creativity as ranging from 'the ability to "perform a restricted range of tasks with zestful initiative to the emergence of brilliantly inventive artistic schemes or penetrating scientific understandings"' (p. 308). Ahn reasons as follows: 'Confucius states, "He who keeps reviewing the old and acquiring the new is fit to be a teacher" (*Analects*, 2.11). This maxim summarizes the Confucian concept of creativity. When the old cannot be applied to the present situation creatively, those who stick to it are just stubborn; when the new does not have any historical foundation, those who apply it to the present are dangerous. Confucius states, "Learning without thinking is fruitless; thinking without learning is perplexing" (*Analects*, 2.15). To learn is primarily to imitate tradition; to think is to

examine it in a new context. Thus, a *junzi* is a person who attempts to recreate tradition in the present context. The recreation of tradition is a paradigmatic form of creativity' (p. 109). Echoing Ahn is Cheng (1972) who posits that a man of *yi* (appropriateness) 'must be a man of creative insights who is able to make appropriate moral judgments in particular situations, judgments which will preserve the totality of goodness and justice' (p. 272). Similarly, Brindley (2011) maintains that 'through the very act of understanding and fulfilling the *Dao*, individuals draw upon their own, unique, particularised contexts, with the result that they may creatively extend the *Dao* in some vital way' (p. 269).

Chapter 6

1 What Confucius exactly means by 'teach without discrimination' (有教無類 *youjiao wulei*) is widely debated. I shall return to this point later when I discuss the role of a teacher. It suffices to note, at this juncture, that despite the controversy, most writers agree that Confucius advocates equal opportunity for everyone to learn and engage in self-cultivation. It is interesting to note that the *No Child Left Behind Act (NCLB) of 2001* signed by President George W. Bush in 2002 has been translated into Chinese as '有教無類法案' (*youjiao wulei faan*, 'Teach without Discrimination' Act). For details, see https://zh.wikipedia.org/wiki/有教無類法案
2 The expression '以致其道' (*yizhi qidao*) is vague, and different translators have rendered it differently. Yang and Sun translate it as 'obtain that way' (獲得那個道) and 'obtain the way' (獲得道) respectively. Lau translates it as 'perfect his way', Ames and Rosemont translate it as 'promote their way', and Slingerland translates it as 'reach the end of his Way'. Despite the differences, all the translators agree that the *junzi* learns for the sake of the Way.
3 Commentator Yang (1980) makes the connection between the process of learning and the Way in his translation of 8.13: 'To firmly believe in our Way, work hard to learn it, resolve to preserve it till death' ('堅定地相信我們的道，努力學習它，誓死保全它') (p. 88).
4 Lai (1996) appears to view 'culture' as primarily an uncritical process of acculturation on at least one occasion. Referring to 7.3 where Confucius claims that he excels in culture (*wen*) but is still not a *junzi*, she claims that Confucius is emphasizing 'critical differences between acculturation (*wen*) – a primarily uncritical process – and cultivation' (p. 75). While I agree that learning about culture is part of acculturation, I do not believe that such a process is necessarily uncritical, neither should it be contrasted with cultivation. Rather, I view learning about culture as part and parcel of self-cultivation to become a *junzi*. This process involves *si* (thinking) – critically reflecting on what one

has learned. As I have argued in the section on the characteristics of culture and cultural refinement, the learning of culture results in cultural refinement that, when complimented with the observanceof *li*, provides the balance to appropriateness that helps one to become a *junzi* – someone who seeks to realize the Way by abiding in *ren* constantly and observing *li* faithfully.

5 Gier (2001) rightly points out that '[l]earning *li* begins with physical exercises such as archery and charioteering and extends to the choreographing of every single bodily movement' (pp. 283–4).

6 On the relationship between learning and culture, Hall and Ames (1987) state that learning 'denotes the acquisition and appropriation of the meaning invested in the cultural tradition by those who have done before' and therefore 'provides persons in a society with a shared world on the basis of which they can communicate and interact' (p. 46).

7 Ames and Rosemont (1998) comment on Confucius' curriculum as follows: '[He] provide[s] them not only with book learning, but with a curriculum that encouraged personal articulation and refinement on several fronts. His "six arts" included observing propriety and ceremony (*li*), performing music, and developing proficiency in archery, charioteering, writing, and calculation, all of which, in sum, were directed more at cultivating the moral character of his charges than at any set of practical skills' (p. 3). I agree with Ames and Rosemont's observation, although I think that it is more accurate to say that Confucius aims to cultivate not just 'moral character' but also the spiritual-ethical-aesthetic dimensions of one's personality.

8 Although the word used in the passage is *wen* (文), the context suggests that the subject matter is not simply 'culture' but the refinement that results from one's learning of culture. That is why other translators also translate *wen* not as 'culture' but 'cultural refinement' (Slingerland), 'acquired refinement' (Lau), 'refinement' (Ames and Rosemont) and 'cultural adornment' (文饰 *wenshi*) (Pei).

9 The idea of *zhi* (basic quality) is also mentioned in 3.8 where a disciple of Confucius, Zixia, described the observance of *li* as analogous to painting on plain silk. I have explained in the chapter on *li* that the meaning of the verse is that just as colours are painted on a plain canvas, the observance of *li* is based upon one's basic quality (*zhi*), which is appropriateness. In other words, appropriateness is the foundation upon which one observes *li*; it enables one to do what is proper and expedient for each occasion.

10 Ames and Rosemont (1998) point out that Confucius' concept of learning is not a passive acquisition of facts but 'personalization through reflecting on what we have learned and the application of this learning in an appropriate way to the business of the day', as well as 'inheriting, reauthorising, and transmitting one's cultural legacy' (pp. 59–60).

11 Ames and Rosemont translate *si* in 2.15 as 'reflection' while Lau and Slingerland translate it as 'thinking'. I agree with Ames and Rosemont that *si* involves reflection but I do not think that it is confined to that. As explained in the text, *si* encompasses a range of advanced thought processes such as understanding, reflection, analysis, synthesis, evaluation, making connections, drawing analogies, making inferences, forming judgements and so on.
12 Hall and Ames (1987) stress that 'thinking for Confucius is not to be understood as a process of abstract reasoning, but is fundamentally *performative* in that it is an activity whose immediate consequence is the achievement of a practical result' (p. 44, italics in the original).
13 Commenting on 3.15, Hagen (2010) notes that 'Confucius's conduct was ritually appropriate (*li*) in the sense that this was a situation in which being inquisitive, and genuinely acting accordingly, expressed a proper sense-of-ritual. More generally, the point could be that one has to be deferential when one is in unfamiliar surroundings. Putting it this way usefully blurs the distinction between rule following and exemplifying a cultivated disposition' (p. 7).
14 It should be acknowledged that Confucius' questions in 3.15 are not critical in nature but fact-finding type of questions that serve to express his interest to learn more about the ceremonial rituals. One may thus deem this example weak, as Confucius' questions do not demonstrate critical thinking in terms of say, questioning assumptions, evaluating evidence and offering alternatives. While I see the validity of this critique of Confucius' questions, I think that we should also bear in mind the historical-cultural context of Confucius' time. The very act of asking questions by Confucius was novel and radical in ancient China, as evident from the surprised response of the observer in the same verse. Confucius should therefore be given the credit for promoting and pioneering a culture of inquiry in ancient China that is in accordance with *li*.
15 Lest we think that Confucius concludes that Yanhui is a poor student, we should note that Confucius goes on to praise him for putting into practice what he has learned: 'I speak with Yanhui the whole day, he never disagrees with me and seems stupid. When he leaves and I examine what he does in private, [I find that] he is able to illustrate [what I have said], Yanhui is not stupid at all' (吾與回言終日，不違，如愚。退而省其私，亦足以發，回也不愚) (2.9). Confucius' point is that he prefers his students to be actively engaged in learning by asking questions *as well as* applying what they have learned in their lives.
16 Highlighting the importance of Confucius' conception of *si* for oneself, Hall and Ames (1987) point out that *si* involves 'both the acquisition and entertainment of existing meaning and the creative adaptation and extension of this meaning to maximise the possibilities of one's own circumstances' (p. 48).

17 Chan (2000) similarly notes that 'the Confucian approach to *li* necessitates reflection that brings to light the ethical content of *li* and the need to critically assess *li* performance. . . . At the level of performance, the Confucian gentleman steeped in *li* must of course be genuine and make every effort to bring that genuineness across to his audience' (pp. 250–1).

18 Ames and Rosemont (1998) point out that the seat of *si* is the heart-and-mind and hence such reflection is not solely a cognitive process, but an affective one as well (p. 60). Tan (2005) adds that 'Confucian thinking (*si*) not only combines imagination and reason, but also includes emotions. In both the *Analects* and the *Mencius*, *si* used in the sense of "thinking of" is an emotion of longing, incorporating within itself a value judgment that something is desirable as well as a desire to obtain and achieve it' (pp. 420–1).

19 Kim (2003) maintains that Confucius' concept of learning consists of two phases: 'The first is the accumulation of the materials of knowledge. Such materials are collected from first-hand experience – observing, listening and paying attention to life – and indirect or second-hand experience – reading and memorizing the wisdom of others. The second is reflection [*si*] on the materials of knowledge so collected and reflection on oneself. Such dual reflection is needed in order to synthesise and systematise the raw materials into a comprehensible whole, and to integrate them into oneself as wisdom' (p. 80). Kim appears to demarcate the process of accumulating knowledge (the first phase of learning) from *si* as reflection (the second phase of learning). However, I think that it is more accurate to interpret Confucius as advocating the need of *si*, understood as a broad term that encompasses a wide range of thought processes from memorizing to reflection, for all stages of learning.

20 On the relationship between learning, practice and *si*, Lai (2006) asserts that *si* with a view to improvise an instance of *li* comes after learning and practice. She writes, '[T]he process of self-cultivation must include a phase of acquaintance and familiarisation during which one practises the behavioural norms appropriate in a range of situations. There is little room for improvisation because one does not have the requisite resources to do this. To insist on the opportunity for critical assessment in the case of a person not capable of reflective and critical thought is a misplaced move. For all learners, the proper understanding of the meaning and context of ritual behaviour [*li*] comes only after much practice' (pp. 71–2). Another writer, Slingerland (2001), adds that '[i]t is clear that the Confucian process of education (like most initiations into a practice) required a great deal of rote learning in the beginning stages' (p. 102). However, I disagree with Slingerland's view that 'a great deal of rote learning' is required in Confucius' conception of education. While I acknowledge that a critical assessment of an instance of *li* can only come after one has sufficient knowledge of that

instance of *li*, I do not think that we should demarcate the different stages of the components (learning, practice and *si*) too sharply. In some instances of *li* such as when conversing with a guest – something that even a novice of learning would need to do – mere knowledge of the practice of *li*, such as the socially appropriate ways to greet a guest, shake hands and serve drinks, would be insufficient. One also needs to know the appropriate things to say throughout the conversation. As such, one needs to *si* or reflect to improvise this instance of *li*, if one is to be a good conversationalist. Hence, *contra* Slingerland and Lai, the proper understanding of the meaning and context of ritual behaviour [*li*] comes during, not only after, the practice.

21 Shim (2008) helpfully points out that the top part of the character for 'learn' (學) comprises two hands that are interlocked in mutual support. This suggests that learning, for the ancient Chinese, involves a combination of studying and teaching another person.

22 There is some ambiguity over what '無類' (*wulei*) means. Slingerland (2003) notes that there are three possible interpretations: (1) there is no difference in the innate endowment and basic educability of all human beings; (2) there is no difference in social classes; and (3) there is no specialization in the subject matter in the sense that the scope of instruction is comprehensive (p. 189). I hold to the second interpretation as this is in line with Confucius' point in 17.2 that it is practice rather than one's birth that sets people apart. It is also consistent with Confucius' statement in 7.7 that he does not turn away anyone who is willing to learn; he posits that teachers should not discriminate in favour of those from the upper echelons of society, but give everyone an opportunity to learn. My interpretation is also shared by Ames and Rosemont, who translate 15.39 as: 'there is no such thing as social classes', and Yang who translates it as: 'no distinction in disparity in wealth, territory etc' (没有［貧富、地域等等］區別).

23 Huang (2011, p. 142) points out that historical records from the *Shiji* [Records of the Historian] (Sima, 2010), *Lü shi chunqiu* [Mister Lü's spring and autumn] (Xu, 2009) and the *Analects* inform us that Zilu was originally 'uncivilised' (*yeren*), Zigong was engaged in commerce (an occupation looked down upon in Confucianism), Zhonggong's father was a 'lowly person' (*jianren*), Zizhang was from a family of low status in the state of Lu, and Yan Zhuju was a robber (also see Cai, 1982, p. 192).

24 Commenting on 7.7, Brindley (2009) asserts that Confucius does not indiscriminately invite all individuals to embark on the Way of the *junzi*. She reasons as follows: 'While it certainly would have been difficult for economically disadvantaged members of the *shi* class to purchase meat, such a gesture would have been even more difficult, if not impossible, for those from more common backgrounds' (p. 50). However, Slingerland (2003) points out that the gift of dried meat refers to 'small, symbolic, rit-

ually-dictated offerings made by a student seeking instruction.... Confucius' door was open to anyone who came willingly and in a ritually correct manner – that is, he did not discriminate on the basis of social status or wealth' (2003, p. 66). That is why Slingerland translates 7.7 as: 'I have never denied instruction to anyone who, of their own accord, offered *as little* as a bundle of silk or bit of cured meat' (italics added). In the same vein, Ames and Rosemont translate the verse as: 'I have never failed to instruct students who, using their own resources, could *only afford* a gift of dried meat' (italics added). Likewise, Lau translates it as: 'I have never denied instruction to anyone who, of his own accord, has given me *so much as* a bundle of dried meat as a present' (italics added).

25 I agree with Wong and Loy's (2001) observation that 'Confucian teaching is much more than a matter of how the Master *transfers* information to a disciple: It is a matter of how the Master in some sense *reshapes pre-existing material*, responding to the particularities of the individual cases' (p. 221) (italics in the original).

26 Confucius' teaching method is similar to that of Socrates in the sense that they both do not spoon-feed but encourage their students to reflect and draw their own conclusions. I have explained elsewhere the parallels between Socrates and Confucius: 'Socrates employed a conversational mode known as the dialectic to educate his students. Drawing on the aspirations and ambitions of the students, the Socratic dialectic sought to expose the ignorance of the students in order to arouse in them a longing for knowledge of those things necessary to fulfil their ambitions. Some of his students came to realise that the pursuit of knowledge of the most important things was itself the most important thing. In a spirit compatible with the Socratic approach, Confucius did not simply impose his views on his students, but instead guided them to discover knowledge for themselves.... Through their methods and by setting an example, Socrates and Confucius helped foster the desire in their students to pursue learning for the sake of their moral and intellectual development' (Tan & Wong, 2008, p. 7).

27 The word *shi* (士) has been variously translated as 'gentlemen' (Lau), 'scholar-apprentices' (Ames and Rosemont), and 'scholar-officials' (Slingerland). Given the context of the verse on the need to make friends with those who are *ren*, I have translated it generally as 'scholar'.

Part 3

The Relevance of Confucius' Work Today

Chapter 7
Confucius and Twenty-First-Century Education

My visit to the Confucius Temple in Taiwan in 2012 was a surreal experience. The temple magically transported me back to the ancient world where Confucius lived. But once I stepped out of the temple, I was instantly reminded that I'm living in the twenty-first century, surrounded by skyscrapers, motorized vehicles, Western-style clothes and modern gadgets. The Chinese students I saw around me were not memorizing ancient classical texts but learning from modern textbooks with the help of Information and Communication Technology (ICT). Indeed, 'Confucius' and 'twenty-first-century education' appear to be strange bedfellows at first glance. However, as I shall argue in this chapter, Confucius' work is important for and highly applicable to twenty-first century education.

To make the connection between Confucius' teachings and education in the twenty-first century, I shall first identify a set of attributes that are deemed by many policymakers and educators today to be essential for graduates in a modern, digital and globalized world. This set of attributes is popularly known as 'twenty-first-century skills', 'twenty-first-century competencies', or 'twenty-first-century competences' (Trier, 2003; European Parliament, 2007; Silva, 2008; Ananiadou & Claro, 2009; Partnership for 21st Century Skills, 2009; Binkley et al., 2010; National Research Council, 2012; Voogt & Roblin, 2012). Some clarifications regarding 'skills', 'competencies' and 'competences' are necessary at the outset. A 'skill' essentially refers to an ability or capacity to do something well. A 'competency' is more than a skill, as explained by Rychen and Hersch (2003):

> A competency is more than just knowledge and skills. It involves the ability to meet complex demands, by drawing on and mobilizing

psychosocial resources (including skills and attitudes) in a particular context. For example, the ability to communicate effectively is a competency that may draw on an individual's knowledge of language, practical IT skills and attitudes towards those with whom he or she is communicating. (as cited in Ananiadou & Claro, 2009, p. 8)

The terms 'competencies' (plural form of 'competency') and 'competences' (plural form of 'competence') appear to be used synonymously in the literature on twenty-first-century education. For example, Ananiadou and Claro (2009) use the two terms interchangeably. Likewise, OECD (2005)'s definition of 'competency' is identical to that of 'competence' used by Rychen and Hersch (2003) cited above.[1] In view of the overlapping meanings of 'skills', 'competencies' and 'competences', I shall use the term 'twenty-first-century skills' to refer collectively to 'twenty-first-century skills, competencies and competences' for the rest of the chapter.

Frameworks for twenty-first-century skills

The frameworks for twenty-first-century skills have been formulated by various governments and organizations across the world. Some prominent organizations and the frameworks they have developed are as follows:

- The Organization for Economic Co-operation and Development (OECD) developed *21st Century Skills and Competences for New Millennium Learners* (OECD, 2005)
- P21 – a national organization in the United States that was formed in 2001 comprising the US government and several private organizations – produced *Partnership for 21st Century Skills* (Partnership For 21st Century Skills, 2009a, 2009b)
- The Council and European Parliament approved a European reference framework known as *Key Competences for Lifelong Learning* (European Parliament, 2007)
- ATC21S – an international project sponsored by Cisco, Intel and Microsoft – launched *Assessment and Teaching of 21st Century Skills* (Binkley et al., 2010)

In a recent review of 32 major frameworks for twenty-first-century skills, Voogt and Roblin (2012) observe that these skills are generally characterized as being (a) transversal (i.e. they are not directly linked to a specific field but are relevant across many fields), (b) multidimensional (i.e. they include knowledge, skills and attitudes) and (c) associated with higher-order skills and behaviours that represent the ability to cope with complex problems and unpredictable situations (p. 300). Based on their analysis of the major frameworks, Voogt and Roblin (2012) conclude as follows:

> [O]ur analysis reveals that there are strong agreements on the need for competences in the areas of communication, collaboration, ICT [Information and Communication Technology] related competences, and social and/or cultural awareness. Creativity, critical thinking, problem-solving, and the capacity to develop relevant and high quality products are also regarded as important competences in the 21st century by most frameworks. (p. 308)

To enable students to acquire and master twenty-first-century skills, many frameworks advocate major changes to the curriculum, pedagogy, assessment and teacher education in schools today. Policymakers and educators are advised to promote 'modern' approaches such as problem-based learning, cooperative learning, experiential learning, formative assessment and comprehensive use of ICT (Voogt & Roblin, 2012, p. 310). In terms of teacher education, the emphasis is on expanding the teachers' repertoire of innovative teaching methods and enabling them to make use of relevant ICT tools to create learning environments that accommodate twenty-first-century learning (p. 311).

The *P21 framework*

To further understand the frameworks on twenty-first-century skills, I shall examine one representative framework, namely the *Partnership for 21st Century Skills by P21* (Partnership for 21st Century Skills, 2009a, 2009b) (I shall henceforth call this the *P21 framework* for short).

Although my focus is on the *P21 framework*, I shall also make references to the other frameworks where applicable. The *P21 framework* aims to develop a vision for student success in the new global economy (Partnership for 21st Century Skills, 2009a, p. 1). The framework comprises four broad domains or areas:

- Core Subjects and Twenty-first-Century Themes
- Learning and Innovation Skills
- Information, Media and Technology Skills
- Life and Career Skills

I shall elaborate on each of these four domains.

Core subjects and twenty-first-century themes

At the centre of the *P21 framework* is the domain of 'Core Subjects and Twenty-first- Century Themes'. The 'Core Subjects' are school subjects such as English, Reading or Language Arts, World languages, Arts, Mathematics, Economics, Science, Geography, History, and Government and Civics (Partnership for 21st Century Skills, 2009a, p. 2). These core subjects are to be infused with 'Twenty-first-Century Themes' that are interdisciplinary in nature. The content of the twenty-first-century themes is as follows (Partnership for 21st Century Skills, 2009a, pp. 2–3):

Global awareness

- Using twenty-first -century skills to understand and address global issues.
- Learning from and working collaboratively with individuals representing diverse cultures, religions and lifestyles in a spirit of mutual respect and open dialogue in personal, work and community contexts.
- Understanding other nations and cultures, including the use of non-English languages.

Financial, economic, business and entrepreneurial literacy

- Knowing how to make appropriate personal economic choices.
- Understanding the role of the economy in society.
- Using entrepreneurial skills to enhance workplace productivity and career options.

Civic literacy

- Participating effectively in civic life through knowing how to stay informed and understanding governmental processes.
- Exercising the rights and obligations of citizenship at local, state, national and global levels.
- Understanding the local and global implications of civic decisions.

Health literacy

- Obtaining, interpreting and understanding basic health information and services, and using such information and services in ways that enhance health.
- Understanding preventive physical and mental health measures, including proper diet, nutrition, exercise, risk avoidance and stress reduction.
- Using available information to make appropriate health-related decisions.
- Establishing and monitoring personal and family health goals.
- Understanding national and international public health and safety issues.

Environmental literacy

- Demonstrating knowledge and understanding of the environment and the circumstances and conditions affecting it, particularly as related to air, climate, land, food, energy, water and ecosystems.
- Demonstrating knowledge and understanding of society's impact on the natural world (e.g. population growth, population development, resource consumption rate, etc.).

- Investigating and analyzing environmental issues, and making accurate conclusions about effective solutions.
- Taking individual and collective action towards addressing environmental challenges (e.g. participating in global actions, designing solutions that inspire action on environmental issues).

Encompassing the core subjects and interdisciplinary themes are three other domains: 'Learning and Innovation Skills', 'Information, Media and Technology Skills', and 'Life and Career Skills'. The content of these skills is as follows (Partnership for 21st Century Skills, 2009a, p. 2, 2009b, pp. 3–7):

Learning and Innovation Skills

- Creativity and Innovation
  - Think creatively
  - Work creatively with others
  - Implement innovations
- Critical Thinking and Problem Solving
  - Reason effectively
  - Use systems thinking
  - Make judgements and decisions
  - Solve problems
- Communication and Collaboration
  - Communicate clearly
  - Collaborate with others

Information, Media and Technology Skills

- Information Literacy
  - Access and evaluate information
  - Use and manage information
- Media Literacy
  - Analyse media
  - Create media products

- ICT (Information, Communications and Technology) Literacy[2]
  - Apply technology effectively

Life and Career Skills

- Flexibility and Adaptability
  - Adapt to change
  - Be flexible
- Initiative and Self-Direction
  - Manage goals and time
  - Work independently
  - Be self-directed learners
- Social and Cross-Cultural Skills
  - Interact effectively with others
  - Work effectively in diverse teams
- Productivity and Accountability
  - Manage projects
  - Produce results
- Leadership and Responsibility
  - Guide and lead others
  - Be responsible to others

Accompanying the teaching and learning of the above-mentioned twenty-first-century skills are five support systems involving standards, assessments, curriculum and instruction, professional development, and learning environments (for details, see Partnership for 21st Century Skills, 2009a, b).

Like the *P21 framework*, other major frameworks also emphasize comparable skills, although they might describe them differently. I shall briefly compare three other frameworks with the *P21 framework*. First, 'Learning and Innovation Skills' is also mentioned in the *Assessment and Teaching of 21st Century Skills* that is developed by ATC21S (Binkley et al., 2010), as follows:

(A) *Ways of Thinking*
   - Creativity and Innovation
   - Critical Thinking, Problem Solving, Decision-Making
   - Learning to Learn, Metacognition

(B) *Ways of Working*
- Communication
- Collaboration (teamwork)

The *Key Competences for Lifelong Learning* proposed by the Council and European Parliament also lists similar skills as key competences (European Parliament, 2007), namely,

- Learning to Learn
- Communication in the Mother Tongue
- Communication in Foreign Languages

OECD (2005) also underlines the same set of skills in its *21st Century Skills and Competences for New Millennium Learners*. These skills are listed under the 'Interacting in heterogeneous groups' category that is sub-divided as follows:

- Relate Well to Others
- Cooperate, Work in Teams
- Manage and Resolve Conflicts

Besides 'Learning and Innovation Skills', 'Information, Media and Technology Skills' in the *P21 framework* is also emphasized in all the other three documents. These skills are variously described as follows:

- Digital Competence (European Parliament, 2007)
- Tools for Working (Information Literacy and ICT Literacy) (Binkley et al., 2010)
- Use technology interactively (OECD, 2005)

Finally, 'Life and Career Skills' listed in the *P21 framework* is also highlighted in the other three frameworks. The *Key Competences for Lifelong Learning* focuses on three categories as follows (European Parliament, 2007):

- Social and Civic Competences
- Sense of Initiative and Entrepreneurship
- Cultural Awareness and Expression

The OECD framework classifies these skills under 'Acting autonomously' with the following sub-sections (OECD, 2005):

- Act within the Big Picture
- Form and Conduct Life Plans and Personal Projects
- Defend and Assert Rights, Interests, Limits and Needs

Moving in parallel with the above frameworks is the framework by ATC21S that spotlights the skill of 'Living in the world' that comprises the following (Binkley et al., 2010):

- Citizenship (Local and Global)
- Life and Career
- Personal and Social Responsibility (including Cultural Awareness and Competence)

Assessment of the frameworks for twenty-first-century skills

Guided by the desire to make education relevant to the realities, demands and challenges of the twenty-first century, all the frameworks stress the need for higher-order thinking and innovation skills, interdisciplinary learning, integration of ICT into the curriculum, and life skills that prepare the young for global competition (e.g. see Law, Pelgrum & Plomp, 2008; Ananiadou & Claro, 2009; Binkley et al., 2010). The aim to inculcate these skills in students is laudable as mere acquisition of knowledge is no longer adequate in the twenty-first century; what students need are an array of dispositions and abilities to interpret, critique, create and apply knowledge in a fast changing world. I also concur with policymakers and educators that the current assessment models in many schools are insufficient for assessing twenty-first-century skills as they are largely focused on measuring discrete knowledge; instead, what we need are new assessments grounded in authentic and complex tasks (Voogst & Roblin; Koh, Tan & Ng, 2012).

Notwithstanding the objective and merits of the frameworks, there are four main shortcomings in the major frameworks for twenty-first-century skills.

An overemphasis on technical rationality

The first shortcoming is a tendency to overemphasize skills (that include competences and competencies) *at the expense of ethical values and attitudes*. Most of the frameworks underscore the need for skills in creativity, innovation, critical thinking, problem solving, communication, collaboration, ICT literacy, cross-cultural awareness and so on. The accent on skills reflects the international trend towards 'technical rationality' in education. A person who possesses technical rationality is one who applies her technical knowledge and skills to routinizable and pre-specifiable procedures and strategies (Schon, 1987). This form of knowledge is 'rationalist' in the sense that it focuses on applying scientific theory and external research to solve the problems faced in practice.

The critique of technical rationality is well established in the literature. Roberts (1996), for example, argues that technical rationality is inadequate to develop students' understanding of the conditions and consequences of their practice as managers (also see Schon, 1983; Grant, 1999). Other writers have criticized the skills model for higher and professional education (Barnett, 1994), teacher education (Jordon & Powell, 1995), research paradigm (Schultze & Leidner, 2002), and Information Systems (Avgerou & McGrath, 2007). What are inadvertently neglected are non-technical and non-rationalist qualities such as ethical values, beliefs, assumptions, worldviews, attitudes and dispositions.

I need to clarify that I am not arguing against skills, competencies and competences per se. There is no doubt that technical rationality, especially information, media and technology skills, is essential to prepare students to be active participants in a digital age. But what is equally important, if not more important, are the ethical values and attitudes needed to guide students in their worldview, identity-formation, decision-making and life choices. Ethical values and attitudes are especially needed in the twenty-first century, where the young are constantly bombarded with (mis)information from the internet and various social media platforms. Hence students need to be grounded in a personal system of ethical values and moral reasoning in order to use their 'twenty-first-century skills' autonomously, responsibly and meaningfully.

To be sure, ethical values and attitudes are not totally absent from the frameworks. For example, in the *P21 framework*, certain ethical values and attitudes are mentioned or alluded to (Partnership for 21st Century Skills, 2009b, pp. 4, 7):

- Deal positively with praise, setbacks and criticism
- Demonstrate integrity and ethical behaviour in using influence and power
- Understand, negotiate and balance diverse views and beliefs to reach workable solutions, particularly in multicultural environments
- Respond open-mindedly to different ideas and values
- Act responsibly with the interests of the larger community in mind
- Respect cultural differences and work effectively with people from a range of social and cultural backgrounds
- Work positively and ethically

However, these values and attitudes are listed under 'Life and Career Skills', where the focus is on the skills rather than the personal ethical values and attitudes one should possess. In other words, the emphasis is still on technical rationality (expressed through words such as 'abilities', 'techniques' and 'strategies') rather than one's ethical character, philosophy and life goals. Ethical values and attitudes are primarily viewed as part of the 'skills' package needed by the graduates to succeed at work.

Compounding the de-emphasis on ethical values and attitudes is the ambiguity surrounding ethical values and attitudes. Even in cases where these values and attitudes are mentioned – for example, 'integrity', 'ethical behaviour', and 'work positively and ethically' in the *P21 framework* – they are not defined or elaborated on in the documents that accompany the framework. As a result, these values and attitudes remain unclear and difficult to apply in real life. It is therefore challenging for these ethical values and attitudes to contribute towards shaping and enabling a person to become a moral/ethical agent beyond economic considerations.

Another framework, one by OECD (2005), highlights 'shared values' as the basis for its framework of competencies:

> Insofar as competencies are needed to help accomplish collective goals, the selection of key competencies needs to some extent to be

informed by an understanding of *shared values*. The competency framework is thus anchored in such values at a general level. All OECD societies agree on the importance of *democratic values and achieving sustainable development*. These values imply both that individuals should be able to achieve their potential and that they should respect others and contribute to producing an equitable society. This complementarity of individual and collective goals needs to be reflected in a framework of competencies that acknowledges both individuals' autonomous development and their interaction with others. (p. 7, italics added)[3]

The document defines 'shared values' as 'democratic values and achieving sustainable development'. But this leads to a question of what is meant by 'democratic values', 'sustainable development' and 'equitable society' – terms that may mean different things to different people. It is also not explained in the document how 'democratic values' could help the individuals achieve their potential and contribute towards attaining an 'equitable society'.

Overall, not enough attention is devoted to getting students to formulate and clarify their own values, worldviews and life goals so as to find fulfilment in one's life. By emphasizing technical rationality, many frameworks for twenty-first-century skills may have unwittingly perpetuated the Cartesian or 'mind-body' dualism where one's values and attitudes are viewed as separate from one's actions. A suitable framework to prepare the young for the realities, demands and challenges of the twenty-first century should be one that acknowledges and integrates our values, attitudes and behaviours.

A predominantly functionalist view of education

Related to an overemphasis on skills is a predominantly functionalist view of education. The spotlight of the twenty-first-century frameworks on 'skills', 'competencies' and 'competences' takes place in the context of a *knowledge society* (also known as a *knowledge-based economy*). A knowledge society is one where ideas and knowledge function as commodities (Anderson, 2008, cited in Voogt & Roblin, pp. 299–300). A knowledge economy is characterized by rapid obsolescence of knowledge coupled with an accelerated pace of technical and scientific advance through knowledge-intensive activities (Powell & Snellman, 2004; Tan, 2005). Such an economy values intellectual capital in an environment where knowledge is constantly being created and exploited in a dynamically changing future (Shapiro & Varian, 1999). Successful individuals are those who possess the ability – or more specifically, the *technical rationality* – to continuously innovate and learn (Nonaka & Takeuchi, 1995; Prusak, 1997; Ryan, 2000; OECD, 1996; Tan, 2008). Against a backdrop of intense international competition, many states are turning to education as a means to upgrade their human capital and equip their graduates with the aforementioned twenty-first-century skills.

There is nothing wrong with using education as a vehicle for attaining economic success, both for oneself and one's country. However, there is a cause for concern, in my view, if education is *only or primarily* valued for its utilitarian purpose. A likely outcome is that students may be motivated to study purely or predominantly for extrinsic, material and short-term rewards, usually measured in terms of one's academic qualifications, job titles or a country's Gross Domestic Product (GDP). Again, there is nothing wrong in wanting to study for the above incentives. But surely there are other and justifiably more desirable motivations for learning, such as the love for and joy of learning? How about learning for the sake of human flourishing – what Aristotle calls *eudemonia* or living well? Or studying so as to contribute towards the betterment of humanity? Unfortunately, these alternative aims of education are rarely underlined in the major framework for twenty-first-century skills.

Insufficient focus on the roles of the family and community

There is also an insufficient focus on the roles of the family and community in supporting a person's quest to acquire the attributes needed for the twenty-first century. Most of the frameworks centre on the skills needed by an individual without situating her in a society of which she is a member. Although most frameworks stress the skills in communication and collaboration in human relationships – competencies that presuppose the existence of one's family and community – these skills are largely skewed towards the pragmatic end of achieving success at work. For the same reason, although 'cultural awareness' is highlighted as necessary for one to understand another ethnic community, it is valued primarily for its contribution to economic success. An example is the stated goal in the *P21 framework* for 'Social and Cross-Cultural Skills' for students to 'leverage social and cultural differences *to create new ideas and increase both innovation and quality of work*' (Partnership for 21st Century Skills, 2009b, p. 7, italics added).

Not much is said about the direct roles of the family and community in acculturating and shaping an individual's values, beliefs, worldviews, attitudes and behaviours. It is arguable that many frameworks are underpinned by a liberal and atomistic view of the individual, rather than a communitarian perspective where individuals are part of a larger community (I shall elaborate on communitarianism later). A case in point is the framework proposed by OECD on the need for personal autonomy:

> Individuals must *act autonomously* in order to participate effectively in the development of society and to function well in different spheres of life including the workplace, family life and social life. This is because *they need to develop independently an identity and to make choices, rather than just follow the crowd*. In doing so, they need to reflect on their values and on their actions. (OECD, 2005, p. 14, italics added)

The dominant tradition of individualism in Anglophone societies may explain why the OECD document highlights the competency of 'Acting Autonomously'. It appears that the framework sees the individual as independent of her membership in a family unit, community or country. On the one hand, I agree that we need to construct and own our personal identity, rather than just follow the crowd. On the other hand, I think that we need to *also* acknowledge the indelible influences our respective traditions have on us, whether consciously or unconsciously. An individual's concept and exercise of personal autonomy simply *cannot* be separated from her tradition. This means that it is difficult, if not impossible, for one to 'develop independently an identity and to make choices' without considering the developmental effect and sociocultural influence of one's family and community. While it is true that we should not 'just follow the crowd', I do not think that we can completely isolate ourselves from the crowd and not be influenced by others, especially if 'the crowd' comprises one's family members and others in the community. Our worldview is not formed in a vacuum but arises from, interacts with and evolves from, the culture in which we are born in and socialized into. To borrow an expression from Thomas Nagel (1986) and Hans-Georg Gadamer (1990), there is simply no 'view from nowhere'. Fox (1997) explains the significance of the 'view from nowhere':

> [L]ike it or not, we are all the creation of our own historical traditions, both in our acceptance and our rejection of them. The 'prejudices' of history is what gives us a world within which we may think, act, judge, critique, and commit to one or another direction or set of beliefs; without a linguistic and historical 'fore-structuring,' creative and critical thought would be an impossibility. (p. 578)[4]

Inadequate teacher education

The last critique concerns teacher education. An overemphasis on technical rationality and a functionalist view of education have a direct impact on the frameworks' vision of teacher education. The *P21 framework* outlines teacher professional development as follows (Partnership for 21st Century Skills, 2009b, pp. 8–9):

Twenty-first-century professional development

- Highlights ways teachers can seize opportunities for integrating twenty-first-century skills, tools and teaching strategies into their classroom practice – and help them identify what activities they can replace/de-emphasize.
- Balances direct instruction with project-oriented teaching methods.
- Illustrates how a deeper understanding of subject matter can actually enhance problem solving, critical thinking and other twenty-first-century skills.
- Enables twenty-first-century professional learning communities for teachers that model the kinds of classroom learning that best promotes twenty-first-century skills for students.
- Cultivates teachers' ability to identify students' particular learning styles, intelligences, strengths and weaknesses.

- Helps teachers develop their abilities to use various strategies (such as formative assessments) to reach diverse students and create environments that support differentiated teaching and learning.
- Supports the continuous evaluation of students' twenty-first-century skills development.
- Encourages knowledge sharing among communities of practitioners, using face-to-face, virtual and blended communications.
- Uses a scalable and sustainable model of professional development.

We can see from the list above that the priority for teachers, as in the case for students, is on skills as expressed through words such as 'ways', 'methods' and 'ability'. While there is no doubt that these skills are essential for teachers, these skills need to be undergirded by an *ethical dimension of teaching*, which unfortunately is missing from most frameworks. Questions that highlight the ethical dimension of teaching include: What do we mean by a 'good teacher'? What is the moral/ethical duty of a teacher? What values, attitudes, aspirations and worldviews do we want to see in educators? How could educators help their students to live ethically and purposefully? These questions, of course, do not yield straightforward answers and are subject to a variety of interpretations, ideologies and sociocultural contingencies. Given the significant role of teachers in nurturing the future generations, policymakers and educators need to urgently address the above questions before they jump on the bandwagon to train the teachers with 'skills', 'competencies' and 'competences'.[5]

An alternative: A Confucian framework for twenty-first-century education

In response to the three major shortcomings of the twenty-first-century skills discussed earlier, I would like to propose an alternative framework for twenty-first-century education by applying key Confucius' concepts. I should clarify that I do not claim that my framework is the best or the only acceptable one for twenty-first-century education. Neither am I asserting that my Confucian framework is the only Confucian model; it is entirely plausible for other writers to formulate different frameworks

Confucius and Twenty-First-Century Education 207

based on the same set of Confucius' ideas. My Confucian framework is represented by the diagram below (Figure 7.1).

Readers would have noticed that my framework is modified from the *P21 framework*. The domain of 'Core Subjects and Twenty-first-Century Themes' remains unchanged. However, the thrust of the three domains – 'Learning and Innovation', 'Information, Media & Technology' and 'Life and Career' – goes beyond skills (that include competences and competencies) to emphasize the importance and integration of values, attitudes and behaviours. Although not illustrated in the diagram, the framework includes the support systems in standards, assessment, curriculum and instruction, professional development, and learning environments. I shall not elaborate on these support systems, as they are not the focus of my critique of the *P21 framework*; I shall instead elucidate the four domains as presented in the diagram.

The framework consists of four concentric circles, each containing one or more Confucian concepts. Two preliminary observations are

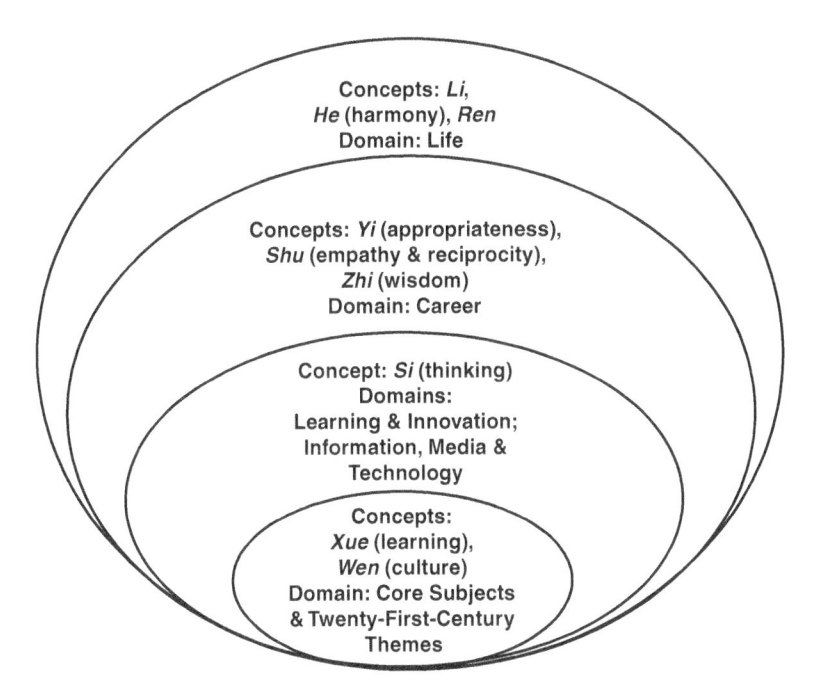

Figure 7.1 A Confucian framework for twenty-first-century education

necessary regarding Confucius' concepts mentioned in the framework. First, not all of Confucius' concepts discussed in this book are listed in the diagram; for example, I have left out *dao* (道 Way) and *zhengming* (正名 rectification of names). The omission does not mean that they are unimportant or that they are excluded from the framework. On the contrary, they are intertwined with and implied in the other Confucius' concepts, as I shall explain later.

Second, the association of particular Confucian concepts with specific domains (e.g. 文 *wen* (culture) is paired with 'Core Subjects and Twenty-first-Century Themes') does not mean that the concept is *only* applicable to that domain. It also does not mean that the various Confucian concepts in the different concentric circles are unrelated and mutually exclusive. The reverse is true: all the concepts are necessarily linked and inseparable in practice. For example, *yi* (appropriateness) is intertwined with *ren* since the former is an expression of loving others by doing what is appropriate for a specific situation. My purpose of explicitly associating certain Confucian concepts with specific domains is to highlight the central roles played by these Confucian concepts in the respective domains.

I would like to explain the framework by starting with the innermost circle. The **innermost circle** comprises the domain of 'Core Subjects and Twenty-first-Century Themes'. Following the *P21 framework*, the Core Subjects are likely to include English, reading or language arts, World languages, Arts, Mathematics, Economics, Science, Geography, History, and Government and Civics. The Twenty-first-Century Themes, on the other hand, may include topics such as Global Awareness, Financial, Economic, Business and Entrepreneurial Literacy, Civic Literacy, Health Literacy, and Environmental Literacy.

The key Confucius' concepts here are 'learning' (學 *xue*) and 'culture' (文 *wen*). The concept of learning, as explained earlier, refers to bringing up or instructing a person in her thoughts, feelings and actions through providing a cornucopia of educational experiences. Confucius highlights the need to enjoy and love learning so as to fulfil heaven's mandate and promote the Way for the good of humankind. It is through unceasing and passionate learning that one acquires *ren* (仁) and other virtues in one's self-cultivation to achieve the Way. The concept of culture refers to a broad-based and interdisciplinary curriculum; Confucius advocates learning the 'six arts': *li*, music, archery, charioteering, calligraphy or writing and mathematics. Whether one is engaging in sports or enjoying a piece of music, one learns to love and find joy in such learning, and appreciate their spiritual-ethical-aesthetic value.[6] The learning of culture enables a person to acquire the wherewithal to be knowledgeable, confident, well mannered and refined. More importantly, a cultured person is one who has achieved internal and external harmony, and is inspired to contribute to the world by broadening the Way.

What then are the implications that arise from the application of Confucius' concepts of learning and culture to the domain of Core Subjects and Twenty-first-Century Themes? I would like to suggest five major implications for policymakers and educators in their endeavours to promote twenty-first-century education. The first is that the focus of learning should not be for the sole or overriding purpose of enriching oneself and succeeding in a competitive world; rather, it should be *to broaden the Way for the good of humankind*. I have argued in my critique of the current frameworks for twenty-first-century skills that a dominant assumption is a liberal and atomistic view of the self coupled with an individualistic' view of education. While there is nothing wrong in wanting to be educated for one's own benefit, a possible negative consequence is that it may foster excessive self-centredness and unhealthy competition rather than peaceful coexistence and altruistic collaboration among people. From Confucius' perspective, it is impossible for anyone to separate oneself from one's community, and unethical for anyone to seek her own interests without considering those of others. Like two sides of a coin, to help oneself, according to Confucius, *is* to help others.

Second, the emphasis on finding joy in and loving learning implies that we need to assist students and educators to *appreciate the non-utilitarian function of education*. The Confucian framework requires schools to (re)craft their curricula so as to encourage students to go beyond mere paper chase to appreciate ideals such as love, beauty, simplicity and joy. An effective way to introduce students to these ideals is for schools to promote the arts and humanities in their curriculum. By learning about great classical works in literature, philosophy, painting, music and other related fields, students are likely to appreciate the aesthetic and ethical value of these works.

The third implication concerns the inclusion of the core subject of *sports* into the curriculum. In view of Confucius' emphasis of the integration of one's mind and body, sports – surprisingly omitted in the *P21 framework* – should be included as a compulsory subject in the framework.[7] The sporting activities, of course, need not include or be confined to archery and charioteering that are mentioned in the *Analects*. They should instead comprise a variety of physical exercises and games that match the students' interests and developmental growth. The aim is to nurture students to appreciate and observe *li* in all aspects of their lives, including the time spent in the basketball field or other outdoor venues. Through an integration of subjects across the curriculum, from languages to Mathematics, Arts, Music and Sports etc., students will achieve internal harmony in their heart-mind (心 *xin*) and body, as well as external harmony in communicating and collaborating with others in accordance with *li*.

Fourthly, the twenty-first-century theme of *civic literacy*, which is one of the twenty-first-century themes, should be actively promoted in schools. According to the *P21 framework*, this refers to participating effectively in civic life by staying informed and understanding governmental processes; exercising the rights and obligations of citizenship at a local, state, national and global level; and understanding the local and global implications of civic decisions. Civic literacy is essential for the young to contribute actively and meaningfully in public policies, both locally and internationally, for the good of humankind. The prevalence of authoritarian governments in East Asian countries that share a Confucian heritage has given rise to a perception that Confucianism suppresses political and democratic participation (Frederick, 2002). But what does Confucius think of civic participation?

We have seen how Confucius is highly critical of the political rulers of his time; he also believes in actively serving in public office and participating in public discourse.[8] I have elsewhere argued that Confucianism recognizes correlative rights that are premised on the right to human dignity, worth and equality, and attached to individuals in specific social positions (Tan, 2012b).[9] It is therefore reasonable to conclude that Confucius is supportive of civic participation and the teaching of civic literacy in schools. The specific expression of civic literacy, of course, will depend on the localized social, political and cultural conditions. This is where the

Confucian concept of appropriateness (義 *yi*) is applicable to guide a person to participate effectively in civic life, exercise her citizen rights and obligations, and understand the local and global implications of civic decisions in a culturally sensitive and contextually appropriate manner. [10]

Finally, I recommend the inclusion of the twenty-first-century theme of *spiritual education* into the curriculum. We have already learned that Confucius' worldview encompasses a distinctive spiritual component that entrusts human beings with the mission to fulfil the mandate of heaven. The spiritual education I have in mind should be distinguished from *religious education*, based on an essential difference between 'religion' and 'spirituality'. Briefly, 'religion' comprises a 'set of ethics, doctrines, organisational hierarchies, and the history of any particular religion' (Minney, 1991, p. 388); 'spirituality', on the other hand, refers to a distinctive capacity for the individual to make sense of oneself within a wider framework of meaning (Tan, 2008, 2009a, 2009b, 2010). Examples of spiritual ideals are feelings of transcendence, knowledge of the divine, a search for meaning, purpose and service, a sense of awe, wonder and mystery, and self-knowledge. Spiritual development is characterized by reflection, attribution of meaning to experience, and an emphasis on a non-material dimension to life and intimations of an enduring reality (OFSTED, 1994). It follows that spiritual education may include, but is not confined to, any set of religious beliefs, an institutionalized belief system, or any realm of worship (Tan & Wong, 2012). Another way of putting it is to see spiritual education as divided into 'religiously tethered' spiritual education (involving one or more religions) and 'religiously untethered' spiritual education (not involving any religion) (Alexander & McLaughlin, 2003; Tan & Wong, 2012).[11]

Confucius' concept of heaven serves as an appropriate framework for spiritual education in schools today. On the one hand, his notion of heaven, with its anthropomorphic characteristics (cf. 2.4, 3.13, 7.23, 14.35), is compatible with a belief in a personal divine being found in some religious systems (see Chapter 3 for a fuller discussion of the concept of heaven). This compatibility could serve as a platform for schools to encourage their students to explore, appreciate and compare different religious beliefs in the world. On the other hand, we have learned that Confucius does not dwell much on the concept of heaven and refuses to engage in a discourse on supernatural matters (cf. 7.21, 11.12). Instead, he emphasizes the ability of human beings to broaden the Way (15.29) through achieving spiritual-ethical-aesthetic harmony within oneself as well as with heaven, other people and the surroundings (cf. 1.12, 2.4). Hence Confucius' spiritual worldview lends itself well to a promotion of spiritual development in students where they acquire insights of enduring worth into their personal existence, attribute meaning to their life experiences, and value a non-material and transcendental (although not necessarily other-worldly) dimension to life. Spiritual education supports the twenty-first-century theme of 'global awareness' since it enables students to appreciate people of diverse cultures, religions and lifestyles at a deeper and sustained manner. It enables and inspires students to view 'the other' empathetically and respectfully against a backdrop of shared humanity and mission to seek the common good. Undergirded by a desire to pursue a united vision for humanity, students are motivated to understand and address global issues by engaging in open dialogue and international collaboration.

The **next outer circle** comprises two other domains for the twenty-first century: 'Learning & Innovation', and 'Information, Media & Technology'. These two domains focus on the attributes needed by students in a knowledge society. Following the *P21 framework*, 'Learning and Innovation' consists of 'creativity and innovation', 'critical thinking and problem solving' and 'communication and collaboration'. 'Information, Media and Technology', on the other hand, consists of 'information literacy', 'media literacy', and 'ICT literacy'. It should be pointed out that the two domains in this circle presuppose that students have learned or are learning the core subjects and twenty-first-century themes found in the innermost circle.

The Confucius' concept associated with the above-mentioned domains is *si* (思 thinking). This concept, as discussed in the previous chapter, is a broad term that encompasses a range of thought processes, such as remembering, understanding, reflection, analysis, synthesis, evaluation, making connections, drawing analogies, making inferences, forming judgements etc. *Si* goes hand in hand with learning (*xue*), with the latter including culture (*wen*). *Si* is crucial in 'leading forth' or nurturing a person by encouraging her to go beyond mere knowledge acquisition to higher-order thinking. The desired outcome here is not just about getting students to learn about their own tradition, but to reflect on, critique and modify their tradition where necessary in accordance with *li* (more on *li* later).[12]

Applying the Confucian concept of *si* to the domains of 'Learning and Innovation' and 'Information, Media and Technology' means that a student does not just accumulate knowledge and skills, such as learning about deductive and inductive reasoning or cutting-edge ICT tools. Important these knowledge and skills may be, the learning should be accompanied by fostering the learner's zeal to actively reflect, ask and seek answers to relevant questions. Examples are getting students to question whether critical thinking as practised in Anglophone societies is culturally appropriate in Asian societies, and the extent to which the utilization of ICT is applicable and beneficial in poor countries.

Si also entails the student extending her learning by applying what she has learned to real life, drawing inferences, forming her own judgements about people and things, and engaging in self-examination. Throughout her inquiry process, she is encouraged to integrate her cognitive and affective faculties in her heart-mind, and translate her learning into normative behaviours. Combining learning and *si*, we have a portrait of a lifelong and life-wide learner who cultivates herself in a pro-active, spontaneous, meaningful and joyful manner. She is on the way to become a *junzi* – an noble or exemplary human being who broadens the Way by observing *li*.

The **second most outer circle** is the domain of 'Career'. This circle presupposes the possession of the aforementioned concepts of learning, culture and *si* in the other smaller circles. Following the *P21 framework*, this domain comprises the sub-topics of 'Productivity and Accountability' (manage projects and produce results) and 'Leadership and Responsibility' (guide and lead others, and be responsible to others). The Confucian qualities central to this domain are *yi* (appropriateness), *shu* (empathy and reciprocity) and *zhi* (wisdom).

The quality of appropriateness (*yi*) is instrumental for one's career advancement as it directs a person to exercise her individual discretion and judgement at work. An employer or employee guided by appropriateness will do what is felicitous in managing projects, producing results, guiding and leading others, and being accountable to others. Accompanying appropriateness is *shu* (empathy and reciprocity) where one learns to live and work harmoniously with people around her. *Shu* is about treating others with respect by not imposing on others what you yourself do not desire. It also stresses reciprocity through cooperation and mutual support – attributes that are especially necessary in a globalized world where human beings are increasingly dependent on one another. Another essential key concept for the workplace is *zhi* (wisdom) that prepares graduates to apply what they have learned to real life. Such applied knowledge comes in the form of knowing how to relate to different types of people, bring out the best in others and help others realize their potentials. In short, a wise person is a responsible person who guides and leads others by appreciating and developing the talents of others. The above illustrates how the Confucian qualities of appropriateness, empathy, reciprocity and wisdom work together to empower an individual to acquire not just skills, competencies and competences but the prerequisite values, attitudes and conduct needed for a successful career.

Finally, the **outermost circle** contains the Confucian concepts of *li*, harmony (*he*) and *ren* that are particularly relevant to the domain of 'Life'. Following the *P21 framework*, this domain comprises the sub-topics of 'Flexibility and Adaptability' (adapt to change and be flexible), 'Initiative and Self-Direction' (manage goals and time, work independently, and be self-directed learners), and 'Social and Cross-Cultural Sensitivity' (interact effectively with others and work effectively in diverse teams).[13] As the biggest circle, it encompasses all the concepts and domains discussed earlier in the other circles.

A central concept in this domain is *li* that refers to the totality of normative human behaviours, accompanied by corresponding attitudes and values in all aspects of life. The observance of *li* requires the harmonization of one's thoughts, feelings and actions so that one can be flexible, adaptable, self-directed, exercise initiative, and demonstrate social and cross-cultural sensitivity. *Li* is a foundational concept in the framework for twenty-first-century education because it is the pattern and discourse for a community of *junzi* who collectively broaden the Way for the good of humankind.[14]

The goal for schools is to go beyond promoting technical rationality and a functionalist view of education by nurturing a generation of *junzi* who internalize and demonstrate the spiritual-ethical-aesthetic dimension of *li* in all aspects of life. Briefly, *li* is 'spiritual' in that it focuses on knowing the divine or other spiritual ideals (religiously tethered or otherwise) and one's place in the universe. It takes one beyond being merely a 'good' or 'useful' person to one that appreciates and pursues non-material and transcendental (although not necessarily otherworldly) goals in life. The ethical dimension of *li* emphasizes the manifestation of normative behaviours with corresponding attitudes and values when we help ourselves as well as others to observe *li*. The aesthetic dimension refers to appreciating harmony by beholding beauty, joy and ethical values in the arts and humanities, especially poetry and music. Clothed with internal and external harmony, students will be able to coexist peacefully, purposefully, and joyfully with themselves, other human beings and the world around them in accordance with *li*.

Another central concept is *ren*; to live a life in accordance with *li* is to possess and exhibit *ren* values, attitudes and behaviours. The achievement of *ren* is particularly evident in one's demonstration of 'Social and Cross-Cultural Sensitivity'; here one is adept at interacting wholeheartedly with others and working effectively in culturally diverse teams. The exercise of *ren* involves the practice of *zhengming* (正名 rectification of names) and *xiao* (孝 filial piety). The rectification of names underlines the need for all people to perform their respective social roles. Filial piety, on the other hand, is the root of *ren* in the sense that one must first love one's parents and family members before one can extend love to other people in society.

It follows from the rectification of names and filial piety that the formation of self-identity cannot be separated from our social functions and responsibilities in the world. This reminds us of my earlier critique of the current frameworks' insufficient focus on the roles of the family and community in contributing towards an individual's success in work and life. I have elsewhere argued that rather than seeing the self as a single, separate individual who stands apart from, or over and against, the community or society, the individual is socially embedded in a web of relations (Tan, 2012b). Self-realization is not just a matter of transforming one's understanding of the self; it requires close communion with others in the common pursuit of *ren*. The importance of the family and community in contributing towards one's life and career means that we need to acknowledge and draw upon the resources of the family and community to enable every individual to succeed in the twenty-first century. In the context of schools, this means that educators need to work closely with the family and community to bring up (i.e. instruct) and lead forth (i.e. nurture) their students in values formation and holistic growth.

It is apparent that my Confucian framework is premised on a communitarian approach to education; the framework acknowledges the central role of the community in shaping and influencing an individual's growth and identity. However, this does not mean that the self is ignored or subservient to the interests of the common good. We have seen how Confucius' concept of harmony is not about homogeneity but diversity in unity. Being a *junzi* is also not about conformity and blind allegiance to rulers but about demonstrating personal autonomy, critical reflection and creativity through self-cultivation.[15]

This concludes our understanding of the Confucian framework for students in the twenty-first century. It is appropriate, at this juncture, to explore the implications of the Confucian framework for **teacher and teacher professional development**. I have noted earlier that the 'twenty-first-century professional development' for teachers in the *P21 framework* overemphasizes skills at the expense of the ethical dimension of teaching. In contrast to the technical focus in the current frameworks, Confucius sees the role of a teacher as primarily that of a nurturer and exemplar to her students. To put it simply, a teacher should strive to be a *junzi*.

In the context of teacher education and professional development, priority should be placed on the *character development* of the teacher and secondarily on teaching methods, assessment abilities or other technical competencies. A Confucian teacher is one who has achieved, or at least strives to achieve, internal and external *he* (harmony) in accordance with *li*. Such a person possesses and manifests harmonized *ren* attitudes, values and behaviours in her relationships with her students, colleagues, parents and others. She is convinced that 'in helping oneself to take a stand, she helps others to take their stand; in desiring to reach a goal, she helps others to reach the goal' (6.30). Since helping one's students presupposes teacher competency, the training and upgrading of a teacher's abilities, techniques and strategies are of course necessary. But more important and fundamental than knowledge and skills training is for the teacher to abide in and demonstrate *ren* by loving her students in accordance with *li*.

Besides character development, teacher education and professional development should also focus on cultivating educators who enjoy, love, and engage in lifelong and life-wide learning. Such a teacher is a passionate learner of multi- and inter-disciplinary curriculum, and proficient in making the connections between what she and her students already know (the old) and what she and her students should know (the new). She is willing to teach anyone who is keen to learn, regardless of the person's family background, individual potential, learning ability and other factors. By patiently guiding her students to learn systematically in a customized manner, such a teacher inspires them to constantly reflect, engage in higher-order thinking and conscientiously apply what they learn in life. Given that a *junzi* is one who draws close to fellow *junzi*, teacher education and professional development should also promote teacher collaboration. This collaboration includes but goes beyond the collaboration mentioned in the *P21 framework* that '(e)ncourages knowledge sharing among communities of practitioners, using face-to-face, virtual and blended communications' (Partnership for 21st Century Skills, 2009b, p. 9). More than just 'knowledge-sharing' that is aimed at improving the teachers' skills, teacher collaboration should centre on mutual encouragement and modelling to abide in *ren* and observe *li*.

Conclusion

A Confucian framework for the twenty-first century is salubrious for schools as it avoids the shortcomings of the major frameworks for twenty-first-century skills. First, it rejects an overemphasis on skills (that includes competences and competencies) at the expense of the students' and teachers' spiritual-ethical-aesthetic values, attitudes and behaviours. By placing *li* in the outermost circle, the framework ensures that all aspects of one's life, be it one's career, study of the core subjects, or relationships with others, are underpinned by the pursuit of harmony and *ren*. Second, the Confucian framework rejects treating education merely as a conduit for economic and material gains in a knowledge-based economy. Instead, it advocates students (and educators) loving and enjoying learning, and motivating them to learn for the sake of the betterment of human beings. Third, the Confucian framework goes beyond a narrow focus on the individual and individual effort by underscoring the significant contributions of the family and community towards an individual's identity, values-formation and life goals. Finally, the framework offers an integrated model where all the domains are interconnected with a shared goal to empower students to observe *li* in school and beyond.

Having looked at the relevance of Confucius' concepts for twenty-first-century education, the next chapter will conclude our study of Confucius' work.

Chapter 8

Conclusion

We have explored Confucius' intellectual biography and key concepts as well as the relevance of his work for twenty-first-century education. This chapter draws our discussion to a close by examining some critiques of and prospects for Confucius' thought.

Critiques of Confucius' thought

Although I have focused largely on the positive aspects of Confucius' work in this book, I do not claim that his teachings are perfect, or that all aspects of his teachings hold contemporary relevance. On the contrary, I am aware that some of his teachings have generated controversy and criticism. This section highlights three main critiques in the current literature of Confucius' educational thought.

Confucius' view of women

The first controversy is Confucius' view on women. There is scant mention of women in the *Analects*; one of the few direct references to women is in the following verse:

> 17.25 子曰：'唯女子與小人爲難養也，近之則不孫，遠之則怨。'
>
> The Master said, 'Only women and petty persons are difficult to provide for; if you are close to them, they become insolent, if you keep them at a distance, they will be resentful.'

Confucius associates women with petty people (小人 *xiaoren*) who are both, in his view, '難養' (*nanyang*). The word '養' (*yang*) refers to the general act of raising, feeding, supporting or nurturing. The expression '難養' (*nanyang*) has been translated variously as 'difficult to provide for' (Ames & Rosemont), 'hard to rear' (Li, 1999), 'difficult to deal with' (Lau), 'difficult to live with' (Yang) and 'hard to manage' (Slingerland). The references to being 'close' (近 *jin*) and 'far' (遠 *yuan*) inform us that the context is about one's uneasy and complicated relationship with women (as well as petty persons). By putting women in the same category as petty persons, Confucius appears to imply that women, like petty persons, are lacking in *ren*, wanting in their observance of *li*, and ultimately incapable of becoming *junzi*. One may also conclude, following the same argument, that the Confucian framework for twenty-first-century education expounded in the previous chapter is and should only be applicable to male and not female students.

Unsurprisingly, Confucius has been criticized for his allegedly derogatory view of women. For example, Rainey (2010) asserts that 'it is not at all clear that Confucius meant to extend education to women' (p. 57). Brindley (2009) makes a stronger claim that the ideal of *junzi* 'certainly was not encouraged as something that would be appropriate or relevant for them [women] to pursue' and that this 'effectively barred such people as women from trying to attain it' (pp. 54–5). Historical developments after Confucius' death further perpetuated the perception that Confucius and Confucianism under-value and oppress women. A significant contributing factor in the third century BCE was the work of a philosopher of law, Han Fei on the 'Three Principal Relationships'. Supposedly based on Confucius' teachings, the three relationships essentially state that the official should serve the sovereign, the son should serve the father and the wife should serve the husband. Wang (2004) explains how the application of these relationships led to the subordination of women (as well as subjects and sons) in the history of China:

> According to this unidirectional idea, an emperor, a father and a husband were the rulers of a subject, a son and a wife. No matter what kind of person the emperor, the father and the husband were, they each had the rights or power that these relationships gave them; their subjects, sons and wives had no rights, only the obligation of unconditional obedience. [. . .] Deeply influenced by the Three Principal Relationships, the concept of the individual person cannot be found

in Chinese culture until the end of the Qing Dynasty (1644–1911). This may be considered the most serious error and legacy of Confucian thinking in relation to moral education. (pp. 433–4, also see Feng, 1985; Li, 1994; Hutton, 2008)

The systemic and widespread subordination of women in ancient China was further entrenched during the Han dynasty through the writings of Confucian scholar Dong Zhongshu in the second century BCE (Chan, 2008).

Before we analyse Confucius' views of women, it is important to keep in mind the milieu Confucius lived in and not evaluate his comments through our modern and/or cultural lens. Ames and Rosemont (1998) rightly remind readers that 'we must refrain from imposing Western concepts of gender on early Chinese thinkers despite the patriarchal structure of classical and imperial Chinese society' (p. 25). Historically, it is true that Confucius did not have any female students and probably did not interact much with women, apart from his female family members. Women during Confucius' time were largely deprived of formal education, kept away from public view, and segregated from men who were unrelated to them. The minority of women who did receive an education were likely to be from the aristocratic class and taught by a private tutor at home. In general, women in ancient China were defined and bound by their social roles as someone's daughter, wife or concubine; it was therefore impossible for *any* woman to learn from Confucius or assume any public office, even if she aspired to do so.

While I agree that 17.25 appears to portray women negatively by mentioning them alongside petty persons, I think it is difficult to infer from this verse that Confucius looks down on and refuses to educate all women. In my view, 17.25 is *descriptive* rather than *prescriptive*: it is about Confucius' lamentation of the behaviour of women (and petty persons) of his time. As argued by Li (1994) regarding 17.25:

> Here Confucius offered an observation of young women rather than a theory about women in general. It probably reflects a social prejudice that already existed in his time. Given Confucius's later illustrious status in China, this short comment on (young) women may have considerably influenced people's view on women in general and

probably reinforced people's prejudice against women. However, there is no reason for one to think that this view is an inherent or essential part of Confucius's thought or an inevitable consequence of his general philosophy. (p. 83)

It is of course plausible that Confucius, as a man of his time, did not hold women in high regard, given the fact that they were largely uneducated, unemployed, voiceless and kept away from public view. Consequently, he probably would not be able to envision women playing a prominent public role in society as scholars, rulers and change agents.[1] But we should not jump to the conclusion that Confucius had intended his teachings (especially on *junzi*, *ren* and *li*) only for males. In particular, we cannot make such an argument from our reading of the *Analects* since this text, like the other classical Chinese texts, does not contain gender-specific pronouns. In fact, there are many verses in the *Analects* that point to the universal appeal and application of Confucius' regardless of gender. These verses include his willingness to teach everyone (cf. 7.7, 15.39), his exhortation for all to strive to be *ren* (7.30, 12.1, 15.35), to be *junzi* (4.5, 15.18), to observe *li* (12.1) and so on.

The *only* distinction made by Confucius regarding human beings in the *Analects* is not about gender, social class, ethnicity or other human differences, but about the extent to which human beings succeed in achieving *ren* in accordance with *li*. In other words, Confucius distinguishes a *junzi* who fulfils heaven's mandate by seeking to broaden the Way according to *li*, from a *xiaoren* (petty person) who is the anti-thesis of a *junzi* (cf. 4.11, 6.13, 13.23, 17.23). Whether male or female (or other human differences), what is most important is the aspiration one holds and effort one puts in that sets such a person apart from other human beings; this is what Confucius means in his observation that 'human beings are similar in their nature, but differ as a result of their practice' (性相近也，習相遠也) (17.2).

We should also differentiate Confucius' teachings from those of his followers such as Han Fei and Dong Zhongshu in the third and second century BCE respectively. It is questionable that Confucius would support Han Fei's Three Principal Relationships if Confucius wishes to be consistent in his teachings as presented in the *Analects*. This is because the principles implied in the Three Principal Relationships –

unconditional obedience, the abuse of power and suppression of individuality – contradict Confucius' teachings on *ren* (loving others), *shu* (empathy and reciprocity) and *zhi* (wisdom). Chan (2008) argues that the subordination of women does not fit comfortably with the major elements in Confucian ethics:

> The first Confucian element that may challenge gender inequality is that females and males are regarded in early Confucianism as being equal in terms of their inborn moral instincts and capacities. Unlike Aristotle, who thinks that women are biologically inferior to men in rational capacities, Mencius is of the view that the most important feature that defines a human being, namely, *ren* as an inborn moral instinct and potentiality to be fully realised, is equally distributed among males and females. The second element is Confucius' famous principle that education should be open to all. He was proud of the fact that, as a teacher, he has never 'denied instruction to anyone who, of his own accord, has given [him] so much as a bundle of dried meat as a present'. (p. 128)

It is also instructive that the history of Confucianism is not totally negative towards women. Slingerland (2001) draws our attention to 'stories from the later Confucian tradition (e.g. the *Lienu Zhuan* or "Biographies of Exemplary Women") [that] credited women with the capacity to reason in the same moral terms as men and often portrayed women as upbraiding their husbands or sons for ritually incorrect or morally questionable behaviour' (p. 117). Li (1994, 2000, 2002) even goes as far as arguing that Confucianism, far from being oppressive to women, is compatible with the feminist ethics of care (for responses to Li's views, see Star, 2002; Yuan, 2002).

Of course, one could question why Confucius did not actively fight for the liberation of women and equal opportunity of learning for them. But I do not think that Confucius sees himself as a social revolutionist; after all, he describes himself as a transmitter of antiquity, not an innovator (7.1). Neither do I think that Confucius is particularly interested in gender issues (or other sociopolitical issues such as class division, political system etc.). Rather, his focus, as evident from the *Analects*, is on restoring the Zhou *li* as *the* solution to the political chaos and flagrant violation of *li* during his time. His primary aim is to fulfil heaven's mandate through the creation and collective efforts of a community of *junzi* who broaden the Way through observing *li*.

Confucius' view on hierarchy and social roles

The second critique concerns Confucius' view of a hierarchical and role-bound society under the leadership of *junzi*. He advocates a social system where the common people, circumscribed by their respective social roles, are expected to obey their ruler (albeit a *junzi*-ruler). This may suggest that Confucius does not believe that the majority of the people should or are capable of becoming *junzi*. A hierarchical and role-based society may in turn foster or condone the development of authoritarian governments coupled with the suppression of individuality and democratic participation. Such a critique is not new as the emphasis on unconditional obedience in dominant Confucian traditions has been blamed (rightly or wrongly) for encouraging dictatorial and corrupt governments. In his survey of governments in the history of East Asia, Frederick (2002) observes that 'Confucian ideas came to be used to subjugate others, and less-than virtuous bureaucrats were much a part of the decline of government by the scholar-rulers'; and 'by the 19th century, the common image of the Confucian was mostly negative, assumed to be the source of many of the ills of totalitarian government in East Asia' (p. 624).

If the above critique holds, it may cast doubt on the egalitarian and meritocratic principles advocated by Confucius, since not everyone should or is capable of becoming a *junzi* or fully virtuous. Sim (2009) identifies the possibility of paternalism in Confucius' teaching:

> Confucius thinks that most people are incapable of becoming fully virtuous and hence being suitable politicians. Consequently, the majority needs to be taken care of and be led well to have their fullest share in the moral life. This seems paternalistic to us: Even if it is true that most people will lack in virtue if we let them run loose in a highly mobile, tradition-criticising society, at least they have their freedom. (p. 90)[2]

Confucius' views on hierarchy and social roles may also imply that the Confucian framework for twenty-first-century education, especially the desired outcomes of civic literacy, critical thinking and innovation, should *not* be taught to all students.

However, the charge that the Confucian tradition promotes authoritarianism and stifles individuality, personal autonomy and innovation applies more to Confucianism as an ideology rather than to the teachings of Confucius. The impression that Confucianism advocates the suppression of self-interest for the sake of societal welfare arises from the politicization of Confucianism where its selective teachings have been utilized for political agendas (Tan, 2012). In this regard, it is helpful to distinguish between *political* Confucianism and *philosophical* Confucianism (Fukuyama, 1995a; Tu, 1998). While the former refers to the attempts of various groups to politicize Confucian ethical values in the service of other, non-ethical purposes, the latter refers to the Confucian intent, as stressed by Confucius himself, to infuse politics with ethics through personal cultivation of the self (Tu, 1984). The teachings of Confucius fall under the category of philosophical Confucianism where he propagates the appointment of *junzi*-rulers who govern their states based on *ren* in accordance with *li*, rather than through harsh laws and punishments.

As for the other question of whether Confucius supports a society that is paternalistic, authoritarian and elitist, it is correct to say that Confucius sees an ideal society as one that is defined by the allocation and performance of specific social roles. But this does not necessarily mean that such a society is paternalistic, authoritarian and elitist. It is not paternalistic in the sense of being interfering and controlling, since the *junzi*-ruler is supposed to govern not by law but by virtue. Far from being authoritarian, a *junzi*-ruler models and encourages the observance of *li* by not being arrogant (20.2), being generous in caring for the common people (5.16) and inspiring the common people to *ren* (8.2). Guided by *yi* (appropriateness), a *junzi*-ruler takes care of and leads the common people, not in a high-handed manner, but by giving them the necessary rights and freedom to live autonomously and participate actively in public policymaking according to *li*. A number of writers have also argued that Confucius does not necessarily advocate authoritarianism, and that Confucianism is potentially compatible with democracy, civil society, human rights, equality and global justice.[3]

Confucius' view of society is also not necessarily elitist, as he believes that everyone has the potential to become a *junzi*. He teaches that we can learn not just from *junzi* but also from everyone (7.22). To further explore the charge of elitism in Confucius' teaching, I shall refer to Daniel Bell (2008)'s critique of a mainland Chinese professor's interpretation of Confucius' work.[4] As mentioned in the introductory chapter, Bell (2008) criticizes Yu Dan for downplaying the elitist dimension of the *Analects*. In his words,

> [I]t's a bit of a stretch to believe that Confucius believed everybody can become an exemplary person [*junzi*]. Quite the opposite, in fact. He takes it for granted that a minority of exemplary people can and should rule over common people (e.g. 12.19, 14.42). Confucius clearly seems to believe that some people, such as Zaiwo, have moral limitations that cannot be overcome (5.10). He also suggests that common people have intellectual limitations (8.9). Nor does everyone have the same level of motivation, and Confucius says that he only instructs those who are driven with eagerness (7.8). Yu Dan doesn't mention such passages, perhaps because such views wouldn't play well with her intended readership. But she may be deviating substantially from Confucius' original views. (2008, p. 167)

For the sake of clarity, I have reproduced Yu Dan's argument on why she thinks that everyone can become a *junzi*:

> Thus, the word 'junzi' appears the most number of times in the *Analects*. His [*junzi*'s] truth is always simple, warm [and] harmonious – something that everyone can adhere to from this moment. The aspiration and goal [of becoming a *junzi*] is lofty yet not unattainable; in fact, it is present at this moment and exists in each of our hearts. Based on this understanding, everyone can become a true *junzi*. (Yu, 2007, p. 74)[5]

In the chapter on *junzi*, Yu Dan (2007) draws out the differences between a *junzi* and a petty person and highlights the ethical qualities of a *junzi* such as being kind, noble, easy-going, action-oriented and firm.

In discussing Bell's critique of Yu Dan, it is helpful for us to refer to three key passages cited by him. First, Bell uses the example of Zaiwo (5.10) to argue that Zaiwo has 'morally limitations that cannot be overcome'. The passage is as follows:

5.10 宰予晝寢。子曰：'朽木不可雕也；糞土之牆不可杇也；於予與何誅'。

Zaiwo was [still] sleeping during the daytime. The Master said, 'Rotten wood cannot be carved and the wall of dung cannot be trowelled. As for Zaiwo, what is the point in reprimanding him?'

In interpreting this verse, we need to understand the specific context that prompts Confucius to compare Zaiwo to a rotten wood that cannot be carved, and wall of dung that cannot be trowelled. Zaiwo chose to sleep in the daytime when he should have been learning from Confucius, which suggests that he was slothful and not interested in working hard to become a *junzi*. In explaining this verse, Chinese commentator Huang Kan notes that 'Confucius' purpose in invoking these metaphors is to tell Zai Wo that if he is the kind of person who sleeps during the daytime then it is impossible to teach him anything' (cited in Slingerland, 2003, p. 43). It is not just this isolated act of sleeping in the daytime that prompts Confucius to pass a seemingly harsh judgement on him. Zaiwo also complained that the three-year mourning period on the death of one's parents was too long (17.21). Confucius concludes from Zaiwo's response that the latter is not-*ren* (不仁 *buren*) because of his lack of filial piety and love towards his parents. But choosing to sleep in the daytime instead of learning from Confucius, and not seeing the need for three years of mourning are not 'moral limitations' that *cannot be overcome*, as claimed by Bell. These shortcomings are not in-born and *can* be corrected if Zaiwo chooses to. Arguing that some people have insurmountable moral limitations contradicts Confucius' belief that *ren* – the mark of a *junzi* – is meant for and lies within everyone (15.35, 12.1, 7.30).

Bell also uses 8.9 to argue that Confucius believes that the common people have intellectual limitations:

8.9 子曰：'民可使由之，不可使知之。'

The Master said, 'The common people can be made to follow [it] but cannot be made to *zhi* [it].'

I have deliberately left the word *zhi* un-translated as it is ambiguous. Some interpret it to refer to one's intellectual ability: Lau and Slingerland translate *zhi* as 'understand' while Yang translates it as 'know' (知道 *zhidao*'). But others such as Ames and Rosemont translate *zhi* as 'realizing' or putting into practice what one knows (see the chapter on *ren* for the discussion on *zhi*). Besides disagreements over the meaning of *zhi*, commentators are also divided on the meaning of 'it'. Commentator Zhang Ping, for example, argues that the first instance of 'it' refers to rule by virtue and the second instance to rule by punishment. Hence he interprets the verse to mean that the common people can be made to follow rule by virtue since 'everyone gets to fulfil their own nature, and everything in the world is put to use without it'; but the common people cannot be allowed to understand rule by punishment since once they 'become aware of these preventive sanctions, they will simply devise more clever ways of being bad (to evade the sanctions)' (cited in Slingerland, 2003, p. 81). Therefore it is not clear, *pace* Bell, that Confucius 'suggests that common people have intellectual limitations' from 8.9 (Bell, 2008, p. 167).

Even if Confucius really believes that the common people are intellectually limited from 8.9, this only shows that everyone has different cognitive abilities. It does not follow from this verse that the common people cannot be *junzi because of* their intellectual limitations. Although a minimal level of cognitive ability (especially in literacy and learning skills) is needed for one to learn the Zhou *li* based on the 'six arts', these skills can be acquired, to differing extents, with the help of a teacher who tailors her teaching to suit the needs of the learner. This is what Confucius means by a teacher who teaches without discrimination (15.39) and practises customised teaching (11.22). It should also be pointed out that a *junzi* is not just an academic scholar; Confucius cautions us against being a petty person *ru* instead of a *junzi ru* (6.13). The former is a specialist who is well versed in traditional rituals and Zhou texts but remains deficient in one's observance of *li*. Beyond intellectual ability, a *junzi* is one who possesses *ren* (4.5), cherishes virtue (4.11), loves learning (1.14), helps others to achieve their goals (6.30), is filial (8.2), shows respect towards her elders (1.2), cultivates herself (14.42) and so on (see chapter on *junzi* for details). All these are personal values and attitudes that may be acquired, to varying degrees of success, if the person is willing to learn and put in hard work to cultivate them.

Finally, Bell also cites 7.8 to support his claim that Confucius does not believe that everybody can become a *junzi*:

7.8 子曰: '不憤不啓, 不悱不發。舉一隅不以三隅反, 則不復也。'

The Master said, 'I do not enlighten a person who is not striving [to understand]; I do not provide [the words to a person] who is not already struggling to speak. If I have raised one [corner] and the person does not come back with the other three [corners], I will not [teach that person] again.'

The content of 7.8 is about Confucius' expectation for his student to have the right attitude and motivation to learn – something that is within the control of every learner. When read in conjunction with 5.10, 7.8 reinforces Confucius' point that everyone *can become* a *junzi*. This claim about everyone's potential to become a *junzi* is different from the claim that everyone *will become* a *junzi*. That not everyone will ultimately succeed in becoming a *junzi* is due to varying aspirations (Zaiwo is an example of one who lacks such an aspiration), opportunities (the common people during Confucius' time were mostly full-time farmers and therefore unlikely to devote much time to studying), character traits and motivations among people. Far from being elitist, Confucius' point is that everyone should aspire to and is capable of becoming a *junzi*. This is what Yu Dan means when she avers that the aspiration of becoming a *junzi* is lofty yet not unattainable by anyone. Besides not promoting elitism through the concept of *junzi*, Confucius also does not advocate the suppression of one's individuality, autonomy and independent thinking. I have already explained in the chapter on *junzi* that such a person possesses personal autonomy, critical reflection and creativity.

If there is any major flaw in Confucius' work, I think it is that Confucius is too optimistic about the transformative power of rule by virtue through the observance of *li* and too critical of the effect of rule by law. I agree with Lai (1995) that 'Confucius' idealism – not unlike that of Plato – [is] in thinking that there could be a philosopher-king, or *chun tzu* [*junzi*], who was a paradigm of virtue and moral responsibility and who could, through his moral achievements, influence the ruled majority' (p. 263). In the real world of flawed human beings, limited resources and cutthroat competition, a good balance of the rule by law and virtue is needed to bring about harmony. It is encouraging to note that such a blend, however incipient, has already been implemented in some East Asian societies. Commenting on constitutionally established democratic governments such as Japan and Korea, Frederick (2002) observes that the 'core Confucian ideas have already been modified to blend the rule of law with the rule of man' and that there is 'good evidence that Confucian bureaucracy and democratic self-government are not only compatible with economic growth, but they may also be a powerful mix of economic, bureaucratic, and democratic ideas' (pp. 624–5, also see Fukuyama, 1995a, b).

Confucius' view on filial piety

A third criticism of Confucius' thought is the primacy he places on *xiao* (filial piety) that prompts him to maintain that a child should cover up for his father's wrongdoing of stealing (13.18). Lai (1995) cautions that the 'example quoted above of concealing wrongdoings, if extended to the sphere of the larger community setting, could lead easily to an unprincipled, subjectively constructed, chaotic community – if that could be termed a community at all – infused with authoritarianism and subjection' (p. 265). Such an act appears to condone parental authoritarianism and threatens to hamper a child's development of autonomy and agency. Some people also maintain that the emphasis on filial piety, by demanding obedience, conformity and stability, inhibits original thinking and is incompatible with modernity (e.g. see Kim, 2005a; Tamney & Chiang, 2002; Ng, 2009).

However, it is questionable that Confucius would encourage everyone to be filial by covering up for one's father's wrongdoing of stealing (or other crimes). A world where individuals think nothing of concealing the transgressions of their parents at the expense of the interests of other members in the community contradicts Confucius' vision of *ren* as loving others. It is also incompatible with other Confucian virtues such as *shu* (empathy and reciprocity) and *zhi* (wisdom) where the focus is on being sensitive to the needs of others, seeking mutual cooperation, and helping others to realize their goals. I have already argued in the chapter on *ren* that 13.18 should be interpreted as Confucius underscoring filial piety as the root of *ren*. He is anxious to preserve the parent–children bond, as the absence of this will threaten the further cultivation of *ren*. This does not mean that Confucius condones all parental transgressions and expects the children's complicity in parental wrongdoing. Elsewhere, Confucius advises children to remonstrate with their parents gently and respectfully for their wrongdoings (4.18).[6]

As for the charge that filial piety fosters obedience, conformity and stability at the expense of original thinking, I agree that Confucius treasures stability and conformity through promoting filial piety in the family and performing one's roles in society. But it does not follow from here that the self is necessarily obliterated or that self-interest should always be subsumed under group interest. Confucius teaches that the development of the self goes hand in hand with the well-being of others. I have argued that a core Confucian teaching is that it is in everyone's self-interest to attain the Confucian ideal of a *junzi* (Tan, 2012a, b). However, becoming a *junzi* does not entail or imply a version of liberal individualism where the self stands apart from, or over and against, the community or society. Rather, the Confucian individual is socially embedded in relationships that constitute and contribute to the development of the self.

Prospects for Confucius' work

It is appropriate, in our closing section, to return to the issues raised at the start of the book regarding some misconceptions in the current literature on Confucius' education.

Confucius, teaching and learning

First, it should be clear by now that Confucius' vision of education is not about textual transmission, rote-memorization and didactic teaching.

Instead, Confucius champions a broad-based education with active and student-centred learning that is characterized by critical reflection and constant application of what one has learned. Far from being authoritarian, Confucius encourages and demonstrates a close personal relationship between the teacher and students based on mutual trust, love and respect. Elstein (2009) dispels the myth that Confucius is an absolute authority figure in the *Analects*:

> One reason that the master is not an absolute authority figure in the *Analects* is that he is not infallible. Later hagiography grew around Kongzi [Confucius] and depicted him as a perfect sage who was never mistaken, but he presents a more human and less idealised figure in the *Analects*. He knows more than his students, but that does not mean he has complete or perfect knowledge. Since his own grasp of the Way is imperfect, this gives his students room to dispute with him and offer different understandings, something Kongzi allows and even encourages. There is not an absolute distinction drawn where the master is an authority figure and the student submits to his authority. Kongzi treats his students as near-equals more than as subordinates. A better understanding of the master-student relationship in the *Analects* will show that there is not an unbridgeable gap between Kongzi and his students: Kongzi can learn from them as well as they from him. (p. 144)

An active and student-centred form of teaching does not, however, mean that Confucius rejects knowledge transmission and memorization. After all, one needs to learn and commit to memory the grammar rules, poems and historical facts when learning the 'six arts'. We have also noted that Confucius advocates *si* (thinking) to be based on a firm foundation of learning. In other words, critical reflection and other forms of higher-order thinking are efficacious only if one has acquired sufficient content knowledge. What Confucius does *not* recommend, rather, are passive learning and rote-memorization as these approaches will not enable a student to take ownership for her own learning, engage in reflective and critical thinking, and consciously apply the lessons learned in her life. Confucius' educational enterprise of living one's life based on *ren* values, attitudes, and behaviours entails that understanding and appropriating what one has memorized are essential.

Knowing Confucius' emphasis on active learning and higher-order thinking enables us to guard against stereotyping Confucian education and students in Confucian Heritage Cultures (CHC). Ryan and Louie (2007), in their analysis of the 'Confucian-Western' dichotomy, caution against viewing terms such as critical thinking, deep learning, lifelong and life-wide learning as the outcomes of 'Western' education, and assuming that students from Confucian Heritage Cultures are passive, dependent, surface/rote learners, prone to plagiarism and lacking critical thinking. The marks of Confucius' teachings – memorization with understanding, and thinking built upon a firm knowledge base – may account for the academic success of East Asian students in international assessments. For example, in the 2009 Programme for International Student Assessment organized by the Organization for Economic Co-operation and Development (OECD), the top four performers were all Confucian Heritage Cultures (Shanghai, Korea, Hong Kong and Singapore) with Finland being the only exception. I have elsewhere argued that Shanghai's impressive achievement in PISA refutes the perception that Chinese students are rote learners lacking understanding (Tan, 2012c, 2013). Instead, Shanghai's teachers are adept at providing a solid foundational knowledge base for their students, as well as developing advanced and independent thinking in their students. Shi (2006), in her empirical study of Mainland Chinese students, also reports that they are active learners who combine an exam-centric approach to learning with an interactive relationship with their teachers. Such a teaching approach is strikingly similar to what Confucius promotes, models and practises for his students.[7]

Confucius, 'moral education' and metaphysics

With reference to the popular perception of Confucius as (just) a moral teacher, I have argued through a textual study of the *Analects* that Confucius' work is not just about 'moral education' or the cultivation of 'moral values'. Of course, Confucius' teachings encompass ethical values, but there is so much more to be gleaned from his teachings. Rather than ethical or moral teaching, it is more accurate to describe his work as *spiritual-ethical-aesthetic teachings* that are concerned with the human existence, condition and vision. That is why Confucius does not just discuss and prescribe ethically right and wrong behaviour, but extends his teachings to spiritual concepts such as *tian* (天 heaven), *dao* (道 Way) and *he* (和 harmony). Confucius' teachings have significant implications not just for moral education but also for all areas of human life, such as politics, aesthetics, sports and religion (see my Confucian framework for twenty-first-century education for details).

A related point is that Confucius' education is not just or predominantly about effective teaching methods, learning strategies, school management and business ethics. Instead, beneath the normative behaviours and corresponding values and attitudes lies Confucius' vision to broaden the Way (*dao*) in order to fulfil the mandate of heaven. For Confucius, spirituality is about going beyond the mundane and temporal to knowing one's place in the universe, and achieving harmony with oneself, other people and the world. Tu (1968) posits that it is 'completely unjustified' to deny the spiritual dimension of Confucianism as it 'performs the comparable functions of an ethico-religious system in Chinese society' (p. 16). It is not surprising that the followers of Confucius, notably the neo-Confucians, later modified and expanded on Confucius' metaphysical teachings in ancient China.

Conclusion

Confucius' work has come a long way since its genesis in the Shandong province in the fifth century BCE. His philosophy has contributed towards the progress of human civilization beyond the shores of China. Neville (2000), in his book interestingly entitled *Boston Confucianism*, maintains that Confucius' teachings are particularly pertinent for the modern world, especially in promoting a multi-cultural philosophy. Indeed, we live in a globalized world where people are more connected than ever before but remain deeply divided along religious, political, social, economic and cultural lines. In this regard, Confucius' work – with its accent on shared humanity and loving others – should be read and put into practice not only in Shangdong and Boston, but also in the rest of the world.

Notes

Chapter 7

1 OECD (2005)'s definition of 'competency' is as follows: 'A competence is more than just knowledge or skills. It involves the ability to meet complex demands, by drawing on and mobilizing psychosocial resources (including skills and attitudes) in a particular context. For example, the ability to communicate effectively is a competence that may draw on an individual's knowledge of language, practical IT skills and attitudes towards those with whom he or she is communicating' (p. 4). As noted in the text, this definition is identical to Rychen and Hersch (2003)'s definition of 'competence'.
2 The *P21 framework* defines ICT as 'Information, Communications and Technology' although ICT is more commonly known as 'Information and Communication Technology' in popular discourses.
3 It may be argued that given that OECD's remit is to promote economic growth, its human capital agenda in education and the economic rationale for its skills strategy simply reflect the purposes of the organization. It is therefore unfair to fault OECD for not emphasizing moral or ethical values. While I agree that the mission of OECD is primarily economic, I also think that economic progress and success *cannot* be pursued without regard for moral values and consideration. Furthermore, OECD itself acknowledges that values are intricately linked to economic considerations: 'All OECD societies agree on the importance of democratic values and achieving sustainable development. These values imply both that individuals should be able to achieve their potential and that they should respect others and contribute to producing an equitable society' (2005, p. 7).
4 Chan (1984) applies Gadamer's hermeneutics to Confucius' teachings by highlighting the role of tradition: 'It is in this sense that the notion of tradition is to be understood in Gadamer (1990)'s hermeneutics. Tradition shapes and "informs" our being and understanding; it is manifested concretely in and through our "prejudices." Tradition serves to provide a horizon from which we may view the world' (p. 434). For a good discussion on the concept of a 'Confucian tradition', see Cua (1992).
5 Another critique of the current frameworks is whether there is a sufficiently strong integrative framework among the various skills. For example, in the *P21 framework*, the three domains of 'Learning and Innovation Skills', 'Information, Media and Technology Skills' and 'Life and Career Skills'

come across as discrete and separate. Although the document states that 'the Partnership views all the components as fully interconnected in the process of 21st century teaching and learning', it is unclear how the various skills are interconnected (Partnership for 21st Century Skills, 2009b, p. 1). For instance, how is 'media literacy' (listed under 'Information, Media and Technology Skills') linked to 'work positively and ethically' (listed under 'Life and Career Skills')? How can one use critical thinking and problem solving (under 'Learning and Innovation Skills') to 'act responsibly with the interests of the larger community in mind' (under 'Life and Career Skills') (Partnership for 21st Century Skills, 2009b, p. 7)? Without a cogent explanation of the connections among the various skills, the various domains of the framework appear disjointed from one another. This may in turn encourage educators to teach and promote these skills as stand-alone abilities rather than harmonized components across the curriculum.

6 Tweed and Lehman (2002) maintain that 'Confucius had a pragmatic orientation to learning; the idea of learning merely for the sake of learning was foreign to him' and that '[a]n acceptable goal of learning, in addition to personal reform, is to competently conduct oneself within a civil service job (13:5), a role Confucius viewed as important for reforming society' (p. 92). However, I disagree with them as Confucius praises the ancient scholars who 'learn for their own sake' (14.24) and extol the virtue of the love for and joy of learning (8.13, 6.20). Tweed and Lehman cite 13.5, but the context of that verse is not about the need to learn for the sake of civil service job, but about the need to put into practice what one has memorized from the *Songs*.

7 Park (2006) posits that Confucius 'possessed a rather holistic and dynamic view of knowledge and learning, in which the different dimensions of individual, social learning, cognitive and practical learning, universal as well as situated learning, etc. are considered' (p. 231). Also stressing the integration of theory and practice, Kim (2004) argues that Confucius' notion of truth offers a more integrated model than the emphasis on truth as corresponding to reality; the latter view is dominant in Anglophone societies. He explains as follows: 'The concept of truth is understood differently between the Western and the Confucian world. In the West, truth is knowledge of reality, basically representations of the world. In the Confucian cultures, truth is performative and participatory. Confucian "truth" is knowledge about the humanistic way, how to live as a person in an interdependent community. The Confucian sense of truth as knowing to live to become a harmonious, integrated person within a community is contrasted with the Western notion of truth as attaining corresponding knowledge of reality.... Compared to correspondence and coherence notions of truth, the notions of "appropriateness or fitness" and "harmony" are emphasised as truth notions in Confucian cultures. What is important in truth notions, for Confucian cultures, is learning to act appropriately and to live harmoniously with others in the community' (p. 118, also see Hall & Ames, 1998).

8 It is evident that Confucius propagates taking an active interest in political affairs. But this does not mean that he believes that the *only* worthy occupation for everyone is public office, or that the *only* purpose of studying is for the sake of political involvement. As noted by Meng (2005), 'Confucius was indeed very concerned about politics, very concerned about society, with strong practical concerns. Furthermore, joining politics was the main employment for someone who pursued studying in ancient society. This is unlike the current situation where there is a variety of occupations and avenues for one to attain life's value. But from Confucius' perspective, joining politics is an important avenue but not the only one, and one should not study for the sake of becoming an official' (pp. 143–4).

9 Sim (2010) rightly argues that Confucius' concept of appropriateness (*yi*) implies certain civil and political rights: '[O]n account of Confucius' emphasis on appropriateness (*yi*) in actions, which actions cannot be achieved without liberty and security, we can imagine his support for the first generation civil and political rights. The right to life, security and liberty are essential not only for acting fairly so that one does not unfairly profit oneself in material goods, honour, power or safety, but also for the other conditions on which Confucius insists for morality, namely, acting with *li*, proper intention, proper respect (*xiao*), and genuine self-investment' (pp. 206–7).

10 Confucius' teaching on achieving *ren* by observing *li* for political leaders could help to address the current problem in many countries, where people increasingly have little trust and respect for government. As argued by Frederick (2002): 'There is widespread evidence of a sharp decline in trust of government officials and a diminished respect for governmental institutions (Nye, Zalikow & King, 1997). The limits of governmental capacity to manage complex social problems by laws and regulations are now apparent. As a consequence, we see the stirrings of the civil society movement and the yearning for community. We witness the relentless calls for a higher morality among our leaders. Western leaders would do well to consider the public morality of the Confucianist good official practicing moral conventions so as to earn the trust and respect of all the people' (p. 625).

11 The concepts of 'religiously tethered' and 'religiously untethered' are borrowed from Alexander and McLaughlin (2003). I have elsewhere used these two terms to describe two types of spiritual ideals (Tan & Wong, 2012). Accordingly, a religiously tethered spiritual ideal is linked to or housed within the tradition of a religious faith. It 'takes its shape and structure from various aspects of religion with which it is associated and that make it possible for us to identify criteria for spiritual development' (Alexander & McLaughlin, 2003, 359). Examples of such spiritual ideals are divinity, prayer and heaven. A religiously untethered spiritual ideal, on the other hand, is concerned with beliefs and practices that are disconnected from religion. This form of spirituality is not associated with any named supernatural power, institutionalized doctrines, or religious

affiliations, and tends to be unstructured, less specific, more open-ended and diffused. Examples are self-knowledge, personal cultivation and the quest for beauty.

12 I share Slingerland (2001)'s view that Confucian training allows room for self-criticism: 'Although the training through which virtues are acquired proceeds according to a general set of rules or principles, the actual decisions made by a person with fully virtuous dispositions are both more flexible and more authoritative than the rules themselves. Thus, once a practice has been mastered, in the sense that the requisite virtues have been fully developed, this mastery brings with it a certain independence from the rules that constitute the practice: *the master is able to reflect upon the rules and may even choose to transgress or revise them* if, in her best judgment, this is what is required to realise the good or goods specific to that practice. Practice mastery thus brings with it a type of transcendence: *the freedom to evaluate, criticise and seek to reform the practice tradition itself* (pp. 102–3, italics added). Characterizing Confucius' approach as a 'critical appropriation of tradition', Chan (2000) adds that 'the sayings of Confucius reflect an essentially "conservative" orientation, finding in tradition a reservoir of insight and truth', coupled with 'a critical dimension to it in that ethical reflection and self-cultivation would enable the individual to challenge particular claims of tradition' (p. 245). Jones and Culliney (1998) also highlight what they call the 'inherent potential for growth' in *li*: 'In Confucius's thought there is an awareness that *li* has an organic aspect, that is, it has the inherent potential for growth or diminution over time. The structure, sustainability, and orderly flow of information within the system could and would change. Confucius suggests that observance and affirmation of this orderly flow was crucial to the preservation of society. If the social system's *li* did not respond to the changing needs of society, stability would be lost. Once stability was lost, society's fragile fabric would come one step closer to losing its pattern of order.... Confucius thus allowed for variation in *li* over time, but this variance had to be in harmony with the emergent order of the system' (p. 399).

13 A point of clarification on the sub-topic of 'Social and Cross-Cultural Sensitivity': the original sub-topic in the *P21 framework* is 'Social and Cross-Cultural Skills' but I have replaced the word 'skills' with 'sensitivity' to show how it is not just about abilities but an integration of one's values, attitudes and behaviours.

14 Kim (2004) draws our attention to the communal role of *li*: '"Ritual practice" or "propriety" [*li*] is not composed simply of given standards or rules of action but has a creative dimension. Even though rituals inform the participants of what proper actions are, it is the participants who actually appropriate the rituals through performing them. When performing rituals, participants reformulate rituals to accommodate uniqueness and

quality of the participants: the participants personalise the rituals. Rituals, on the one hand, inform the participants of the shared set of values. On the other hand, rituals offer persons the opportunity to contribute novel meaning to the community and thereby to be integrated in a way enriching to the community' (p. 119).

15 Commenting on the primacy of the self in Confucius' conception, Fingarette (1979) explains: 'We have the concept of the self as a self-observing and self-regulating individual, a self sharply distinct from Others, a self with interests that may in fact conflict with those of Others but that ought ideally to be brought into accord with or even yield to the interests of Others. From this self there arises a kind of directed dynamism-wanting, willing-that characteristically is what mediates the orientation of the self and the actual conduct of the self' (p. 133). Stressing the centrality of the individual, Hall and Ames (1987) assert that a person becomes an 'author' in his creative disposition, in the sense that he becomes 'an "authority" in his deference to and embodiment of existing meanings' in his interaction with heaven (p. 244).

Chapter 8

1 In this sense, Confucius is like Aristotle in overlooking the potential of women. In explaining the apparently derogatory view of Aristotle of women, Gier (2001) asserts that 'Aristotle's conception of woman as an ill-formed and irrational man was almost universally accepted' during his time (p. 282).

2 By citing Sim, I am not implying that she holds that Confucius or Confucianism rejects egalitarian and meritocratic principles, promotes or supports authoritarian governments and suppresses individuality and democratic participation. My focus is strictly on her view that Confucius does not think that everyone is capable of becoming fully virtuous.

3 For a good discussion of Confucianism and democracy, see Bell (1998b); Tan (2004); Collins (2008); Tao (2010); Tan (2010); on Confucianism and a civil society, see Tan (2003); on Confucianism and human rights, see Ames (1997); Chan (1999); Li (1999); Nuyen (2002); Sim (2004); Williams (2006); Chen (2011), pp. 21–34; on Confucianism and equality and global justice, see Nuyen (2001), Nuyen (2003).

4 By supporting Yu Dan's interpretation that Confucius believes that everyone is capable of becoming a *junzi*, I am not thereby claiming that all her interpretations of Confucius' teachings are accurate. For a critique of her exposition of Confucius' views, see 'Yu Dan: defender of traditional culture, force for harmony' (www.danwei.org/scholarship_and_education/yu_dan_defender_of_traditional.php)

5 The English translation is done by me. The original version (in simplified Chinese script) is as follows: '由此可见,"君子"这个《论语》中出现最多的字眼,他的道理永远是朴素的,是温暖的,是和谐的,是每一个人可以从当下做的;而那个梦想,那个目标,既是高远的,又不是遥不可及,它其实就存在于当下,也存在于我们每一个人的内心。从这个意义上喃,我们每一个人都可以成为一个真君子。' (Yu, 2007, p. 74).
6 It should be noted that loyalty to one's close siblings and parents is not just a Confucian idea. Plato (1999) for example, discusses it in his work *Euthyphro*; contemporary political philosopher Michael Sandel (2009) defends it through what he calls the 'obligation of solidarity' to one's family members. I thank Kim-chong Chong for pointing this out to me.
7 The East Asian success in international assessment reminds us of what is known in the academic circle as 'the paradox of the Chinese learner'. John B. Biggs explains the paradox: 'westerners saw Chinese students as rote learning massive amounts of information in fierce exam-dominated classrooms – yet in international comparisons, students in the Confucian heritage classrooms greatly outperformed western students learning in "progressive" western classrooms' (as cited in Chan & Rao, 2009, p. x). This paradox is resolved when we note that memorization and repeated practice for the Chinese students do not necessarily mean that they are learning by rote or that they lack deep understanding of the subject matter. On the contrary, empirical research has shown that memorization and repetition are part of a strategy for the Chinese students to achieve deep understanding, logical thinking and strong application. For further readings on the paradox of the Chinese learner, see Biggs (1996); Biggs and Watkins (1996); Kember (2000); Chan and Rao (2009); Huang and Leung (2004); Marton, Wen and Wong (2005); Jin and Cortazzi (2006); and Morrison (2006).

References

Aguinis, H., & Roth, H. A. (2005). Teaching in China: Culture-based challenges. In I. Alon & J. R. MaIntyre (Eds), *Business and management education in China: transition, pedagogy, and training* (pp. 141–64). Hakensack, NJ: World Scientific Publishing Co. Ltd.

Ahn, H. (2005). *Junzi* as a tragic person: A self psychological interpretation of the *Analects. Pastoral Psychology, 57*, 101–13.

Alexander, H., & McLaughlin, T. H. (2003). Education in religion and spirituality. In N. Blake, P. Smeyers, R. Smith, & P. Standish (Eds), *The Blackwell guide to the philosophy of education* (pp. 356–73). Malden, MA: Blackwell.

Ames, R. (1997). Continuing the conversation on Chinese human rights. *Ethics & International Affairs, 11*, 177–205.

Ames, T. R., & Rosemont, Jr, H., Trans. (1998). *The Analects of Confucius: a philosophical translation*. New York: Ballantine Books.

Ananiadou, K., & Claro, M. (2009). *21st century skills and competences for new millennium learners in OECD countries.* Organisation for Economic Cooperation and Development. Available online at: http://search.oecd.org/officialdocuments/publicdisplaydocumentpdf/?cote=EDU/WKP%282009%2920&docLanguage=En, accessed 22 Oct. 2012.

Aoki, K. (2008). Confucius vs. Socrates: The impact of educational traditions of East and West in a global age. *The International Journal of Learning, 14*(11), 35–40.

Arthur, J. (1998). Communitarianism: What are implications for education? *Educational Studies, 24*(3), 353–68.

Avgerou, C., & McGrath, K. (2007). Power, rationality, and the art of living through socio-technical change. *MIS Quarterly, 31*(2), 295–315.

Bai, B. G. 白炳贵 (2011). 从孔子终身教育思想到成人教育的可持续性 Cong Kongzi zhongshen jiaoyu sixiang dao chengren jiaoyu de kechixuxing [From Confucius' lifelong education to the sustainability of adult education] 黑龙江高教研究 *Heilongjiang gaojiao yanjiu, 2*(202), 165–7.

Barnett, R. (1994). *The limits of competence: knowledge, higher education and society*. London: Open University Press.

Bell, D. A. (2008a). *China's new Confucianism: politics and everyday life in a changing society*. Princeton: Princeton University Press.
— (2010). *Reconciling socialism and Confucianism? Reviving tradition in China*. Dissent, winter, 91–9.
Bell. D. A., Ed. (2008b). *Confucian political ethics*. Princeton: Princeton University Press.
Bi, L., Ehrich, J., & Ehrich, L. C. (2012). Confucius as transformational leader: Lessons for ESL leadership. *International Journal of Educational Management*, 26(4), 391–402.
Biggs, J. (1996). Western misperceptions of the Confucian-heritage learning culture. In D. A. Watkins & J. B. Biggs (Eds), *Teaching the Chinese learner: psychological and pedagogical perspectives* (pp. 46–7). Hong Kong/Melbourne: Comparative Education Research Centre, The University of Hong Kong/Australian Council for Educational Research.
Biggs, J., & Watkins, D. (1996). The Chinese learner in retrospect. In D. A. Watkins & J. B. Biggs (Eds), *Teaching the Chinese learner: psychological and pedagogical perspectives* (pp. 269–85). Hong Kong/Melbourne: Comparative Education Research Centre, The University of Hong Kong/Australian Council for Educational Research.
Binkley, M., Erstad, O., Herman, J., Raizen, S., Ripley, M., & Rumble, M. (2010). *Defining 21st century skills [Draft White Paper 1]. Assessment and teaching of 21st century skills project*. Available online at: http://atc21s.org/index.php/resources/white-papers/#item1, accessed 12 Feb. 2010.
Brindley, E. (2009). 'Why use an ox-cleaver to carve a chicken?' The sociology of the *junzi* ideal in the *Lunyu*. *Philosophy East and West*, 59(1) (Jan.), 47–70.
— (2011). Moral autonomy and individual sources of authority in the *Analects*. *Journal of Chinese Philosophy*, 38(2), 257–73.
Brooks, B. E., & Brooks, T. A. (1998). *The original Analects: sayings of Confucius and his successors*. New York: Columbia University Press.
Cai, R. H. 蔡仁厚 (1996). 论语人物论 *Lunyu renwu lun* [A discussion of the characters in the *Analects*]. 台北：台湾商务印书馆股份有限公司 Taipei: Taiwan shangwu yinshuguan gufen youxian gongsi.
Cai, S. S. 蔡尚思 (1982). 孔子思想体系 *Kongzi sixiang tixi* [Confucius' thoughts]. 上海：上海人民出版社 Shanghai: Renmin chubanshe.
Cai, Y. 才颖, & Sun, X. Y 孙小晕 (2011). 基于历史真实与艺术真实对立统一的视阈看 '孔子' Jiyu lishi zhenshi yu yishu zhenshi duili tongyi de shiyin kan 'Kongzi' [Viewing 'Confucius' from the perspective of the opposition and unity of historical truth and artistic truth]. 影视画外音当代文坛 *Yingshi hua waiyin dangdai wentan*, 1, 187–90.
Cai, Z. (1999). In quest of harmony: Plato and Confucius on poetry. *Philosophy East and West*, 49(3), 317–45.

Chan, A. (1984). Philosophical hermeneutics and the *Analects*: The paradigm of 'Tradition'. *Philosophy East and West*, *34*(4), 421–36.
— (2000). Confucian ethics and the critique of ideology. *Asian Philosophy*, *10*(3), 245–61.
Chan, C. K. K., & Rao, N. (2009). The paradoxes revisited: The Chinese learner in changing educational contexts. In D. A. Watkins & J. B. Biggs (Eds), *Teaching the Chinese learner: psychological and pedagogical perspectives* (pp. 315–49). Hong Kong/Melbourne: Comparative Education Research Centre, The University of Hong Kong/Australian Council for Educational Research.
Chan, G. K. Y. (2008). The relevance and value of Confucianism in contemporary business ethics. *Journal of Business Ethics*, *77*, 347–60.
Chan, J. (1998). Confucian attitudes towards ethical pluralism. In D. A. Bell (Ed.), *Confucian political ethics* (pp. 113–38). Princeton: Princeton University Press.
— (1999). A Confucian perspective on human rights for contemporary China. In J. R. Bauer & D. A. Bell (Eds), *The East Asian challenge for human rights*. Cambridge: Cambridge University Press, pp. 212–37.
— (2002). Moral autonomy, civil liberties, and confucianism. *Philosophy East and West*, *52*(3), 281–310.
Chan, S. Y. (1998). Gender and relationship roles in the Analects and the Mencius. In D. A. Bell (Ed.), *Confucian political ethics* (pp. 147–74). Princeton: Princeton University Press.
Chang, H. 常桦 (2012). 东方沉思录:半部论语开启人生 *Dongfang chensilu: Banbu 'Lunyu' kaiqi rensheng* [Oriental meditation: Half the Analects to open human life]. 台北：人类智库数位科技股份有限公司 Taibei: Renlei zhiku shuwei keji gufen youxian gongsi.
Chen, L. 陈来 (2011). 孔夫子与现代世界 *Kongfuzi yu xiandai shijie* [Confucius and the modern world]. 北京：北京大学出版社 Beijing: Beijing daxue chubanshe.
Chen, S. P. 陈淑萍, & Huang, Z. M. 黄兆铭 (2005). 谈'有教无类'和'因材施教' – 孔子教育思想在实践中的运用 Tan 'youjiao wulei' he 'yincai shijiao' – Kongzi jiaoyu sixiang zai shijianzhong de yunyong [Discuss 'customised teaching' and 'teach without discrimination' – practical application of Confucius' educational thought]'. *Journal of Jiangxi Vocational and Technical College of Electricity*, *18*(1), 50–2.
Chen, W. 陈伟, & Wang, M. 王敏 (2011). 孔子教育本质上是职业教育 *Kongzi jiaoyu benzhishang shi zhiyejiaoyu* [The nature of Confucius' education is vocational education] 长春理工大学学报（社会科学版） *Changchun ligong daxue xuebao (shehui kexueban)*, *24*(5), 112–13.
Cheng, C.-Y. (1972). On *yi* as a universal principle of specific application in Confucian morality. *Philosophy East and West*, *22*(3), 269–80.
— (2000). Confucian onto-hermeneutics: Morality and ontology. *Journal of Chinese Philosophy*, *27*(1), 33–68.

Chin, A. (2007). *The authentic Confucius: a life of thought and politics*. New York: Scribner.
Chong, K.-C. (1998). The aesthetic moral personality: *Li, yi, wen*, and *chih* in the *Analects. Monumenta Serica, 46*, 69–90.
— (1999). *The Practice of Jen. Philosophy East and West, 49*(3), 298–316.
— (2007). *Early Confucian ethics*. Chicago: Open Court.
Clements, J. (2004). *Confucius: a biography*. Gloucestershire: Sutton Publishing.
Collins, M. (2008). China's Confucius and Western democracy. *Contemporary Review, 290*(1689), 161–72.
Creel, H. G. (1949). *Confucius and the Chinese way*. New York: Harper
Csikszentmihalyi, M. (2002). Confucius and the *Analects* in the Han. In B. W. Van Norden (Ed.), *Confucius and the* Analects*: new essays* (pp. 134–62). Oxford: Oxford University Press.
Cua, A. (1978). *Dimensions of moral creativity: paradigms, principles and ideals* (p. 55). University Park and London: Pennsylvania State University Press.
— (1992). Competence, concern, and the role of paradigmatic individuals (Chün-tzu) in moral education. *Philosophy East and West, 42*(1) (Jan.), 49–68.
— (1992). The idea of Confucian tradition. *The Review of Metaphysics, 45*(4), 803–40.
— (1996). The conceptual framework of Confucian ethical thought. *Journal of Chinese Philosophy, 23* (2), 165.
— (2002). The ethical and the religious dimensions of 'li' (rites). *The Review of Metaphysics, 55*(3), 471–519.
— (2005). *Human nature, ritual, and history: studies in Xunzi and Chinese philosophy*. Washington, DC: Catholic University of America Press.
Cummins, R. E. (1983). Lessons of a master teacher-Confucius. *Educational Leadership, 41*(3), 59–62.
Dahlgaard-Park, S. M. (2006). Learning from east to west and west to east. *The TQM Magazine, 18*(3), 216–37.
Dahlin, B., & Watkins, D. (2000). The role of repetition in the processes of memorising and understanding: A comparison of the views of Western and Chinese secondary school students in Hong Kong. *British Journal of Educational Psychology, 70*, 65–84.
Dawson, R. (1982). *Confucius*. Oxford: Oxford University Press.
De Bary, W. M. T. (1995). The new Confucianism in Beijing. *American Scholar, 64*(2), 175–89.
Dirlik, A. (1995). Confucius in the borderlands: Global capitalism and the reinvention of Confucianism. *Boundary 2, 22*(3), (Fall), 229–73.
Du, W.-M. 杜维明 (2008). 儒教 *Rujiao* [Confucianism]. Chen, J. 陈静, Trans. 上海：上海古籍出版社 Shanghai: Shanghai guji chubanshe.

Elliott, J., & Tsai, C. (2008): What might Confucius have to say about action research?, *Educational Action Research, 16* (4), 569–78.

Elstein, D. (2009). The authority of the master in the *Analects*. *Philosophy East and West, 59*(2), 142–72.

European Parliament (2007). *Key competences for lifelong learning: a European reference framework*. Available online at: http://ec. europa.eu/dgs/education_culture/publ/pdf/ll-learning/keycomp_en.pdf, accessed 18 Jan. 2010.

Fan, M. (24 July 2007). Confucius making a comeback in money-driven modern China. *Washington Post*, A01. Available online at: www.washingtonpost.com/wp-dyn/content/article/2007/07/23/AR2007072301859_pf.html, accessed 12 Aug. 2012.

Feng, Y. L. 冯友兰 (1985). 中国哲学史新编 *Zhongguo zhexueshi xinbian* [New edition of the history of Chinese philosophy], Vol. III. 北京：人民出版社 Beijing: People's Press.

Fernandez, J. A. (2004). The gentleman's code of Confucius: Leadership by values. *Organisational Dynamics, 33*(1), 21–31.

Fingarette, H. (1972). *Confucius – the secular as sacred*. New York: Harper and Row.

— (1979). The problem of the self in the *Analects*. *Philosophy East and West, 29*(2), 129–40.

Fox, R. A. (1997). Confucian and communitarian responses to liberal democracy. *The Review of Politics, 59*(3), 561–92.

Frederickson, H. G. (2002). Confucius and the moral basis of bureaucracy. *Administration & Society, 33*, 610–28.

Fu, C. W. (1978). Fingarette and Munro on early Confucianism: A methodological examination. *Philosophy East and West, 28*(2), 181–98.

Fu, P. R. 傅佩荣 (2002). 孔子新说－在考验中成长 *Kongzi xinshuo – zai kaoyanzhong chengzhang* [New interpretations of Confucius – growth through testing]. 台北：幼狮文化事业股份有限公司 Taibei: Youshi wenhua shiye gufen youxian gongshi.

— 傅佩荣 (2010). 原来孔子这样说 *Yuanlai Kongzi zheyangshuo* [So this is what Confucius says]. 台北：九歌出版社有限公司 Taibei: Jiuge chubanshe youxian gongsi.

— 傅佩荣 (2011a). 我读'论语' *Wodu 'Lunyu'* [I read the *Analects*]. 北京：北京理工大学出版社 Beijing: Beijing ligong daxue chubanshe.

— 傅佩荣 (2011b). 孔门十弟子 *Kongzi shidizi* [Ten disciples of Confucius]. 台北：连经出版事业股份有限公司 Taibei: Lianjing chuban shiye gufen youxian gongsi.

Fu, P. R. 傅佩荣, Guo, Q. Y. 郭齐勇, & Kong, X. L. 孔祥林 (2008). 孔子九响 *Kongzi jiujiang* [Nine talks on Confucius]. 北京：中华书局 Beijing: Zhonghua shuju.

Fukuda, K. (2012). 萌译论语 *Mengyi Lunyu* [Manga *Analects*]. 石玉风 Shi, Y. F., Trans. 台北：三彩文化出版事业有限公司. Taibei: Sancai wenhua chuban shiye youxian gongsi.

Fukuyama, F. (1995a). Confucianism and democracy. *Journal of Democracy*, *6*(2), 20–33.
— (1995b). *Trust: the social virtues and the creation of prosperity*. New York: Free Press.
Gadamer, H.-G. (1990). *Truth and method* (2nd ed.), Ed. and Trans. J. Weinsheimer & D. G. Marshall. New York: Crossroad Publishing Company.
Gao, M. 高敏 (2011). 学孔子当老师的智慧 *Xue Kongzi dang laoshi de zhihui* [Learn to have the wisdom of a teacher like Confucius]. 北京: 中国纺织出版社 Beijing: Zhongguo fangzhi chubanshe.
Gier, N. F. (2001). The Dancing *Ru*: A Confucian aesthetics of virtue. *Philosophy East and West*, *51*(2), 280–305.
Gordon, J., Halsz, G., Krawczyk, M., Leney, T., Michel, A., Pepper, D., Putkiewicz, E., & Wisniewski, W. (2009). *Key competences in Europe. Opening doors for lifelong learners across the school curriculum and teacher education*. Available online at: http://ec.europa.eu/education/more-information/moreinformation139_en.htm, accessed 5 Apr. 2010.
Graham, A. C. (1989). *Disputers of the Tao*. Chicago, IL: Open Court.
Grange, J. (2004). *John Dewey, Confucius and global philosophy*. Albany: State University of New York.
Grant, J. (1999). The incapacitating effects of competence: A critique. *Advances in Health Sciences Education*, *4*(3), 271–7.
Hagen, K. (2010). The propriety of Confucius: A sense-of-ritual. *Asian Philosophy*, *20*(1) (Mar.), 1–25.
Hahm, C. (2004). The ironies of Confucianism. *Journal of Democracy*, *15*(3), 93–107.
Hall, D. L., & Ames, R. T. (1987). *Thinking though Confucius*. Albany: State University of New York.
Han, K., & Scull, W. (2010). Confucian culture in the mainstream classroom: A case study of an Asian American student. *The International Journal of Learning*, *17*(1), 601–16.
Hofstede, G., & Bond, M. H. (1988). The Confucius connection: From cultural roots to economic growth. *Organisational Dynamics*, *16*(4), 5–21.
Huang, R., & Leung, K. S. F. (2004). Cracking the paradox of the Chinese learners: Looking into the mathematics classrooms in Hong Kong and Shanghai. In L. Fan, N.-Y. Wong, J. Cai & S. Li (Eds), *How Chinese learn mathematics: perspectives from the insiders* (pp. 348–81). Singapore: World Scientific Publishing.
Huang, Y. (2011). Can virtue be taught and how? Confucius on the paradox of moral education. *Journal of Moral Education*, *40*(2), 141–59.
Hui, L. (2005). Chinese cultural schema of education: Implications for communication between Chinese students and Australian educators. *Issues in Educational Research*, *15*(1), 17–36.
Hutton, E. L. (2008). Han Feizi's criticism of Confucianism and its implications for virtue ethics. *Journal of Moral Philosophy*, *5*, 423–53.

Ip, P. K. (2009). Is Confucianism good for business ethics in China? *Journal of Business Ethics, 88*, 463–76.

Ivanhoe, Philip J. (1990). Reweaving the 'one thread' of the *Analects*. *Philosophy East and West, 40*(1), 17–33.

— (1991a). Character consequentialism: An early Confucian contribution to contemporary ethical theory. *The Journal of Religious Ethics, 19*(1), 55–70.

— (1991b). Review of *Thinking through Confucius*, by D. L. Hall and R. T. Ames. *Philosophy East and West, 41*(2), 341–54.

— (1993). *Confucian moral self-cultivation*. New York: Peter Lang.

— (2007). The shade of Confucius: Social roles, ethical theory, and the self. In M. Chandler & R. Littlejohn (Eds), *Polishing the Chinese mirror: essays in honor of Henry Rosemont Jr.* (pp. 33–49). New York: Global Scholarly Publications.

Ji, X. S. 季旭昇, Ed. (2010). 孔子家语：中文经典100句 *Kongzi jiayu: zhongwen jingdian 100ju* [The words of Confucius: 100 Classical Chinese sentences]. 台北：商周出版，城邦文化出版 Taipei: Shangzhou chuban, Chengbang wenhua chuban.

Jiang, W. Y. 江文也 (2009). 孔子的乐论 *Kongzi de yuelun* [The music theory of Confucius]. 杨儒实 Yang, R. S., Trans. 台北：国立台湾大学出版社 Taibei: Guoli taiwan daxue chubanshe zhongxin.

Jin, L., & Cortazzi, M. (2006). Changing practices in Chinese cultures of learning. *Learning, Culture and Curriculum, 19*(1), 5–20.

Jones, D., & Culliney, J. (1998). Confucian order at the edge of chaos: The science of complexity and ancient wisdom. *Zygon, 33*(3), 395–404.

Jordon, R., & Powell, S. (1995). Skills without understanding: A critique of a competency-based model of teacher education in relation to special needs. *British Journal of Special Education, 22*(3), 120–4.

Kember, D. (2000). Misconceptions about the learning approaches, motivation and study practices of Asian students. *Higher Education, 40*(1), 99–121.

Kim, H.-K. (2003). Critical thinking, learning and Confucius: A positive assessment. *Journal of Philosophy of Education, 37*(1), 71–87.

— (2005a). Cultural influence on creativity: The relationship between creativity and Confucianism. *Roeper Review, 27*, 186.

— (2005b). Learning from each other: Creativity in East Asian and American education. *Creativity Research Journal, 17*(4), 337–47.

Kim, H. P. (2006). Confucius's aesthetic concept of noble man: Beyond moralism. *Asian Philosophy, 16*(2), 111–21.

Kim, K. H. (2004). An attempt to elucidate notions of lifelong learning: *Analects*-based analysis of Confucius' ideas about learning. *Asia Pacific Education Review, 5*(2), 117–26.

Koh, K., Tan, C., & Ng, P. T. (2012). Creating thinking schools through authentic assessment: The case in Singapore. *Educational Assessment, Evaluation and Accountability, 24* (2), 135–49.

Kohut, H. (1971). *The analysis of the self*. New York: International Universities Press.
Kramers, R. P. (1950). *K' ung tzu chia yu: The school sayings of Confucius*. Leiden: Brill.
Kuang, Y. M. 匡亞明 (1990). 孔子评传 *Kongzi pingzhuan* [A critical biography of Confucius]. 南京: 南京大学出版社 Nanjing: Nanjing daxue chubanshe.
Kyung, H. K. (2009). Appropriating Confucius' conception of lifelong learning: Reconsidering neoliberal perspective. *KEDI Journal of Educational Policy*, 6(2), 141–60.
Lai, Karyn L. (1995). Confucian moral thinking. *Philosophy East and West*, 45(2), 249–72.
— (2006). *Li* in the Analects' training in moral competence and the question of flexibility. *Philosophy East and West*, 56(1), 69–83.
Lau, D. C., Trans. (1979). *Confucius: the Analects*. Harmondsworth, Middlesex: Penguin Books.
Law, N., Pelgrum, W. J., & Plomp, T. (2008). *Pedagogy and ICT use in schools around the world. Findings from the IEA SITES 2006 study*. Hong Kong: Comparative Education Research Centre, The University of Hong Kong, & Dordrecht: Springer.
Legge, J. (1960). *The Chinese classics*, Vol. V. *The Ch'un Ts'ew, with the Tso Chuen*. Hong Kong: Hong Kong Chinese University Press.
Li, B. 李彬 (2010). 孔子教育思想对当代素质教育的启示 *Kongzi jiaoyu sixiang dui dangdai suzhi jiaoyu de qishi* [The implications of Confucius' educational thought for quality-oriented education today]. 新课程研究 *Xinkecheng yanjiu*, 176(Feb.), 15–17.
Li, C. (1994). The confucian concept of *Jen* and the feminist ethics of care: A comparative study. *Hypatia*, 9(1), 70–89.
— (1999). *The Tao encounters the West: explorations in comparative philosophy*. Albany: The State University of New York Press.
— (2002). Revisiting Confucian Jen ethics and feminist care ethics: A reply to Daniel Star and Lijun Yuan. *Hypatia*, 17(1), 130–40.
— (2006). The Confucian ideal of harmony. *Philosophy East and West*, 56(4), 583–603.
— (2007). *Li* as cultural grammar: On the relation between *li* and *ren* in Confucius' Analects. *Philosophy East and West*, 57(3), 311–29.
Li, C., Ed. (2000). *The sage and the second sex: Confucianism, ethics, and gender*. La Salle, IL: Open Court.
Li, J. (2003). The core of Confucian learning. *American Psychologist*, 58, 146–7.
— (2005). Mind or virtue: Western and Chinese beliefs about learning. *Current Directions in Psychological Science*, 14(4), 190–4.
Li, L. (2009–10). Gentlemen and petty men. *Contemporary Chinese Thought*, 41(2), 54–65.

Lin, S. F. 林淑芬, Ed. (2012). 悦读论语十分钟 *Yuedu Lunyu shifenzhong* [Enjoy reading the *Analects* for 10 minutes]. 台北：五南图书出版股份有限公司. Taibei: Wunan tushu chuban gufen youxian gongsi.

Lin, Y. T. 林语堂 (2009). 林语堂中英对照孔子的智慧 *Lin yutang zhongying duizhao kongzi de zhihui* [Lin yutang's Chinese-English edition on the wisdom on Confucius]. 台北：中正书局股份有限公司. Taibei: Zhongzheng shuju gufen youxian gongsi.

Lin, Y. Z. 林义正 (1987). 孔子学说探微 *Kongzi xueshuo tanwei* [Exploration of the doctrine of Confucius]. 台北：东大图书公司印行 Taibei: Dongda tushu gongsi yinxing.

Liu, D. J. 刘殿爵, & Yang, B. J. 杨伯, Trans. (2009). 论语 *Lunyu* [*Confucius: The Analects*]. Chinese-English edition. Taipei: Lianjin chuban.

Liu, S. L. 刘胜良 (2010). 孔子教育管理伦理思想探微 *Kongzi jiaoyu guanli lunli sixiang tanwei* [Exploration of Confucius' thought on educational management] 辽宁工业大学学报（社会科学版） *Liaoning gongye daxue xuebao (Shehui kexueban), 12*(1), 41–4.

Liu, X. X. 刘小霞 (2011). 孔子教育思想对当代中国教育的启示 *Kongzi jiaoyu sixiang dui dangdai zhongguo jiaoyu de qishi* [The implications of Confucius' educational thought for contemporary education in China]. 陕西教育（高教）*Shaanxi Jiaoyu (Gaojiao), 7–8,* 28–9.

Louie, K. (1984). Salvaging Confucian education (1949–1983). *Comparative Education, 20*(1), 27–38.

— (2011). Confucius the chameleon: Dubious envoy for Brand China. *Boundary 2, 38*(1), 77–100.

Low, P. K. C. (2010). Teaching and education: The ways of Confucius. *Educational Research, 1* (12), 681–6.

Loy, H.-C. (2003). *Analects* 13.3 and the doctrine of 'correcting names'. *Monumenta Serica, 51,* 19–36.

Luo, C. L. 骆承烈 (2011). 孔子：至圣先师的思想精华 *Kongzi: Zhisheng xianshi de sixiang jinghua* [Confucius – The essence of the thought of the sage and teacher]. 台北:龙图腾文化 Taipei: Longtuteng wenhua.

Luo, S. (2010). A defence of *ren*-based interpretation of early Confucian ethics. In K. Yu, J. Tao & P. J. Ivanhoe (Eds), *Taking Confucian ethics seriously* (pp. 123–44). Albany: State University of New York Press.

— (2011). Is *yi* more basic than *ren* in the teachings of Confucius? *Journal of Chinese Philosophy, 38*(3), 427–43.

Lü, S. (1982). *Lü Simian's notes for reading histories*, vol. 1. Shanghai: Guji Press.

MacIntyre, A. (1988). *Whose justice? Which rationality?* Notre Dame: University of Notre Dame Press.

Marton, M. A. (2006). The cultural politics of curricular reform in China: A case study of geographical education in Shanghai. *Journal of Contemporary China, 15*(47), 233–54.

Meng, P. Y. 蒙培元 (2005). 蒙培元讲孔子 *Meng peiyuan jiang kongzi* [Meng peiyuan talks about Confucius]. 北京：北京大学出版社 Beijing: Beijing University Press.

Minney, R. (1991). What is spirituality in an educational context? *British Journal of Educational Studies*, *39*(4), 386–97.

Morrison, K. (2006). Paradox lost: Towards a robust test of the Chinese learner. *Education Journal*, *34*(1), 1–30.

Mou, B. (2004). A Reexamination of the structure and content of Confucius' version of the golden rule. *Philosophy East and West*, *54*(2), 218–48.

Na, L. (2012, 7 May). Top 30 Confucius institutes in 2011. *China.org.cn*. Available online at: www.china.org.cn/top10/2012-05/07/content_25252751.htm, accessed 5 Nov. 2012.

National Research Council. (2012). *Education for life and work: developing transferable knowledge and skills in the 21st century*. Available online at: www.nap.edu/catalog.php?record_id=13398, accessed 7 Aug. 2012.

Neville, R. C. (2000). *Boston Confucianism: portable tradition in the late-modern world*. Albany: State University of New York Press.

Ng, R. M. (2009). College and character: What did Confucius teach us about the importance of integrating ethics, character, learning, and education? *Journal of College & Character*, *10*(4), 1–7.

Nonaka, I., & Takeuchi, H. (1995). *The knowledge-creating company*. New York: Oxford University Press.

Nuyen, A. T. (2001). Confucianism and the idea of equality. *Asian Philosophy*, *11*(2), 61–71.

— (2002). Confucianism and the idea of citizenship. *Asian Philosophy*, *12*(2), 127–39.

— (2003). Confucianism, globalisation and the idea of universalism. *Asian Philosophy*, *13*(2/3), 75–86.

Nye, J. S., Jr, Zalikow, P. D., & King, D. C. (1997). *Why people don't trust government*. Cambridge, MA: Harvard University Press.

Nylan, M., & Wilson, T. (2010). *Lives of Confucius*. New York: Doubleday.

Office for Standards in Education [OFSTED] (1994). *Spiritual, moral, social and cultural development*. An OFSTED discussion paper. London: Author.

Organization For Economic Co-Operation and Development [OECD] (1996). *The Knowledge-based economy*. Paris: Author.

— (2005). *The definition and selection of key competencies [Executive Summary]*. Available online at: www.oecd.org/dataoecd/47/61/35070367.pdf, accessed 7 Jan. 2010.

Partnership for 21st Century Skills. (2009a). *Framework for 21st century learning*. Available online at: www.p21.org/documents/P21_Framework.pdf, accessed 21 May 2012.

— (2009b). *P21 framework definitions*. Available online at: www.p21.org/storage/documents/P21_Framework_Definitions.pdf, accessed 21 May 2012.

Peng, H. Q. 彭海芹 (2010). 孔子教育思想中的教师心理素质分析 Kongzi jiaoyu sixiangzhong de jiaoshi xinli suzhi fenxi [An analysis of the teacher's psychological quality in Confucian thought]. 成人教育 *Chengren jiaoyu*, 8(283), 15–16.

Ping, F. 平飞 (2011). 论孔子教育思想对当代素质教育的意义 Lun Kongzi jiaoyu sixiang dui dangdai sushi jiaoyu de yiyi [A discussion of the value of Confucius' educational thought on contemporary quality-oriented education] 南昌航空大学学报版 *Nanchang hangkong daxue xuebao (shehui kexueban)*, 13(1), 91–7.

Powell, W. W., & Snellman, K. (2004) The knowledge economy. *The Annual Review of Sociology*, 30, 199–220.

Prusak, L. (1997). *Knowledge in organisations*. Boston, MA: Butterworth-Heinemann.

Radcliffe, R. J. (1989): Confucius and John Dewey. *Religious Education*, 84(2), 215–31.

Rainey, L. D. (2010). *Confucius and Confucianism: the essentials*. West Sussex: Wiley-Blackwell.

Reid, T. R. (1999). *Confucius lives next door: what living in the East teaches us about living in the West*. New York: Vintage Books.

Roberts, J. (1996). Management education and the limits of technical rationality: The conditions and consequences of management practice. In R. French & C. Grey (Eds), *Rethinking management education* (pp. 54–75). London: Sage Publications.

Robertson, C. J., & Hoffman, J. J. (2000). How different are we? An investigation of Confucian values in the United States. *Journal of Managerial Issues*, 12(1), 34–47.

Romar, E. J. (2002). Virtue is good business: Confucianism as a practical business ethic. *Journal of Business Ethics*, 38(1/2), 119–31.

— (2004). Managerial harmony: The Confucian ethics of Peter F. Drucker. *Journal of Business Ethics*, 51(2), 199–210.

Rosemont Jr, H. (2001). *Rationality and religious experience: the continuing relevance of the world's spiritual traditions*. Chicago, IL: Open Court.

Rowbotham, A. H. (1945). The impact of Confucianism on seventeenth century Europe. *The Far Eastern Quarterly (pre-1986)*, 4(3), 224–32.

Ryan, J., & Louie, K. (2007). False dichotomy? 'Western' and 'Confucian' concepts of scholarship and learning. *Educational Philosophy and Theory*, 39(4), 404–17.

Ryan, T. (2000). The new economy's impact on learning. *The 21st Century Learning Initiative 2000*. Available online at: www.21learn.org/acti/prime%20economics.pdf, accessed 7 February 2005.

Sandel, M. (1981). *Liberalism and the limits of justice*. Cambridge: Cambridge University Press.
Schiller, D. R. (2011). *Confucius: discussions/conversations, or, the Analects (Lunyu)*. Charlton, MA: Sage Virtual Publishers.
Schon, D. A. (1983). *The reflective practitioner: how professionals think in action*. United States: Basic Books.
— (1987). *Educating the reflective practitioner*. San Francisco: Jossey-Bass.
Schultze, U., & Leidner, D. E. (2002). Studying knowledge management in information systems research: Discourses and theoretical assumptions. *MIS Quarterly, 26*(3), 213–42.
Schwartz, B. I. (1985). *The world of thought in Ancient China*. Cambridge: The Belknap Press.
Shandongsheng ruxue yanjiu jidi 山东省儒学研究基地, & Qufu shifan daxue kongzi wenhua xueyuan 曲阜师范大学孔子文化学院 (Eds) (2001). 孔子：儒学研究文丛（1）*Kongzi: Ruxue yanjiu wencong (1)* [Collection on research in Confucianism]. 济南：齐鲁书社出版发行 Jinan: Qilu shushe chuban faxing.
Shapiro, C., & Varian, H. R. (1999). *Information rules: a strategic guide to the network economy*. Boston, MA: Harvard Business School Press.
Shi, L. (2006). The successors to Confucianism or a new generation? A questionnaire study on Chinese students' culture of learning English. *Language, Culture and Curriculum, 19*(1), 122–47.
Shi, S. Z. 石毓智 (2010). 非常师生：孔子和他的弟子们 *Feichang shisheng: Kongzi he tade dizimen* [Paradigmatic teacher and student: Confucius and his disciples]. 北京：商务印书馆. Beijing: Shangwu yinshuguan.
Shim, S. H. (2008). A philosophical investigation of the role of teachers: A synthesis of Plato, Confucius, Buber, and Freire. *Teaching and Teacher Education, 24*, 515–35.
Shun, K.-L. (1993). *Jen* and *li* in the 'Analects'. *Philosophy East and West, 43*(3), 457–79.
— (2002). *Ren* and *li* in the *Analects*. In B. W. Van Norden (Ed.), *Confucius and the* Analects: *new essays* (pp. 53–72). Oxford and New York: Oxford University Press.
Silva, E. (2008). *Measuring 21st century skills*. Available online at: www.educationsector.org/sites/default/files/publications/MeasuringSkills.pdf, accessed 23 May 2012.
Sim, M. (2004). A Confucian approach to human rights. *History of Philosophy Quarterly, 21*(4), 337–56.
— (2007). *Remastering morals with Aristotle and Confucius*. New York: Cambridge University Press.
— (2009). Dewey and Confucius: On moral education. *Journal of Chinese Philosophy, 36*(1), 85–105.

— (2010). Rethinking virtue ethics and social justice with Aristotle and Confucius. *Asian Philosophy*, *20*(2), 195–213.
Sima Qian 司马迁 (2010). 史记 *Shiji* [Records of the historian]. 北京：中华书局 Beijing: Zhonghua Shuju.
Slingerland, E. (2000). Why philosophy is not 'extra' in understanding the analects. *Philosophy East and West*, *50*(1), 137–41, 146–7.
— (2001). Virtue ethics, the 'Analects,' and the problem of commensurability. *The Journal of Religious Ethics*, *29*(1), 97–125.
Slingerland, E., Trans. (2003). *Confucius Analects: with selections from traditional commentaries*. Indianapolis, IN: Hackett Publishing Company, Inc.
Slote, W. H., & De Vos, G. A., Eds (1998). *Confucianism and the family*. Albany: State University of New York.
Smart, N. (1989). *The world's religion*. Cambridge: Cambridge University Press.
Star, D. (2002). Do Confucians really care? A defense of the distinctiveness of care ethics. *Hypatia*, *17*(1), 77–106.
Starr, D. (2009). Chinese language education in Europe: The Confucius institutes. *European Journal of Education*, *44*(1), 65–82.
Starr, F. (1930). *Confucianism: ethics, philosophy, religion*. New York: Covici-Friede Publishers.
Sun, J. Q. 孙钦善 (1993). 论语 *Lunyu* [*Analects*]. 台北：锦绣出版事业股份有限公司 Taibei: Jinxiu chuban shiye gufen youxian gongsi.
Sun, Q. (2008). Confucian educational philosophy and its implication for lifelong learning and lifelong education. *International Journal of Lifelong Education*, *27*(5), 559–78.
Tamney, J. B., & Chiang, L. H. (2002). *Modernization, globalization, and Confucianism in Chinese societies*. Westport: Praeger Publishers.
Tan, C. (2005). The potential of Singapore's ability driven education to prepare students for a knowledge economy. *International Education Journal*, *6*(4), 446–53.
— (2008a). Globalization, the Singapore state and educational reforms: Towards performativity. *Education, Knowledge and Economy*, *2*(2), 111–20.
— (2008b). The teaching of religious knowledge in a plural society: The case for Singapore. *International Review of Education*, *54*(2), 175–91.
— (2009a). Reflection for spiritual development in adolescents. In M. D. Souza, L. Francis, J. O'Higgins-Norman, & D. Scott (Eds), *International handbook of education for spirituality, care and wellbeing* (pp. 397–413). Dordrecht: Springer.
— (2009b). Taking faith seriously: Philosophical thoughts on religious education. *Beliefs and Values*, *1*(2), 209–19.
— (2010). Dialogical education for inter-religious engagement in a plural society. In K. Engebretson, M. de Sousa, G. Durka & L. Gearon (Eds), *Interna-

tional handbook of inter-religious education (pp. 361–76). Dordrecht: Springer.
— (2011). Framing educational success: A comparative study of Shanghai and Singapore. *Education, Knowledge and Economy, 5*(3), 155–66.
— (2012a). For group, (f)or self: Communitarianism, Confucianism and values education in Singapore. *Curriculum Journal, iFirst article, DOI:10.1080/09585176.2012.744329*, 1–16.
— (2012b). 'Our shared values' in Singapore: A Confucian perspective. *Educational Theory, 62*(4), 449–63.
— (2012c). The culture of education policy making: Curriculum reform in Shanghai. *Critical Studies in Education, 53*(2), 153–67.
— (2013). *Learning from Shanghai: lessons on achieving educational success.* Dordrecht: Springer.
Tan, C., & Mokhtar, I. A. (2010). Communitarianism, the Muslim identity, and Islamic social studies in Singapore. In M. S. Merry & J. A. Milligan (Eds), *Citizenship, identity and education in Muslim communities: essays on attachment and obligation* (pp. 147–65). New York: Palgrave Macmillan.
Tan, C., & Wong, B. (2008). Classical traditions of education: Socrates and Confucius. In C. Tan (Ed.), *Philosophical reflections for educators* (pp. 3–12). Singapore: Cengage Learning.
Tan, C., & Wong, Y.-L. (2012). Promoting spiritual ideals through design thinking in public schools. *International Journal of Children's Spirituality, iFirst Article, DOI:10.1080/1364436X.2011.651714*, 1–13.
Tan, S. (2010). Authoritative Master Kong (Confucius) in an authoritarian age. *Dao, 9*, 137–49.
Tan, S.-H. (2003). Can there be a Confucian civil society? In K.-C. Chong, S.-H. Tan & C. L. Ten (Eds), *The moral circle and the self* (pp. 193–218). Chicago: Open Court.
— (2004). *Confucian democracy: a Deweyan reconstruction.* Albany: State University of New York Press.
— (2005). Imagining Confucius: Paradigmatic characters and virtue ethics. *Journal of Chinese Philosophy, 32*(3), 409–26.
Tan, J. Z. 谭家哲 (2006). 论语与中国思想研究 *Lunyu yu zhongguo sixiang yanjiu* [The *Analects* and research on Chinese thought]. 台北：唐山出版社 Taibei: Tangshan chubanshe.
Tang, H. 汤化 (1997). 论语漫谈 *Lunyu mantan* [A discussion on the *Analects*]. 台北：顶渊文化事业有限公司 Taibei: Dingyan wenhua shiye youxian gongsi.
Tao, J. (2010). Trust within democracy: A reconstructed Confucian perspective. In K. Yu, J. Tao & P. J. Ivanhoe (Eds), *Taking Confucian ethics seriously* (pp. 99–122). Albany: State University of New York Press.
Taylor, C. (1985). *Philosophy and the human sciences: philosophical papers 2.* Cambridge: Cambridge University Press.

— (1989). *Sources of the self: the making of modern identity*. Cambridge, MA: Harvard University Press.
Ten, C. L. (2003). The moral circle. In K.-C. Chong, S.-H. Tan & C. L. Ten (Eds), *The moral circle and the self* (pp. 17–25). Chicago: Open Court.
Thomas, N. (1986). *The view from nowhere*. New York: Oxford University Press.
Tian, C. (2009). The ideological development of Confucianism in the global age. *New Political Science*, 31(4), 515–27.
Trier, U. (2003). Twelve countries contributing to DeSeCo: A summary report. In D. Rychen, L. Salganik & M. McLaughlin (Eds), *Definition and selection of key competences. Contributions to the second DeSeCo symposium* (pp. 7–59). Neuchatel: Swiss Federal Statistical Office.
Tu, W.-M. (1968). The creative tension between Jen and li. *Philosophy East and West*, 18(½), 29–39.
— (1979a). *Humanity and self-cultivation: essays in Confucian thought*. Berkeley, CA: Asian Humanities Press.
— (1979b). Ultimate self-transformation as a communal act. *Journal of Chinese Philosophy*, 6, 237–46.
— (1984). *Confucian ethics today: the Singapore challenge*. Singapore: Curriculum Development Institute of Singapore and Federal Publications.
— (1985). *Confucian thought: selfhood as creative transformation*. Albany, NY: State University of New York Press.
— (1993). Confucian traditions in East Asian modernity: Exploring moral authority and economic power in Japan and the four mini-dragons. *Bulletin of the American Academy of Arts and Sciences*, 46(8), 5–19.
— (1996a). *Confucian traditions in East Asian modernity: moral education and economic culture in Japan and the four mini-dragons*. Cambridge: Harvard University Press.
— (1996b). Confucian traditions in East Asian modernity. *Bulletin of the American Academy of Arts and Sciences*, 50(2), 12–39.
— (1998). Probing the 'three bonds' and 'five relationships' in Confucian humanism. In W. H. Slote & G. A. De Vos (Eds), *Confucianism and the family* (pp. 121–36). Albany: State University of New York Press.
Tweed, R. G., & Lehman, D. R. (2002). Learning considered within a cultural context: Confucian and Socratic approaches. *American Psychologist, 57*, 89–99.
Van Norden, B. W. (Ed.) (2002). *Confucius and the Analects: new essays*. Oxford: Oxford University Press.
Van Norden, B. W. (2003). Virtue ethics and Confucianism. *Comparative Approaches to Chinese Philosophy*, 99–12.
Voogt, J., & Roblin, N. P. (2012). A comparative analysis of international frameworks for 21st century competences: Implications for national curriculum policies. *Journal of Curriculum Studies*, 44(3), 299–321.

Wang, B. W. 王邦雄, Zeng, Z. X. 曾昭旭, & Yang, Z. H. 杨祖汉 (1982). 论语义理疏解 *Lunyu yili shujie* [A philosophical interpretation of the *Analects*]. 台北：鹅湖出版社 Taibei: Ehu chubanshe.

Wang, D. H. 汪大海, & Hu, W. H.胡卫红 (2010). 跟老子学无为领导，跟孔子学有为管理 *Gen Laozi xue wuwei lingdao, gen Kongzi xue youwei guanli* [Learn 'wuwei' management from Laozoi, learn 'youwei' management from Confucius]. 北京：石油工业出版社 Beijing: Shiyou gongye chubanshe.

Wang, F. (2004). Confucian thinking in traditional moral education: Key ideas and fundamental features. *Journal of Moral Education*, 33(4), 429–47.

Wang, G. X. 王国轩, & Wang, X. M. 王秀梅 (2011). 孔子家语 *Kongzi jiayu* [The words of Confucius]. 北京：中华书局 Beijing: Zhonghua shuju.

Wang, J. L. 王鈞林 (2011). 最想问孔子老师的１０１个问题 *Zuixiangwen Kongzi laoshi de 101ge wenti* [101 most sought-after questions to ask teacher Confucius]. 台北：如果出版社 Taibei: Ruguo chubanshe.

Wang, Y. H. 王言红 (2006). 论孔子教育思想对现代教育的启示 *Lun Kongzi jiaoyu sixiang dui dangdai jiaoyu de qishi* [A discussion of the implications of Confucius' educational thought on modern education]. 大学时代论坛 *Daxue shidai luntan*, 3, 47–8.

Watanabe, M. (2011). 读论语，有什么用？ *Du Lunyu, youshenme yong?* [What's the use of reading the *Analects*?] 刘宗德 Liu, Z. D., Trans. 台北：大是文化有限公司 Taibei: Dashi wenhua youxian gongsi.

Watson, B. (1958). *Ssu Ma Ch' ien Grand historian of China*. New York: Columbia University Press.

Wawrytko, S. A. (1982). Confucius and Kant: The ethics of respect. *Philosophy East and West*, 32(3), 237–57.

Williams, C. (2006). International human rights and Confucianism. *Asia-Pacific Journal on Human Rights and the Law*, 1, 38–66.

Wilson, S. A. (1995). Conformity, individuality, and the nature of virtue: A classical Confucian contribution to contemporary ethical reflection. *The Journal of Religious Ethics*, 23(2), 263–89.

Wong, B., & Loy, H.-C. (2001). The Confucian gentlemen and the limits of ethical change. *Journal of Chinese Philosophy*, 28(3), 209–34.

Wong, J. (2004). Are the learning styles of Asian international students culturally or contextually based? *International Education Journal*, 4(4),154–66.

Wong, K. (1998). Culture and moral leadership in education. *Peabody Journal of Education*, 73(2), 106–25.

— (2001). Culture and educational leadership. In K. C. Wong & E. Colin (Eds), *Leadership for quality schooling: International perspectives* (pp. 36–53). London: Routledge/ Falmer.

Wong, M. (1998). A comparison between the philosophies of Confucius and Plato as applied to music education. *Journal of Aesthetic Education*, 32(3), 109–12.

Woods, P. R., & Lamond, D. A. (2011).What would Confucius do? – Confucian ethics and self-regulation in management. *Journal of Business Ethics*, *102*, 669–83.

Wu, E. H. (2006). Nurture over nature: A reflective review of Confucian philosophy on learning and talented performance. *Gifted Education International*, *21*(2/3), 181–9.

Wu, G. L. 吴甘霖 (2010). 亲爱的孔子老师：子贡的十堂智慧课 *Qinai de Kongzi laoshi: Zigong de shitang zhihuike* [Dear teacher Confucius: ten lessons on wisdom by Zigong]. 台北：漫游者文化事业股份有限公司 Taipei: Manyouzhe wenhua shiye gufen youxian gongsi.

Xu, W. Y. 许维遹 (2009). *Lüshi chuqiu jishi* 吕氏春秋集释 [Collected interpretation of Mister Lü's spring and autumn]. 北京：中华书局 Beijing: Zhonghua shuju.

Yang, B. 杨伯峻 (1980). 论语译注 *Lunyu yizhu* [Annotation of the *Analects*]. 北京：中华书局 Beijing: Zhonghua shuju.

— (1990). 春秋左传注 *Chünqiu zuozhuanzhu* [Annotation of *Zuozhuan Chünqiu*]. 北京：中华书局 Beijing: Zhonghua shuju.

Yang, H.-Y., & Yang, G., Trans. (1974). *Records of the historian*. Hong Kong: Commercial Press.

Yang, M. Y. 杨明宇 (2010). 心通 '论语' *Xintong 'Lunyu'* [The *Analects* through the heart]. 合肥：安徽文艺出版社. Hefei: Anhui wenyi chubanshe.

Yao, X. (1999). Confucianism and its modern values: Confucian moral, educational and spiritual heritages revisited. *Journal of Beliefs & Values*, *20*(1), 30–40.

— (2000). *An introduction to Confucianism*. Cambridge: Cambridge University Press.

Yu, D. 于丹 (2007). 于丹 '论语' 心得 *Yudan 'Lunyu' xinde* [Yudan's insights from the *Analects*]. 台北：连经出版事业股份有限公司. Taibei: Lianjing chuban shiye gufen youxian gongsi.

—. 于丹 (2008). 于丹 '论语' 感悟 Yudan 'Lunyu' ganwu [Yudan's sentiments from the *Analects*]. 北京：中华书局 Beijing: Zhonghua shuju.

Yu, J. (1998). Virtue: Confucius and Aristotle. *Philosophy East and West*, *48*(2) 323–47.

— (2009). The influence and enlightenment of Confucian cultural education on modern European civilisation. *Frontiers of Education in China*, *4*(1), 10–26.

Yu, K., Tao, J., & Ivanhoe, P. J. (Eds) (2010). *Taking Confucian ethics seriously* (pp. 99–122). Albany: State University of New York Press.

Yuan, L. (2002). Ethics of care and concept of *jen*. *Hypatia, 17*(1), 107–29.

Zhang, H. L. 张惠丽 (2007). 试论孔子教育思想对新课程改革的启示 *Shilun Kongzi jiaoyu sixiang dui xinkecheng gaige de qishi* [On the implications of Confucius' educational thought for the new curriculum reform]. 读与写集志 *Duyuxie jizhi*, *4*(11), 68, 74.

Zhang, J. 张军 (2008). 大师说儒 *Dashi shuoru*. [Great teachers talk about Confucianism]. 汕头：汕头大学出版社 Shantou: Shantou daxue chubanshe.

Zhang, Q. S. 张秋升, & Wang, H. J. 王洪军 (2004). 中国儒学史研究 *Zhongguo ruxueshi yanjiu [Research on history of Confucianism in China]*. 济南：齐鲁书社出版发行 Jinan: Qilu shushe chuban faxing.

Zhang, T., & Schwartz, B. (1997). Confucius and the cultural revolution: A study in collective memory. *International Journal of Politics, Culture, and Society, 11*(2), 189–212.

Zhou, Y. 周勇 (2008). 跟孔子学当老师 *Gen Kongzi xuedang laoshi [Learn to be a teacher like Confucius]*. 上海：华东师范大学出版社. Shanghai: East China Normal University Press.

Zhou, Z. W. 周振微 (2005). 谈孔子的因材施教与素质教育 Tan Kongzi de yincai shijiao yu suzhi jiaoyu [A discussion of Confucius' customised teaching and quality-oriented education. 当代教育论坛 *Dangdai jiaoyu luntan, 20*, 52–3.

Zhu, F. (2009). A study on James Legge's English translation of *Lun Yu. Canadian Social Science, 5*(6), 32–42.

Index

ability
  cognitive 228
  intellectual 228
acculturation 182n. 4
aesthetics/aesthetic 3, 58, 60–1, 63–4, 69–70, 81, 82, 83, 160n. 21, 161n. 23, 163n. 36, 166n. 7, 168n. 14, 174n. 4, 177n. 18, 215, 234
  ethico-aesthetical 160n. 21
  moral-aesthetic 160n. 21
  spiritual-ethical-aesthetic 4, 61, 64, 72, 82, 132, 150, 154n. 14, 160n. 21, 165n. 4, 180n. 28, 183n. 7, 209, 212, 214, 217, 233
Ames, Roger T. 7–8, 10, 10–11, 12n. 2, 16–17, 89, 152n. 8, 155nn. 19–20, 156n. 1, 157nn. 4, 158nn. 10–12, 159n. 16, 160nn. 18, 21, 22, 162n. 27, 163n. 31, 166n. 7, 167n. 10, 168–7nn, 170n. 23, 171n. 27, 174nn. 4–5, 176n. 12, 177n. 20, 178n. 24, 182n. 2, 183–4nn, 184n. 18, 186nn. 22, 24, 187n. 27, 221, 228
Analects (論語 *Lunyu*)3, 7–11, 10, 11–12, 12n.1, 14n. 11, 17–21, 25–6, 27nn. 3, 5, 31, 32, 37, 39, 48, 50, 55, 56, 60, 63, 67, 69, 74, 77–8, 80, 83, 86–8, 100, 103–4, 105, 110, 113, 129–31, 134, 137, 144–5, 148–9, 152n. 1, 153–4nn, 156n. 24, 157n. 3, 158n. 7, 159n. 18, 160n. 22, 161n. 24, 162nn. 27–8, 163n. 36, 164n. 2, 166n. 8, 167n. 10, 170nn. 24, 26, 171n. 28, 173n. 1, 176n. 14, 177n. 16, 181n. 34, 185n. 18, 186n. 23, 210, 219, 222–3, 226, 232
antiquity 51, 52, 121, 145, 147, 223
appropriateness (義 *yi*) 35, 45, 103, 108, 109–10, 118, 120–1, 133–5, 141, 149, 158n. 12, 175nn. 10–11, 176nn. 11–12, 177n. 18, 181n. 34, 182n. 4, 183n. 9, 207–9, 210, 213–14, 225, 236n. 7
archery (射 *she*) 24, 39, 106–7, 131–2, 135, 146, 183nn. 5, 7, 209–10
aristocrat/aristocrats 19, 23–4, 33, 74, 103–4, 149, 164n. 1, 173n. 2, 174n.3, 221
Aristotle 6, 175n. 9, 203, 223, 239n. 1
arts 24, 64, 131–2, 135, 146, 183n. 7, 209, 228, 232
  see also humanities
Asian 2, 178n. 24, 213
authority 27n. 3, 105, 171n. 31, 180–1n 31, 232, 239
autonomy 12n. 2, 108, 111, 121, 179n. 26, 180nn. 29, 31, 204, 216, 225, 229–30

barbarians 120, 167n. 12, 180n. 28
basic quality (質 *zhi*) 66–7, 109, 133–4, 176n. 12, 183n. 9

Bell, Daniel 12n. 3, 13n. 9, 27n. 6, 28n. 7, 162n. 28, 226–9, 239n. 3
benevolence 74, 166n. 7, 174n. 7
Bentham, Jeremy 100
Bible 88, 169n. 20
Boniu 21
Book of Changes (易 *Yi*) 27n. 5
Book of Documents (書 *Shu*) 21
Book of History see *Book of Documents*
Book of Odes see *Book of Songs*
Book of Rites (禮 *Li*) 27, 171n. 29
Book of Songs (詩 *Shi*) 21, 27n. 5, 39, 64, 93, 132, 136, 139, 140, 141, 163n. 30, 164n
Book of the Spring and Autumn Annals (春秋 *Chunqiu*) 27n. 5
Boyu 20, 65
Buddhism 24, 25

calculation 183n. 7
calligraphy (書 *shu*) 24, 131–2, 209
categorical imperative 101
ceremony 32, 35, 155n. 17, 161n. 24, 183n. 7
charioteering (御 *yu*) 7, 24, 131–2, 183n. 5, 209–10
Chinese imperial exam 25
chung see dutifulness
circle 99–100, 107, 172n. 34, 207, 208, 212–14, 217, 240n. 7
  concentric circles 99, 107, 172n. 34, 207–9
  family 14n. 11
conduct (行 *xing*) 24, 129, 146
Confucian Heritage Cultures 2, 25, 233
Confucianism 1, 7–9, 13nn. 6, 8–9, 14n. 10, 24–6, 27nn. 4, 6, 28n. 8, 102, 154n. 12, 162n. 28, 167n. 12, 173n. 36, 186n. 23, 210, 220, 223, 225, 234, 239nn. 2–3
  philosophical 225
  political 225

Confucius Institute 1, 26, 50
Confucius Temple 1, 50, 51, 191
consequentialist 100
courage (勇 *yong*) 43, 47–8, 71, 77, 79, 80, 85, 91, 106, 110, 127, 168n. 13, 173n. 36, 174n. 7
courageous 80, 106, 115
creativity 2, 121, 155n. 20, 181n. 34, 193, 196, 197, 200, 212, 216, 229
criticality/critical
  contrasted with uncritical 117
  etymology of 121
  in relation to Confucius 34, 184n. 14, 210, 229
  in relation to culture 182n. 4
  in relation to *junzi* 181nn. 32, 34
  in relation to *li* 154n. 15, 176n. 14, 181n. 32, 185nn. 17, 20
  in relation to reflection 121, 139, 182n. 4, 216, 229, 232
  in relation to thinking 2, 145, 193, 196–7, 200, 205, 212–13, 225, 233, 235n. 5
  in relation to tradition 238n. 12
  the state of 121
culture 26, 69, 117, 159n. 14, 161n. 25, 169n. 21, 178n. 22, 179n. 28, 205
  Chinese 180n. 28, 221
  Confucian 2, 11, 236n. 7
  Culture (文 *wen*) 24, 53, 56–7, 96–7, 116, 124–5, 129–31, 133–5, 147, 157n. 5, 182n. 4, 183n. 6, 207–10
  diversity of 194, 212–13
  in relation to *junzi* 134
  in relation to *li* 134
  in relation to the six arts 131
  in relation to Zhou 117, 130
    see also Zhou
  of the sage-kings 130, 149

deference (讓 *rang*) 43–5, 48–9, 63, 71, 79, 82, 106, 118, 152n. 8, 156n. 23, 167n. 12, 239n. 15
democracy/democratic 7, 171n. 31, 202, 210, 224–5, 230, 236n. 3, 239nn. 2–3
didactic teaching 2, 5, 135–6, 231
discernment 42, 72, 108–9, 141
  see also discretion; judgement
discourse 37, 51, 54, 101, 210–11, 235n. 2
discretion 38–40, 42, 44–5, 71, 73, 84, 108–9, 112, 133, 137, 141, 149, 151, 176n. 13, 213
  see also discernment; judgement
disposition 35, 44, 78, 92, 156nn. 21–2, 166nn. 7, 9, 173n. 36, 184n. 13, 199, 200, 238n. 12, 239n. 15
Doctrine of the Mean (中庸 *Zhongyong*) 27n. 5
Dong Zhongshu 221–2
Drucker, Peter F. 6, 13n. 6
Duke Chu 20
Duke Ding 128
Duke Jing 91
Duke Ling 20
Duke of Lu 20
Duke of Wei 92
Duke of Zhou (周公 *Zhougong*) 33, 53, 157n. 3
dutifulness (忠 *zhong*) 24, 76, 77, 80, 118, 129

East Asian/East Asia 7, 25, 178n. 24, 210, 224, 230, 233, 240n. 7
educare 154
education
  communitarian approach to 216
  Confucian 2, 13, 233–4
  of Confucius 2, 3, 4, 6, 8, 11, 23, 150, 154, 185n. 20, 223, 231, 232, 234

cultural 135
in culture 97
ethical 179n. 27, 180n. 29
formal 124, 131, 149, 221
functionalist view of 200, 209
higher and professional 200
informal 124, 131
meaning of 124–5
modern 5
moral 3–4, 26, 178n. 23, 221, 233
non-formal 124, 131
performance-based 4
private 24
quality-oriented 5
in relation to human experiences 145, 149
in relation to knowledge-based economy and globalization 5
in relation to *li* 125
in relation to OECD 235n. 3
in relation to *si* 136, 145
in relation to technical rationality 200
in relation to twenty-first century 8, 11, 191–2, 199, 203, 206, 209, 214, 218, 219–20, 225
in relation to women 14n. 11, 104, 220–1
religious 211
student-centred 135
spiritual 211–12
for talented performance 5
teacher 193, 200, 205, 216–17
teacher-centred 135
vocational 5
Western 2, 233
educere 124
empathy *see shu*
exemplar/exemplars 150, 216

feminist ethics of care 223
filial piety (孝 *xiao*) 34, 95–7, 99–100, 103, 107–8, 215, 230, 237n. 9
Fingarette, Herbert 155n. 20, 161n. 24, 239n. 15
Five Classics (五經 *Wujing*) 27n. 5
Former Kings 58–9, 64
  see also sage-kings
Four Books (四書 *Sishu*) 25, 27n. 5
free will 179n. 26

Gadamer, Hans-Georg 207, 235n. 4
Gao Yao 87
gentleman 8–9, 21, 104, 173n. 2, 174–5nn, 181n. 32, 185n. 17
ghosts 17, 23, 62
golden age 157nn. 2, 6
golden rule 88, 169n. 20
Gongye Chang 111
government 19, 20, 22, 26, 43–4, 88, 92–3, 97, 119, 153n. 10, 170. 26, 224, 237n. 10
  authoritarian 224, 239n. 2
  and Civics 195, 208
  corrupt 224
  democratic 230
  in East Asia 212, 224
  in the history of East Asia 224
  officials 237n. 10
  self-government 230
  of US 192
Great Learning (大学 *Daxue*) 27n. 5
Guan ju 68

Han dynasty 17, 18, 24–5, 221
Han Fei 220, 222
Han Wudi 24
harmonization 50, 59, 63, 72, 78, 99, 129, 135, 214
harmony (和 *he*) 19, 51, 57–64, 67, 68, 70–1, 82, 84–5, 95, 97, 106–8, 112, 120, 121, 159n. 16, 160n. 20, 162n. 28, 163nn. 35, 36, 174n. 8, 214–17, 230, 234, 236n. 7, 238n. 12
  external 59–60, 63, 66, 74, 82, 107, 209–10, 215–16
  internal 58–60, 66, 74, 82, 107, 209–10, 215–16
  spiritual-ethical-aesthetic see aesthetic
heart-mind (心 *xin*) 56, 61, 114, 120–1, 143, 160n. 22, 210, 213
heaven (天 *tian*) 7, 17, 22–3, 33, 54–5, 57, 59–62, 71–2, 82–3, 105, 107, 121, 125, 127, 129–30, 135, 157n. 5, 158nn. 8–10, 160n. 21, 168n. 14, 169n. 18, 174n. 8, 180n. 31, 208, 211–12, 222, 224, 234, 237n. 11, 239n. 15
hermeneutics 235n. 4
hierarchy 171n. 31, 178n. 23, 224–5
human nature 7, 172n. 35, 176n. 12
humanities 24, 64, 67, 132, 215
humanity 158n. 8, 172n. 33, 203, 212, 234
  co-humanity 74, 85
  as *ren* 23

individualism 179n. 26, 204, 231
individuality 2, 113, 121, 159n. 16, 223–5, 239n. 2
Information and Communication Technology (ICT) 191, 193, 197–200, 212–13, 235n. 2
innovation 8, 173n. 36, 193, 196–200, 204, 207, 212–13, 225, 235n. 5, 235n. 5
inquiry 4, 169, 184n. 14, 213
internet 1, 200

Ji family 33
Joy (樂 *le*) 22, 58–60, 64, 67–8, 70–3, 74, 81, 92, 107, 118, 127, 135, 146, 159n. 19, 173n. 1, 203, 209, 215, 236n. 6

the state of 106, 125, 148, 213, 215
judgement 38–40, 44, 72–3, 108–9, 112, 121, 133, 136–8, 141–2, 144, 155n. 19, 172n. 35, 175n. 11, 176n. 13, 184n. 11, 196, 212–15, 227
  see also discernment; discretion
junzi (君子) 1–6, 12n. 3, 21, 23, 55, 62, 92, 95, 101–2, 103–22, 125, 127, 129–30, 132–3, 137, 141, 143, 148, 149–50, 162n. 28, 163n. 38, 168n. 15, 169n. 18, 171n. 30, 173–4nn, 177nn. 19–20, 178nn. 22, 23, 179n. 25, 181nn. 32, 34, 182nn. 2, 4, 186n. 24, 213, 216–17, 220, 222, 224–31, 239n. 4
  see also *xiaoren*

Kant, Immanuel 100–1, 172n. 35
  Kantian 169n. 21, 172n. 35
  Kantianism 100, 177n. 15
  post-Kantian ethics 12n. 2
King Wen 53, 57, 129–30, 157n. 3
King Wu 53, 68
knowledge-based economy 5, 202
knowledge society *see* knowledge-based economy
Kong Fuzi (孔夫子) 18
Kongqiu (孔丘) 19
Kongzi (孔子) 4–5, 17–18, 27n.3, 232
Kuang 20, 57, 129

language 10, 26, 41–2, 64, 67, 93, 120, 132, 146, 159n. 14, 171n. 27, 192, 194, 198, 208, 210, 235n. 1
Lau, D.C. 10, 41, 89, 152nn. 4, 6, 156n. 1, 157n. 4, 158nn. 10–11, 159nn. 18–19, 163n. 31, 164n. 3, 165n. 7, 169n. 17, 170n. 23, 174n. 4, 176n. 12, 177n. 15, 182n. 2, 183nn. 8, 10, 186n. 24, 187n. 27, 220, 228
learning 2, 5, 20, 22–4, 60–1, 71–2, 75–6, 83, 93–4, 116–17, 122, 124, 146, 149–51, 159n. 18, 174n. 8, 178n. 24, 183nn. 7, 10, 184n. 15, 186n. 21, 187n. 26, 191, 193–4, 196–9, 203, 205–9, 212–13, 217, 227–8, 231–4, 235nn. 5–7
  lifelong 5, 71, 102, 192, 217, 233
  in relation to culture 129–34, 182n.4, 183nn. 6, 8, 185n. 19, 208, 212
  in relation to harmony 60
  in relation to *li* 71–2, 154n. 16, 180n. 28
  in relation to practice 146–9, 185n. 20
  in relation to the Way 127, 182n. 3
  in relation to thinking 138–45, 181n. 34
  rote 2, 139, 163n. 38, 185n. 20, 240
  student-centred 232
    see also thinking
  for women 223
  as *xue* (學) 124–36
legalism 24
Li (禮)
  of Confucius 32, 36, 38, 45, 50, 78, 153n. 9
  prevailing 32, 34–6, 46, 49–50, 78, 131, 167n. 11
libation 32
Lienu Zhuan 223
literature 2–3, 5–6, 8, 64, 67, 93, 146, 192, 200, 219, 231
literacy 195–8, 200, 208, 210, 212, 225, 228, 236
Lu family 39

Lu state 19, 32, 53, 64

mandate of heaven (天命 *tian-ming*) 55, 59–61, 71, 82–3, 107, 127, 158nn. 8, 10, 160n. 21, 211, 234
mathematics (數 *shu*) 24, 131
May Fourth Movement 25
memorization 2, 5, 24, 116, 136, 232–3, 240n. 7
   rote 2, 231–2 *see also* learning
Mencius (孟子 *Mengzi*) 7–8, 24, 160n. 22, 223
   the book of *Mencius* 27nn. 2, 5, 185n. 18
Mill, J.S. 100
minister/ministers 20, 87, 91, 93, 105, 112, 118, 170n. 23, 173n. 38, 173n. 2
Modern New Confucianism *see* New-Confucianism
modesty (儉 *jian*) 46, 48–9, 52, 63, 109, 111, 133
Moism 24
moral law 158n. 8, 172n. 35
multitude 87, 90, 94, 96, 117, 130, 141, 179n. 25
music 21–2, 38–9, 58, 102, 118, 153n. 11, 159n. 16, 163nn. 30–3, 36, 177n. 18, 210, 215
   of *shao* 20, 53, 68
   as 樂 (*yue*) 24, 59, 64, 67–70, 83, 92–3, 131–2, 146, 163n. 37, 170n. 25, 183n. 7, 209

Nanzi 20
Neo-Confucianism 25
New-Confucianism 25
Nine Barbarian Tribes 120
1911 revolution 25
norm/norms 37, 45, 50, 51–2, 60, 71, 74, 111, 152n. 7, 156n. 22, 157n. 5, 163n. 34, 167n. 12, 175n. 11, 176n. 13, 178n. 22, 180n. 30, 185n. 20
normative 9–10, 19, 22–4, 36–7, 41, 43, 48–50, 51–2, 54, 56, 60, 64, 71–2, 74, 76–7, 80, 92–3, 101, 110, 125, 137, 153n. 9, 158n. 7, 166–7nn, 180n. 28, 213–14, 215, 234
normativity 23, 37, 77, 78, 82, 142, 167n. 11

Organization for Economic Co-operation and Development (OECD) 192, 198–9, 201–4, 233, 235nn. 1–3

paradox of the Chinese learner 240n. 7
Partnership for 21st Century Skills 191–4, 196–7, 201, 204–5, 217, 235n. 5
performance 4, 37–8, 44, 102, 114, 160n. 21, 163n. 36, 178n. 24
   in relation to *li* 154n. 15, 155n. 19, 181n. 32, 185n. 17
   in relation to social roles 67, 225
   in relation to talent 5
person/persons
   exemplary 55, 104, 125, 177n. 20, 226
   ideal 23, 162n. 28
   noble 95, 104, 171n. 30
   paradigmatic 60, 177n. 19
   see also junzi; xiaoren
phronesis 175n. 9
poetry 21, 24, 64–7, 132, 163n. 30, 215
Post-Confucianism 25
Postmodern Neo-Confucianism 25
problem solving 193, 196–7, 200, 205, 212, 235n. 5
professional development 197, 205–7, 216–17

Programme for International Student Assessment (PISA) 233
propriety 6, 19, 32, 36, 153n. 9, 156n. 22, 158n. 12, 164n. 2, 174n. 8, 183n. 7, 238n. 14

Qing dynasty 25, 220
Qu Bo-yu 107

Ranyou 19, 40–1, 69, 149
reciprocity see *shu*
Records of the Historian (史記 *Shiji*) 17–20, 27n.2, 186n. 23
rectification of names (正名) 24, 26–8, 67, 86, 91–5, 99–100, 105, 112, 170–1nn, 208, 215
religion 62, 194, 211–12, 234, 237n. 11
  see also spirituality
respect (敬 *jing*) 21, 34–5, 45, 48, 63, 76–8, 80, 88, 95–8, 110, 115n. 4, 117–19, 128, 130, 167nn. 10–12, 179n. 25, 212, 214, 228, 231–2
reverence (恭 *gong*) 43, 76, 77, 80, 82, 90–1, 94, 142
rightness 45, 100, 176n. 12
rights 195, 198, 210–11, 220, 225, 237n. 9, 239n. 3
rites 17, 19, 21, 32, 34, 36, 51, 78, 108, 152n. 4, 154n. 12, 159–60nn, 163n. 37, 176n. 13
  see also rituals
ritual/rituals 228, 238n. 14, 238n. 14
  ceremonial 24, 31, 32, 33, 34, 36, 38, 42, 43, 44, 45, 49, 51, 52, 112, 131, 139, 175n. 11, 184n. 14
  sense of 153n. 9
Rosemont, Jr, Henry 7–8, 10, 10–11, 12n. 2, 16–17, 89, 152n. 8, 155nn. 19–20, 156n. 1, 157nn. 4, 158nn. 10–12, 159n. 16, 160nn. 18, 21, 22, 162n. 27, 163n. 31, 166n. 7, 167n. 10, 168–7nn, 170n. 23, 171n. 27, 174nn. 4–5, 176n. 12, 177n. 20, 178n. 24, 182n. 2, 183–4nn, 184n. 18, 186nn. 22, 24, 187n. 27, 221, 228
ruler/rulers 14n. 10, 19, 24, 33–4, 43–5, 49, 52–5, 61, 63, 69, 71, 74, 78, 88, 91–4, 97, 101, 105, 112, 128, 130, 135, 155n. 19, 156n. 23, 162n. 28, 164n. 1, 170n. 23, 171n. 30, 173n. 2, 210, 216, 220, 222, 224
  junzi-ruler 104–5, 119–20, 179n.25, 224–5

sage-king/sage-kings 19, 52, 54, 56–7, 60, 71, 74, 87, 113, 121, 130–2, 149, 157n. 5, 157n. 6, 175n. 11
  see also Former Kings
sagehood 178n. 21
sameness 63, 120
scholar/scholars (士 *shi*) 117, 126, 149, 222, 228, 236n. 6
  scholar-apprentices 187n. 27
  scholar-officials 81, 173n. 38, 174n. 6
  scholar-rulers 224
self
  centredness 21, 110, 209
  Confucian 172n. 34
  conscious 61, 72, 106, 162n. 29
  control 110
  criticism 238n. 12
  cultivation 13n. 8, 23, 25, 31–2, 67, 71, 73, 100, 107, 114, 116–18, 120, 126, 140, 179n. 25, 180–1nn, 182nn. 1, 4, 185n. 20, 208, 216, 225, 228, 238n. 12
  direction 197, 214
  examination 142–3, 213
  expression 163n. 38

government 230
identity 215, 231
improvement 142–3, 147
interest 225
investment 237n. 9
knowledge 175n. 10, 213, 237n. 11
legislation 180
motivation 4, 139
observing and regulating 239n. 15
overcoming 88, 101, 164nn. 2–3, 165n. 5
realization 215
reflection 181n. 32
regulating 59, 68, 155n. 19
restraint 127
sacrifice 52
self-help books 4
transformation 165n. 5
shao music 20, 53, 68, 145
Shaonan (召南) 65, 93
shared values 201–2
shu (恕) 20–2, 88–91, 94, 99–100, 121, 131, 138, 169–70nn, 213, 223, 231
Shun (舜) 52, 56, 68, 87, 113, 117, 157n. 2
Sima Qian (司马迁) 18
sincerity 47, 49, 76, 77–8, 80, 118, 167n. 10
six arts (六藝 *liuyi*) *see* arts
Slingerland, Edward 8–10, 23, 67–8, 89, 116, 152nn. 3–4, 6, 154nn. 12, 16, 156n. 1, 158nn. 9–11, 159nn. 18–19, 163n. 31, 165nn. 3, 7, 168n. 14, 169nn. 17–18, 170n. 23, 171n. 32, 173n. 36, 174n. 4, 175n. 9, 176n. 12, 177n. 17, 179n. 25, 182n. 2, 183n. 8, 184n. 11, 185n. 20, 186nn. 22, 24, 187n. 27, 220, 223, 227–8, 238n. 12
Socrates 6, 187n. 26

spirituality 62, 211, 234, 237
  see also religion
Spring and Autumn period 17, 19
subjects
  as domains of learning 24, 131–2, 194, 196, 207–10, 212, 217
  in relation to rulers 94, 164n. 1, 220

Tang (湯) 87
  see also Shun
Taoism 24–5
teacher/teachers 2–5, 19, 22, 24, 47, 81, 124, 131, 135, 139, 141, 145, 148–50, 171n. 32, 179n. 27, 181n. 34, 182n. 1, 186n. 22, 205, 206, 223, 228, 232–3
  education 193, 200, 205–6
  professional development 216–17
  teacher-centred 2, 135
textual transmission 2, 5, 231
thinking 145, 159n. 16, 178n. 24, 179n. 27
  Confucian 221
  critical 2, 184n. 14, 193, 200, 205, 212, 225, 233, 235n. 5
  ethical 171n. 32
  higher-order 2, 5, 138, 199, 212–13, 217, 232, 233
  independent 108, 141, 229, 233
  inferential 139–41
  innovative 121
  original 230–1
  reflective 147, 182n. 4
  in relation to feeling and doing 82, 108, 168n. 16
  in relation to learning 181n. 34
  in relation to the heart-mind 143
  as 思 (*si*) 124–45, 182n. 4, 184nn. 11–12, 185n. 18, 212, 232, 240n. 7
systems 196
tradition/traditional 11, 12n. 1, 23, 50, 100, 145, 153. 9, 154n. 15,

155nn. 19–20, 157n. 6, 158n. 12, 162n. 26, 163n. 34, 179n. 26, 181n. 32, 181n. 34, 204–5, 212–13, 224, 235n. 4, 238n. 12
Chinese 145
Confucian 12n. 2, 13n. 8, 103, 143, 223–5, 235n. 4
cultural 183n. 6
Greek 158n. 8
living 25
normative 158n. 7
practice 42, 142
religious 237n. 11
rituals 32, 51, 116, 157n. 5, 228
sources 17
texts 97, 130
traditionalism 157nn. 5, 6
Western 12n. 4, 100, 143, 171n. 32, 204
Trustworthiness (信 xin) 24, 77, 82, 90–1, 94, 111, 127, 129
truth/truthful 156n. 1, 175n. 10, 178n. 24, 226
Confucian notion of 158n. 13, 236n. 7
in relation to tradition 238n. 12
Western notion of 236n. 7
Tu, Wei-Ming 13n. 8, 25, 164n. 2, 167nn. 10, 11–12, 172n. 34, 173n. 37, 225, 234
Twenty-first-century 2, 7–8, 151, 193, 199, 200, 202–3, 215–16, 217, 219
competences 191–2
competencies 191–2
domains 214
education 11, 191–2, 206, 209, 213–14, 218, 219–20, 225
learning 193
professional development 205, 216
professional learning communities 206
skills 191–4, 196–206, 209, 212, 217, 235n. 5
skills development 206
teaching and learning 235n. 5
theme of global awareness 212
theme of spiritual education 211
themes 194, 207–10

utilitarianism 100, 177n. 15

virtue/virtues 46, 49, 97, 99, 101, 103, 112, 114, 127, 146–7, 153n. 9, 162n. 26, 163n. 31, 166n. 7, 170n. 26, 178n. 24, 179n. 26, 200, 224, 230, 236n. 6, 238n. 12
Confucian 171n. 32, 177n. 18
in Confucius 55
as 德 (de) 19, 23–4, 44, 63, 71, 115, 131, 158nn. 8–9, 225, 228–9
of a junzi-ruler 119
in relation to heaven 55, 82
in relation to ren 12–14, 74, 78–9, 167–8nn, 174n. 7
thief of 46
virtue ethics 100–1, 173n. 36
of Zhou 52

Way (道 dao) 54, 58, 65, 88, 106, 126–7, 151, 158nn. 7, 11–13, 159n. 19, 172n. 35, 175n. 10, 180n. 31, 181n. 34, 208, 234
West/Western/Westerners 2, 12nn. 2, 4, 100, 143, 154n. 12, 160nn. 21–2, 162n. 29, 171nn. 27, 32, 177n. 15, 179n. 26, 180n. 28, 191, 221, 233, 236n. 7, 237n. 10, 240n. 7
Confucian-Western dichotomy 233
wisdom see zhi

women
  woman 14n. 11, 22, 104, 219–23, 239n. 1
writing *see* calligraphy
wu music 73, 145

Xia dynasty 53–4, 145, 157n.4
xiao (孝) *see* filial piety
xiaoren (小人) 110, 116, 119, 174n. 4, 178n. 23, 219–22, 26
  see also *junzi*
Xunzi (荀子) 7–8, 24, 160n. 22
  the book of *Xunzi* 27n. 2

Yanhui 20–1, 59, 102, 137, 147, 157n. 6, 184n. 15
Yang, Bojun 10, 33–4, 68, 87, 149, 152n. 6, 156n. 1, 159nn. 18–19, 163n. 31, 165nn. 2, 3, 169n. 18, 170n. 23, 171n. 29, 176n. 12, 182nn. 2–3, 186n. 22, 220, 228
Yao 52, 54–6, 82, 113, 117, 157n. 2
yi *see* appropriateness
Yin dynasty 53, 145
Yong ode 33, 38
Yu 52, 56, 157n. 2
Yu Dan (于丹) 3, 12n. 3, 226–7, 229, 239n. 4

Zaiwo 96, 226–7, 229
Zengxi 68–70, 163n. 37
Zheng state 53
zhengming *see* rectification of names

zhi (知) 85–7, 99–100, 105, 121, 168n. 16, 207, 213–14, 223, 228, 231
zhong (忠) *see* dutifulness
Zhongni (仲尼) 19
Zhongyong (中庸) see *Doctrine of the Mean*
Zhou
  culture 59, 117, 157n. 5
  dynasty 19, 33, 52–5, 74, 158, 180n. 28
  li 55–6, 60, 62, 71–2, 97, 121, 125, 130–1, 145, 145, 169n. 18, 175n. 11, 180n. 28, 223, 228
  texts 228 *see also* culture
Zhougong (周公) *see* Duke of Zhou
Zhounan (周南) 65, 93
Zichan 21, 119
Zigong 67, 84, 88, 113, 115, 134, 138–1, 186n. 23
Zihua 69
Zilu 22, 40–1, 47–8, 55, 68–9, 92, 110, 117, 148–9, 186n. 23
zither 67–8, 70
Zixia 66, 86–7, 116, 126, 140–1, 183n. 9
Ziyou 22, 35
Zou village 22, 47, 137
Zuo Commentary (左傳) 17–18, 21, 24, 27n. 2, 162n. 28
Zuozhuan see *Zuo Commentary*